TEXAS AFTER THE CIVIL WAR

Number Fourteen: Texas A&M Southwestern Studies

TEXAS after the CIVIL WAR

The STRUGGLE of RECONSTRUCTION

CARL H. MONEYHON

Texas A&M University Press
College Station

The paper used in this book meets the minimum requirements
of the American National Standard for Permanence
of Paper for Printed Library Materials, z39.48-1984.
Binding materials have been chosen for durability.
∞

Library of Congress Cataloging-in-Publication Data

Moneyhon, Carl H., 1944–
    Texas after the Civil War : the struggle of Reconstruction / Carl H. Moneyhon.—1st ed.
        p. cm.—(Texas A&M southwestern studies ; no. 14)
    Includes bibliographical references and index.
    ISBN 1-58544-361-1 (alk. paper)
    ISBN 1-58544-362-X (pbk. : alk. paper)
    1. Reconstruction—Texas. 2. Texas—Politics and government—1865–1950.
    3. Texas—Social conditions—19th century. 4. Texas—Economic conditions—
    19th century. I. Title. II. Series.
    F391.M636 2004
    976.4'05—dc22
                                    2004003675

For John Hope Franklin, whose scholarship remains
a continuing influence on my own.
And in memory of Robert A. Calvert, who wanted this book done.

Contents

ILLUSTRATIONS

PHOTOGRAPHS

MAPS

Acknowledgments

Abook of this character necessarily owes much to the many scholars whose pioneering works have revised our attitudes toward the Reconstruction era. I owe a debt to all of those students of Texas history whose studies have reshaped the story of post–Civil War Texas. A number of people have helped me produce this book, providing useful criticism of both my ideas concerning Reconstruction and the manuscript in its various stages and sharing their expertise. In particular, I wish to thank James Smallwood, now emeritus at Oklahoma State University, who has offered frequent comments on my work. The late Barry Crouch of Gallaudet University unselfishly shared the results of his research in the Freedmen's Bureau Papers and forced me into frequent reevaluations of my own views of that agency. Alwyn Barr of Texas Tech University patiently listened to me expound on my views about Reconstruction on more than one occasion, responding with suggestions that also shifted my interpretations. I owe a special debt to Mike Campbell of the University of North Texas, with whom I have engaged in a continuing dialogue about the meaning of Reconstruction in Texas. I would also like to thank the staff at Texas A&M University Press for its encouragement and assistance in the preparation of this book.

Over the years, as I have carried out research projects on Texas Reconstruction, the staffs of numerous institutions have provided invaluable assistance. In particular, I wish to thank Donally Bryce at the Texas State Archives, who has shared his invaluable knowledge of the collections there. Ralph Elder always has had an answer for whatever question I have asked at the Center for American History at the University of Texas at Austin, an institution that will always be the Barker Texas History Center.

And, as usual, I am indebted to my wife, Patricia, who has always been supportive of my research and writing efforts.

Texas after the Civil War

INTRODUCTION

Texans at the end of the Civil War existed in a world with an uncertain future. As a result of the war, changes had taken place that had the potential of revolutionizing the state's economic and social order. The emancipation of the slave population, the blow to prosperity produced by economic destabilization, and the breakdown of traditional political relations among the state's elite produced a situation that made maintaining the society that had existed before the war impossible. As a result, at least potentially, blacks might achieve the ability to control their own economic destinies as well as equal civil and political rights in addition to emancipation. A more diversified economy might grow in the place of one that had relied almost solely on cotton culture and ranching. A viable two-party political system might emerge to replace the single party that had dominated the state during the antebellum years. In 1865 what the character of postwar Texas would be remained unknown.

Between 1865 and 1874, the years of Reconstruction, the new Texas emerged. The potential for a revolution remained throughout much of the period. The presence of the Freedmen's Bureau and the U.S. Army during the first years promised protection to the freedmen as they attempted to assert their economic and personal freedom. Then Congressional Reconstruction politicized the freedmen when it gave them the vote. A Republican state government, in office from 1870 to 1874, introduced measures that also threatened to produce significant change. Nevertheless, a radical revolution never took place. Texas in 1874 was different. Still, it resembled the Texas of 1861 more than anyone might have predicted at the war's end. African Americans were no longer slaves, but they found themselves constrained by a new bondage of poverty and racism that seriously limited the freedom they might have enjoyed. The state's economy recovered, but it looked little different from that of the antebellum years, with agriculture, cotton in particular, dominating the scene. One party still controlled state and local government, the one that had monopolized power before the war and had led the state into secession in 1861.

The potential for change inherent during the Civil War and Reconstruction and the eventual triumph of the status quo have long held the interest of students of Texas history. Charles W. Ramsdell, one of the earliest professional scholars to write on the history of the state, addresses the topic in his *Reconstruction in Texas,* published in 1909. Examining Texas between 1865 and 1874, he concludes that the failure of change could be attributed to those who sought to bring it about. Responsibility lay with Congress and the Republican party of Texas. Congress took the lead when it imposed a radical and impractical program of Reconstruction on Texas and the rest of the South, enfranchising men who Ramsdell considers had little stake in society and had shown little ability to live as free people, the former slaves. Black enfranchisement brought to power white Republicans who claimed to be reformers but proved to be venal and corrupt politicians seeking little more than furthering their own ends and ignoring the needs and wishes of the people. These Republicans, holding power because of Congress and black voters, provoked the people of Texas to rise up against them in a legitimate uprising, demanding that they surrender power. Ramsdell concludes that, with the return of the Democratic party to power in 1873, the state had returned to the hands of her own citizens. Of course, in drawing his conclusions, Ramsdell never perceives blacks as having a legitimate political interest to be served by the politics of the day.[1]

Decades after the appearance of *Reconstruction in Texas,* most professional historians no longer accept Ramsdell's basic conclusions regarding the cause of Reconstruction's failure, although the popular perception of that era often still clings to this earlier view. Historians have examined many different aspects of the state's postwar past, producing an extensive literature on the era's history. Although they often have disagreed about elements of the story, their work generally has challenged Ramsdell's overarching interpretation.[2] Still, despite this flurry of scholarship, no history exists that attempts to synthesize this literature into a new interpretation of Texas Reconstruction. The only other work besides that of Ramsdell to examine the era comprehensively, W. C. Nunn's *Texas under the Carpetbaggers,* fills in the details of events left untold by the former, covering the period 1870 to 1874; yet despite being published in 1962, it draws on none of the insights provided by the revisionist literature. The present volume seeks to fill this gap in historical studies and provide a new view of Reconstruction that includes not only its political but also its social and economic history and takes into account the findings of recent scholars.

The story that follows is appreciably different from the traditional one. It views the coalition of African Americans and white Republicans that formed in Texas during this period as being every bit as representative of the interests of the people of the state as their Conservative opponents and possessing a legitimate claim to power. Brought together by the refusal of many of the political leaders of antebellum Texas to fully accept the consequences of Confederate defeat, this combination, emerging as the Republican party in 1867, consisted of a wide variety of groups, elements as diverse as African American freedmen, white Unionists, railroad men, and regional interests. The new party's promised change reflected the political demands of its representative parts.

Unfortunately for its future, the Texas Republican party threatened the very survival of the state's antebellum Democratic political leadership, plantation interests, and the racist attitudes that supported both. In such circumstances the opposition used every means at hands to defeat the new party. Violence, intimidation, election fraud, and blatant appeals to racial fears were coupled to more traditional campaign tactics of misinformation and misrepresentation to create a white majority, ultimately organized in the Democratic party, opposed to the state's Republican government. The Republicans, desirous of change but never committed to a revolution, found themselves unable to respond to their opponents in a manner capable of defeating them. Given the Democrats' refusal to accept the course put forward by the Republicans and their willingness to use all means available to prevent the latter's success, they could have done little short of engaging in full-scale civil and racial war to succeed. As a result, antebellum leaders, not the whole of the people, kept the state on its old road, leaving Texans a legacy of a single-crop agricultural system that dominated the economy and racial repression that lasted into the next century.

This book represents an effort at synthesizing the views of a generation of scholars and introduces little new detail. As a result, notes have not been used unless citing direct quotes, identifying less-well-known information, or discussing topics where major differences of interpretation exist among historians. Information on the secondary literature that provides the narrative's underpinnings may be found in the annotated bibliography.

I intend this work to offer an interpretation of the Reconstruction era that takes into account the knowledge generated by the revisionist literature produced over the last three decades and an alternative picture to that of the traditional literature. In writing it, the need for a vast amount of additional research in areas ranging from the response of African Americans to freedom to the effect of Republican programs became apparent. Hopefully, this book will provoke and challenge others to ask new questions of Texas history and set the stage for even more scholarship on this critical era.

Chapter 1

TEXAS IN 1865

O n June 2, 1865, at Galveston, Lt. Gen. Edmund Kirby Smith, commander of the Confederate Trans-Mississippi Department, surrendered the military forces under his command and brought an end to the Civil War in the West. The department at the time consisted of little more than Texas, but Smith still gave up reluctantly. The state, even though its people had sacrificed much in providing manpower and resources to sustain the Confederacy, had remained virtually untouched by the war and still had the military forces to continue the fight for a time. With this in mind, the general, some of his officers, and local political officials believed that it would be possible to keep fighting, to force better peace terms if nothing else. Few common soldiers or civilians agreed. The surrender of the Army of Northern Virginia and the subsequent submission of the Army of Tennessee in the East had destroyed morale. Many soldiers in Texas made it clear that they had no interest in continuing the fight; they simply abandoned their units and went home. Without an army, Smith had no choice but to quit. Many Confederate leaders in Texas either fled to Mexico or followed their men home.

The collapse of the Confederacy confronted Texans with an uncertain future. In June, 1865, few whites believed that the future promised anything good, though the exact implications of defeat remained unclear. In 1860 and 1861 most of the state's political leaders had warned that a national government dominated by northern politicians and the Republican party meant catastrophe for the South and for Texas. They equated Republicanism with radical abolitionism and predicted that the triumph of Abraham Lincoln, the Republican candidate for president of the United States at that time, would produce not only an end to slavery but also economic disaster and social disruption. Now, in 1865, Lincoln was dead at the hands of an assassin, but the Republicans still controlled the national government that had conquered the South. Most Texans feared that the dire predictions of 1860 would now come true.

By the middle of the month, federal officials initiated the first steps into that uncertain future when they issued two critical proclamations relative to affairs in the state. Each had potentially revolutionary implications for the people of Texas. Pres. Andrew Johnson began the process in Washington, D.C., on June 17 when he made public his appointment of a provisional governor for Texas. He sent Andrew J. Hamilton, an old Texan and Unionist politician, to the state, cloaked with powers to take all steps necessary to restore civil authority and to ensure a loyal and republican government. Johnson's proclamation provided that the governor call a convention of men elected by loyal voters. The president asked, but did not demand, that the convention also ratify the Thirteenth Amendment ending slavery, repudiate the state's Confederate war debt, renounce secession, and provide for statewide elections. Afterward, the newly seated loyal government could then return Texas to its normal relationship within the Union.

President Johnson defined the loyal voters in his Amnesty Proclamation, issued in May, as those southern men who took an oath of allegiance administered after the war. He excepted certain Confederate officials, state governors, and military officers—those above the rank of colonel in the army and lieutenant in the navy. He also excluded from the general amnesty men who had previously sworn an oath of allegiance to the United States and then supported the Confederacy. Lastly, he left unpardoned those who had owned taxable property of more than twenty thousand dollars in 1860. Even those exempted from the general pardon could secure an individual pardon by a special application to the president, however.

This proclamation established the basic framework for a return to the Union, but it did not define clearly the means to achieve that end. Johnson left the process of administering the oath of allegiance and calling a convention to the discretion of the governor. This provided Hamilton with a considerable amount of power in determining who voted and also allowed him to set the timetable for Reconstruction. In short, the president's lack of clarity gave the governor an opportunity to mold postwar Texas politics into a shape that differed from that of the antebellum years. Persecuted for his Unionism during the war, Hamilton's appointment only underscored the possibility for political upheaval feared by many of the state's former leaders.

A second measure, issued on June 19, may have had a more immediate effect on most Texans and raised even more concerns among the white citizens of the state. Gen. Gordon Granger arrived at Galveston that day as commander of the first elements of Union troops sent to ensure that Kirby Smith carried out the conditions of the surrender. Granger also had the responsibility of enforcing the Emancipation Proclamation within the state. In General Orders No. 3, he declared all slaves in Texas free. His directive also provided specific definitions of the meaning of that freedom, insisting that future labor relationship between masters and their former slaves would be as between employers and hired laborers. Further, it explained that freedom gave blacks the same personal and property rights as whites. With this order, the labor system that had been the basis for the state's plantation economy disappeared, which raised critical questions about the economic and social future of Texas. Could landowners continue to grow profitable cotton crops without slave labor? If not, what would happen to the antebellum elites who depended on plantation wealth? In addition, what did freedom mean to a social hierarchy that had long placed blacks in subordination to whites?

The actions of Johnson and Granger opened up the possibility of an extensive transformation of the state's economic, social, and political life, adding greater uncertainty to a community already unsettled by the war. Reconstruction, with its purposes of guaranteeing loyal government and emancipation, ensured that some sort of change ultimately would take place. No matter what the intent of the federal government, however, from the beginning, forces at work within Texas helped define the meaning of loyal government and emancipation in ways acceptable locally. The fact that the Civil War had shaken the community that had existed in Texas before the war but not destroyed it made the resistance to changes in government and society even greater than elsewhere in the South. Pressure existed for change, but it had to work against an economic and social order that remained essentially intact. In 1865 Texas remained much as it had been in 1861.

The relative stability of conditions in Texas derived in large part from the state's geographic position on the far western boundary of the Confederacy, distant from the critical theaters of battle east of the Mississippi. But the war unquestionably devastated the lives of individuals and families. Texas may have contributed as many as ninety thousand troops to the Confederacy, though at least one scholars has suggested that the number may have been considerably smaller.[1] Based on the larger number, and assuming that Texans suffered casualty rates similar to those of other states, as many as nineteen thousand men may have died in the service. An equal number suffered wounds, disease, or captivity; the latter survived, but they often suffered physical and psychological effects resulting from their experiences for years afterward.[2] In addition, families that financially invested in the Confederate cause lost fortunes. The end of slavery also visited a heavy toll on the state's wealthy citizens, liquidating without compensation millions of dollars in assets through emancipation. Still, Texas had remained largely untouched by battle. Union troops had occupied Galveston for a short time in 1862, and an invasion force had moved along the Lower Gulf Coast in 1864, but most Texans never saw a Union soldier until U.S. troops began to arrive following the surrender. In addition, Texas never saw the physical destruction visited on most of the other Confederate states. As a result the local economy endured and in some cases actually prospered. In turn, social and political relations also persisted and invariably played a role in defining the course of Reconstruction.

The Texas that existed in 1865 appeared especially stable economically, and economic issues underlay many of the future struggles of Reconstruction. At the end of the war, the state's economy remained in good shape, relative to the rest of the South. Livestock raising and the cultivation of cotton, the two most important components of this economy, survived the war with few setbacks.

Of the principal aspects of agricultural production, the popular imagination usually associates nineteenth-century Texas with ranching, and ranchers were prospering at the war's end. Before secession, the rich coastal prairie lands of the state promised what many newcomers hoped would be an effortless rise to wealth by producing livestock for sale, and the hopeful came in great numbers to raise cattle, sheep, and horses. The size of the ranching industry may be understood in census reports of 1860, which indicated that Texans owned 2,761,736 head of beef cattle, 753,363 sheep, and 325,698 horses.[3]

Ranches produced different types of animals, but most principally raised cattle, and cattle and their byproducts generated the greatest income for Texans. Beef ranching took place in most antebellum counties, and even farmers often ran small herds to supplement their planted crops. The center of production, however, lay largely within what is known as the Gulf Coastal Plain, stretching from Nueces County in the west to the eastern border with Louisiana. The largest herds ran on the lower parts of the numerous rivers that cut across this flatland, but sizeable operations extended inland as far as Travis County along the Colorado River and Ellis County on the upper Trinity. A steady market for Texas beef encouraged this emphasis on ranching before the war. The $4,835,284 reported for cattle slaughtered in 1859 in the 1860 census represented a significant part of the state's economic productivity. Ranchers drove their herds to coastal towns such as Indianola or Galveston, where local packing houses slaughtered the animals, salted the beef, and packed it for shipment. Local packers also shipped a variety of byproducts, including hides, tallow, horns, and bone. While local slaughterhouses handled some of the cattle, those of New Orleans processed even more. Live animals went to the Crescent City in overland drives or aboard ship, and that city served as the principal market for Texas beef.

The war produced problems for ranchers. Secession had cut them off from their primary eastern market. The withdrawal of the U.S. Army from the western and Rio Grande frontiers and the inability of the Confederacy to replace its presence opened up ranches to increasing raids by outlaws and Indians. The appearance of lawless bands of draft dodgers and deserters in frontier areas added to the banditry. A drought that began in 1862 and lasted throughout the war years created further problems. Still, local markets for livestock remained good, and ranchers also found an additional outlet through Mexico. The existence of such markets meant that, though profits suffered relative to the antebellum years, cattlemen still had an income during the war. By the summer of 1865, most ranchers remained solvent, and figures gathered by the editors of the *Texas Almanac* indicate the state's cattle herds had surpassed figures for 1860 by nearly half a million head. High prices after the war promised renewed profits for ranchers. Cattle sold locally for between three and five dollars per head, but if they could be driven to New Orleans, they could bring in between twenty-five and thirty-five dollars per head. The future actually looked bright for an industry that had survived the war in a relatively healthy condition.[4]

While ranching often dominated even the contemporary view of the Texas economy, the cultivation of crops ultimately constituted an even more important part of antebellum economic life. The state's farmers grew a large number of products of considerable value that flowed into local, regional, and national markets. Corn, often consumed by the animals and workers of its producer, also entered local markets as a supplement for those unable to produce enough foodstuffs for their own needs. Grains such as rye, oats, and wheat thrived in the state's upper Grand Prairie and Blackland Prairie and moved primarily to market at Shreveport, Louisiana. By 1859 the state's wheat harvest, based on an average price of $1.50 per bushel, reached a value of $2,217,517, an amount equal to half the value of slaughtered cattle. Sixteen of 151 counties grew more than a thousand pounds of tobacco, another crop with a good market. In Sabine County rice farming proved commercially successful before the war, and local planters marketed 20,840 pounds in 1859. Another regionally important product, sugar cane and the cane molasses manufactured from it, provided its growers with good profits. The latter industry centered in Brazoria County, which produced 346,640 gallons of the statewide total 408,358 gallons of molasses.

Ultimately, however, one crop dominated the farm economy. Cotton commanded a ready cash market around the world. Its importance to the Texas economy grew through the 1850s at least in part because it had virtually no geographic limitations on its cultivation. About 39 percent of the state's 42,891 farms grew some cotton in 1859. That same year these farms and plantations produced 431,463 bales. With the price of cotton at the time averaging eleven cents per pound, these four-hundred-pound bales provided an income of roughly $19,000,000. This amount made it the single-most-valuable agricultural product grown in Texas. The revenue it generated represented more than half of the value of all agricultural goods, both crop and animal, produced in the state.

This agricultural output came from two distinctive types of operations. The large commercial farm, called the plantation, was one. An exact definition of a plantation does not exist, but it usually possessed several unique characteristics. First, it focused on growing one of the state's great cash crops, often to the neglect of subsistence crops. Second, it usually relied heavily on slave labor for its workforce. Typically, contemporaries considered a farmer with twenty or more slaves to be a planter. He could count on having roughly twenty bales of cotton for sale each year, based on figures for Harrison County, Texas, indicating an average productivity of one bale of cotton per slave each year. Achieving planter status also required one to have at least forty acres of land devoted to cotton, since much of the land in Texas averaged only half a bale per acre. An additional eighty acres would be needed to grow food grains, particularly corn, or to pasture livestock. Based on cotton prices of around ten to eleven cents per pound just before the war, a small planter grossed a little less than a thousand dollars per year, a substantial amount for the time. Using the figure of twenty bales of cotton per year to define a plantation, 9.4 percent of all Texas farms in 1859 fit within the category, yet, as shown by historians Randolph Campbell and Richard Lowe, they produced nearly 80 percent of that year's crop. Plantations existed throughout the state, though the rich bottomlands of the Colorado and Brazos Rivers to the west of Houston and along the Sabine River in the northeastern part of the state contained most of them.[5]

Texans usually called the second type of operation unit simply a farm. These grew some crops for market, but generally their owners practiced more diversified agriculture and aimed at greater self-sufficiency. While farmers might have some slave workers, they more often relied on family members for labor. Farms composed the vast majority of agricultural units in the state before the war, and in 1859, 90.6 percent of them grew either less than twenty bales of cotton or none at all. A writer for the *Texas Almanac* described a hypothetically successful farm operated by a man with two or three sons. Once the original land had been cleared and a farm established, a family of this size could actually cultivate between fifty and seventy-five acres. Over half of this would be devoted to growing the corn needed to feed livestock and to grind into meal, with additional land dedicated to pasturage and possibly grains such as wheat, barley, oats, or rye. While such an operation might have the land necessary to grow a considerable amount of cotton, the lack of laborers meant it could produce only about four bales per year, a cash value of less than two hundred dollars. Still, by being self-sufficient, profits could be made on the cotton, grain, and perhaps the sale of some animals and then invested in additional land or in the purchase of a slave to supplement the family workforce. The hope of becoming a planter helped integrate even the smallest cotton farmer into the slave-labor system.[6]

As in the case of ranching, the war caused problems for both planters and farmers, but generally these Texans fared better than their counterparts elsewhere in the South. The relative strength of the state's agriculture did not diminish its problems. Of the two unit types, the small farm probably experienced worse hardships than the plantation because they relied more heavily on white workers, who were called away to fight in the army. On many small farms the cultivation of crops languished throughout the war years. Plantations had different problems. Some planters believed that, with the absence of white men, the slave labor force did not work as hard as it had before the war. In addition, both types of operations suffered whenever markets were disrupted.

Still, in some areas an influx of refugee slaveowners, who sometimes rented their slaves to local farmers or rented their land, alleviated the problems caused by the loss of white workers. In addition, as in the case of the cattle industry, Mexico provided an outlet for Texas farm products, especially cotton, throughout the conflict. Gold and silver flowed into the local economy from this cross-border trade. Income might have been down, and the war certainly ruined some individual families, but as with ranchers, the state's planters and farmers emerged from these years relatively undamaged. High prices for produce, particularly cotton, encouraged many in agriculture to look optimistically toward the future and a quick recovery.

For planters, the stability of the slave-labor force throughout the war and at its end added to positive outlook. Elsewhere in the South, the nearness of Union lines enticed thousands of slaves to flee their masters. In the wake of advancing northern armies, even more had left. In Texas, however, Union forces never made inroads into the parts of the state with the largest slave populations. Some planters worried that their slaves knew that the war offered them potential liberation and feared this knowledge might encourage either resistance or uprisings. Some thought that they recognized this in an unwillingness of some workers to take orders. Yet while slaves may have recognized the revolutionary implications of the war, few managed to escape to Union forces when they occupied Galveston for a short time or when they entered southern Texas. The great mass of them remained at work until the very end, even planting a crop in the spring of 1865.[7]

Other elements of the economy had not fared as well during the war. Wholesale and retail businesses and marketing operations had suffered serious losses during the war as demand for goods diminished. Even though trade continued during the war, it often utilized new lines. Commerce that had moved east into Louisiana or through Galveston shifted to the south and Mexico due to the federal blockade of Texas ports. As a result, businesses in Galveston and Houston declined. Galveston suffered the most, for many businessmen fled to the mainland when federal forces occupied the city and did not return until the war's end. Good agricultural prospects in June, 1865, however, promised a rapid recovery for these merchants. Most seem to have expected just such a recovery. A burst of business activity that summer indicated that many of these businessmen believed that there would be a rapid return to good times. At Galveston, the city that endured the worst effects of the war, newspapers reported old firms reestablishing themselves and new ones opening. Construction boomed along the town streets. Similar reports indicated a revival of business in the other major towns of the state.

The future of the state's modest transportation industry also depended on agricultural prospects, and expectations appeared high in 1865. Railroad construction had not begun in earnest in Texas until the 1850s. By the outbreak of the Civil War, eight companies had begun actual operations, but only four hundred miles of track had been built. Except for the San Antonio and Gulf road and another known as the Southern Pacific, between Marshall and Caddo Lake, all of these companies radiated outward from Galveston and Houston and tied those cities to the surrounding countryside so their agricultural produce would move over them. Freight cars loaded with cotton provided the greatest revenue for the roads. Declining trade with these cities necessarily reduced revenues, and the blockade kept railroads from securing the iron and machinery necessary to maintain their tracks and equipment, though trains continued to run. Only the San Antonio line suffered serious damage when Confederate forces destroyed it in 1863 in order to keep a federal invasion force from using it. Further encouraging optimism, Texas had passed favorable legislation during the war that allowed many of the railroads to reduce their indebtedness by paying off loans from the state's school fund in Confederate paper money, which had to be accepted at face value. This left the companies relatively debt free and the school fund bankrupt. The railroads already in operation stood ready to begin again their antebellum expansion in the postwar world.

Manufacturing constituted only a small part of the antebellum economy, and its character made recovery relatively easy. Before the war only four companies, all producing cotton textiles, could be considered highly mechanized and operating on the basis of the factory system. Other prewar manufacturers worked in small shops to fabricate goods such as carriages and wagons, saddles and harnesses, a variety of wood products, and metal wear for local and regional markets. These shops, owned by artisans, usually employed only a few workers, used little machinery to create their wares, and only sold locally. The war actually encouraged an expansion of larger enterprises, when the Confederate state and national governments encouraged the development of enterprises to make textiles, hats, uniforms, accoutrements, powder, and weapons, but these state-owned enterprises did not survive the surrender, however; home-bound soldiers or local civilians looted most of these factories. Still, since most manufacturers did not rely heavily on machinery, they could start up production rapidly when craftsmen returned to work. The connection of most of these businesses to the agricultural economy meant that the optimistic outlook in the latter promised a rapid return to the prosperity of prewar days.

The fact that the war did not have a catastrophic effect on the state's economy meant that the social world that grew out of it remained largely intact as well. During the antebellum years, a key element of society, its system of status and the prestige and power that accompanied each rank, had mirrored that in the other slaveholding states. Contemporaries recognized a hierarchy of status among whites that generally placed at the top an elite that included prosperous planters and businessmen. Beneath this upper class existed a middle class of smaller planters, landowning farmers, businessmen, and craftsmen and a lower class of the landless poor. Status derived largely from economic resources and occupation in this world, and the dominant agrarian economy helped define its roles.

In the antebellum years this social hierarchy did not create sharply different class ideologies or outlooks within the state. In 1860, with status based largely on wealth, a booming economy led most people to believe that they had a chance to move upward, even if fact did not always match the dream. Especially in the newer counties, more equitable divisions of wealth and the existence of even more economic opportunity contributed to a unity of identity not found in older and more established communities in the eastern part of Texas. In addition, the agrarian character of the community meant that from the richest planter to the poorest farmer, all shared a mutual world of endeavor that allowed men to meet on common ground. Some antebellum politicians attempted to play upon jealousies that might exist between the rich and poor, usually on the grounds that the rich and powerful sought to cut off access to their status; Sam Houston used such appeals in his 1859 gubernatorial campaign. Little evidence exists, however, that these arguments attracted great numbers of voters.

The presence of a large number of German immigrants and a sizeable Mexican American population complicated antebellum society to some extent. Generally, economically successful Mexican Americans associated easily with their Anglo counterparts and became accepted as a part of society. Whites tended to identify the vast majority of Mexican American poor, however, as not only of a lower status but also a separate and inferior class, with their identity based on racial characteristics. An equally complex relationship existed for Germans and the larger society. Those who embraced American culture generally became a part of the dominant social order and integrated into status positions corresponding with their wealth. Those who remained isolated on the western frontier or preserved their German cultures, however, remained a class unto themselves, though usually not considered socially inferior.

African Americans, constituting approximately a third of the state's population in 1860, represented a caste apart, doomed by their status as slaves and by race to perpetual inferiority in the minds of most whites. In the 1830s in response to the rise of abolitionism, southerners had developed an elaborate defense of slavery that drew upon religion, classical literature, and other sources to justify bondage. By 1860 most whites considered blacks to be an inferior people because of their race. Their definition of this helped justify slavery, but it produced serious barriers to ever integrating free blacks into the existing social order. By the time of the Civil War, most whites would have described blacks as lazy and shifty. At the same time, ironically, they viewed blacks as potentially violent. Such characteristics they considered as demanding that African Americans' labor and behavior had to be controlled if they were to live in society with whites.

As in the case of the economy, the war had shaken the social status quo but not destroyed it. Nevertheless, serious potential divisions had developed, raising questions of class identity that did not exist earlier. In Texas the poor resented conscription, resisted it, and in time came to view the conflict in the same way poor people did elsewhere in the South—a rich man's war and a poor man's fight. Hundreds of men refused to serve, keeping the Confederate provost marshals busy arresting men and placing them into the service against their will. In some cases men refused to serve and fled from their homes, creating a very unstable situation in areas where draft resisters joined those who had deserted from the army and some outlaws in lawless bands that undermined Confederate authority. The thickets of eastern Texas and the country along the Red River boundary with Indian Territory became virtually lawless, with such bands surviving by carrying off cattle and other livestock. When the war ended, these men remained in those regions, having little reason to return to peaceful living.

In addition, the war also created tensions between the Anglo community and some Germans. A number of Germans opposed the Confederacy for ideological and political reasons, though probably even more simply did not wish to participate in the fighting. They came up against Confederate authority after passage of the first conscription act in April, 1862. German Texans resisted the new law to an even greater degree than the broader population and in some cases actively opposed its enforcement. As a result, Confederate authorities sent troops into some of the German-speaking areas to force compliance and to dragoon men into the service. In the best-known incident between authorities and German Unionists, Confederate soldiers pursued a group of draft resistors from Kendall and Gillespie Counties fleeing to Mexico and killed them in a fight that became known among the Germans as the Massacre on the Nueces River. Other less celebrated events occurred in German communities across the state. Ultimately, the Confederate efforts left considerable ill will in its wake and created potential problems for postwar Texas society.

Still, most Texans remained loyal to the state government and the Confederacy, no matter what misgivings they might have harbored about the war and its consequences for them. The poor did not rise up against the rich. Most Germans did not take up arms against the Confederacy. Indeed, large numbers from both groups went to war willingly to fight for the Confederacy. Most Texans ultimately obeyed the law, no matter what their personal feelings. For those men who went into the army, often the camaraderie such service created among soldiers would actually overcome any feelings of class hostility that may have existed earlier.

War did little to disrupt the antebellum view of social order. The basic array of individuals and families into their appropriate status groups also remained unchanged. After the war the state's old planter elite remained, still controlling a disproportionate share of the wealth, exercising power, and dominating society. New persons who had entered the upper-class world during these years generally came from the same background as those in the antebellum era, though a few more merchants joined the planters among this group. Historian Randolph Campbell's study of Harrison County has shown that the plantation elite there survived the war and held on to its position in that community at roughly the same proportion as it had the 1850s, 52.8 percent to 55.1 percent. In a later work Campbell has shown that in this county not a single member of this upper class died in the war. Indeed, nearly half of the county's military-age population did not serve in the army, and married men composed only a minority of those who went to war. Thus, the county's youth provided most of the soldiers and most of the dead killed by war and disease. While this produced horrible suffering for those families involved, it did not threaten the family's basic survival. Although Campbell's research focuses on only one county, his findings parallel those for many other communities across the South, which suggests that his conclusions might be applied to Texas in general and that, statewide, the war did nothing to undermine the position of the antebellum elite.[8]

If the economy and social order remained largely intact through the war years, the antebellum political order saw deep fissures develop that in 1865 promised continued confrontation in the postwar world. During the 1850s, political differences within Texas had been subordinated to the overarching demand that politicians stand together to protect the South from a combined abolitionist and northern attack upon the region's basic institutions and what contemporaries perceived as the political rights of the states. The interests of Texas elites and the ambitions of most other free men required this unified stand and, for all practical purposes, brought an end to party politics in the prewar decade. The Whig party, with limited regional strength in northern and eastern Texas and some support in towns, disappeared altogether by 1852 as a result of its northern supporters' drift toward abolitionism. The Know-Nothing party emerged in the wake of Whiggery's demise, but it never attracted widespread support in Texas.

By the end of the 1850s, the Democratic party survived as the only viable political organization within the state, and its primary platform being the protection of slavery and the economy based on it. The Democracy's strident demand that the national government protect slavery against the threat of abolitionism unified whites. Its leaders insisted that all Texans stand together in opposition to any threat from the North. In 1857 the editor of the *Galveston Weekly News,* one of the more conservative Democratic newspapers, made clear the party's view of the need for solidarity when he wrote, "Those who are not for us must be against us."[9]

Outward unity did not mean that political struggles ceased. Even though no opposition lined up against the Democrats, the party's leaders faced repeated challenges from within. The Democratic party represented the broader interests of the state's planters, merchants, and increasingly its railroad men, and regional rivalries among these groups often led to disagreements as each sought to use the government for its particular benefit. The usual political struggles involved eastern and western Texas against the economically more powerful interests of the older plantation area along the lower Brazos and Colorado Rivers. Such contests also developed out of the rivalries between Galveston and Houston or between those two cities and the aspirations and interests of businessmen in Austin, San Antonio, Jefferson, and any other town that hoped for economic success.

Political unity began to unravel, however, during the secession crisis, when serious disagreements rose among Texas' political leaders. The push for secession among some southerners had begun during the presidential campaign of 1860, and party leaders held up the prospective election of the Republican candidate, Abraham Lincoln, as the cause for withdrawing from the Union. In Texas, secessionists dominated the leadership of the regular wing of the Democratic party, but all political leaders did not go with the mainstream of opinion. Gov. Sam Houston criticized secession as tantamount to suicide, and he received support from many of politicians who had supported him in the past. In the struggles of 1860 and early 1861, these men began to call themselves Unionists. The secession election proved the Unionists to be a minority, but it showed that strong opposition existed in counties in the northeastern part of the state and also in those with German majorities in central Texas. Texas went to war, though not completely united.

The wartime struggles between secessionists and Unionists produced almost irreparable divisions among the state's political leaders. Many Unionists refused to give their support to the Confederacy. Loyal Confederates proclaimed

Gov. Sam Houston, prewar Unionist leader. Courtesy Texas State Library and Archives

this refusal treason, charging that Unionists had abandoned the people of their state in the crisis. Many Texas Unionists initially tried to sit out the war, but the growing hostility of Texas Confederates made it impossible. While a few managed to remain behind, by about 1863 a steady stream of Unionists, including men as prominent as former congressman Andrew J. Hamilton, fled the state. Many of them actively supported Union efforts at suppressing the Confederacy; President Lincoln later appointed Hamilton military governor of Texas. State judge Edmund J. Davis served as commander of the 1st Texas Cavalry (U.S.) and ultimately as a general in the Union Army.

The treatment these men received did little to make a peaceful Reconstruction possible. Confederate authorities acted against the holdings of those who had fled the state. The government declared such men to be alien enemies, confiscated their property, and then sold it. In the case of George Paschal, a Unionist who refused to pay Confederate taxes, state authorities seized his property and sold it for the taxes, assessed at double the initial amount as a penalty. When the war ended, many of the Unionists returned to the state facing a worse financial situation than their enemies. For those who could not leave, conditions proved even worse. State officials arrested and imprisoned many of these men. In some cases local authorities hunted down and killed those Unionists who openly resisted their authority. Such treatment created hostility that survived long into the postwar era.

These conditions defined the world that Andrew Johnson and Gordon Granger addressed in June, 1865. Their pronouncements posed challenges to the survival of what had been Texas before the war. Granger's represented the greatest threat to the status quo since it concerned the end of slavery and threw into doubt the economic recovery upon which the survival of the old order depended. Slaves had produced most of the cotton grown in antebellum Texas. They had worked not only on the plantations but also on the state's ranches, small farms, and even as laborers in the towns. They played a major role in driving the state's economy. Most white landowners wondered whether or not an economic recovery could be managed with blacks as free laborers. Their racial views led them to believe that black laborers required coercion and had to be controlled. Granger threatened the implementation of any system of control when he indicated that the new relationship between masters and their former slaves would be one of employer and free laborer. Almost no white Texan could conceive of the freedmen working in such a relationship, and they saw the general's proclamation as a virtual death sentence for the state's economy.

If Granger's proclamation threatened the state's economic future, it also put into question the survival of the state's social order. Wealth invested in slaves and created in the fields by slaves served as the basis for status of a large portion of the antebellum elite. The wealthiest 7 percent of antebellum Texans had owned nearly 72 percent of the state's slaves, and that investment totaled at least four hundred million dollars. They might not retrieve that lost capital, but the loss of the labor of their slaves posed an even greater challenge to their position. Planters emerged from the war still in control of their land, but Granger made uncertain their mastery of the labor necessary to make that land productive. The general's action not only destabilized the state's economic future but also challenged the racial views of the community and the personal survival of the state's most powerful individuals.

President Johnson's demand that the provisional governor ensure republican government presented a challenge to the state's political order as great as

Granger's to the survival of its economic and social order. His exclusion of high government officials, military officers, and the wealthiest men in the state from the general amnesty made prospects uncertain, for it banned from government most of the state's antebellum political leaders and certainly those who had led Texas during the war. In turn, it might potentially bring to power a group men who had been bloodily persecuted during the war. If they did secure power, it might bring retribution. It might produce a political revolution.

For old Texas, the summer of 1865 jeopardized much that had existed. But it opened up new prospects and new opportunities for others, especially the freedmen and those whites who had remained loyal to the Union. During the next nine years, the interests of old Texas struggled with those of the new. The conflict determined the extent of the potential revolution of 1865.

Chapter 2

THE PROVISIONAL GOVERNMENT, 1865–66

As the actual process of reconstruction began in June, 1865, enormous problems confronting Texans and the various officials charged with restoring the state to the Union demanded immediate attention. No state government existed to develop and put into place a course of action for administering the oath of allegiance and registering voters in preparation for a constitutional convention. The legitimacy of county and city governments remained unclear. Of more immediate importance, issues concerning the freedmen pressed for solutions. Whites proved reluctant to accept fully the idea of complete independence for their former slaves and often hoped that they could retain some sort of control over them. Blacks insisted on full freedom. Differences between the two sides helped bog down the contracting of labor amid the growing season and the delay threatened the 1865 crop. In the months that followed the surrender of Confederate forces and the arrival of federal troops, the people of Texas, the provisional governor, officers of the U.S. Army, and officials of the Freedmen's Bureau wrestled with these problems, and their actions helped determine the subsequent course of events in the state. Critical decisions taken in the months between June, 1865, and the inauguration of the government of James W. Throckmorton in August, 1866, made this period one of the most important in the state's Reconstruction era.

The complex process of restoration and adjustment began unsteadily that summer. Difficulties arose almost immediately when Gov. Andrew J. Hamilton failed to reach the state until late in July, more than a month after the arrival of the first contingent of federal occupation forces. Gen. Edgar M. Gregory, the officer named to head the Freedmen's Bureau, the agency created by the government specifically to deal with the affairs of the freedmen, in Texas did not arrive until that September, over three months after the surrender. Problems related to emancipation demanded immediate attention, however. Planters and farmers desperately wanted to continue cultivation of the crops planted that spring with their old workforce; the freedmen needed to make a livelihood. High prices for cotton and other agricultural products promised large profits in the upcoming fall. Everyone had a vested interest in a successful harvest. Yet they found themselves with little guidance concerning the form that free labor should take. In the absence of Hamilton and Gregory, those military officials already on the ground stepped in and developed policy.

Officers established guidelines that varied considerably from place to place. These amounted to a patchwork of policies that reflected either the personal views of military commanders or the practical reactions by local authorities to situations they encountered. Gen. C. C. Andrews, who commanded the District of Texas at the time, offered the most authoritative views in several speeches and in official orders. Citing the necessity to cultivate the crops already growing in the fields and to prevent the problems created whenever freedmen crowded into towns and cities, Andrews insisted that African Americans stay with those former masters who would treat them as freedmen. Where landowners refused to contract with their old laborers, he advised the workers to hire themselves out to others. He offered little advice, however, concerning the specific provisions of employment. The general believed that many planters found that paying their workers a share of the crop (he suggested one-tenth) worked well, so he suggested contracts be made on this basis. Otherwise, he demanded nothing but that labor agreements be "reasonable and fair."[1]

Theoretically, emancipation meant that the freedmen might decide not to work at all, but Andrews's policies made it clear that the general did not accept that as a possible alternative. He believed the freedmen had to go to work, and when blacks refused to sign what he considered to be reasonable contracts, the general indicated the army would insist on their finding employment. In the Houston area he ordered the provost marshal to hire out to planters, or any others who would employ them, those freed people who neglected to sign labor agreements or possessed no honest means of support. Andrews also informed Texans that the military would compel, with force if necessary, those who had signed good contracts to fulfill to them.

The edicts of local military commanders added to the confusion concerning contractual relations that summer. The provost marshal at Galveston, for example, issued a circular encouraging former slaves to remain at work with their old masters and insisting that cruel treatment would not be permitted. At the same time, he placed serious restrictions on their freedom when he informed laborers that "no persons formerly slaves will be permitted to travel on the public thoroughfares without passes or permits from their employers." At Houston the post commander issued a similar order, concluding with a statement that any former slaves found in that city without employment would be "put at labor, cleaning the streets, without compensation."

By midsummer some white Texans came to believe, partly as a result of observing the actions of the military, that not just aspects of the old labor system might survive but even slavery itself. Rumors circulated that, having found free labor unworkable, the president had revoked emancipation and restored slave property to the masters. Another report receiving wide circulation speculated that emancipation had been considered a wartime measure and would have no force now that the war had ended.[2] Even among those who realized that such hopes had no foundation, the statements of General Andrews and other military officers led them to believe that federal authorities would accept some degree of compulsion within the new labor system, that some aspects of the old system could be salvaged. They perceived Andrews's phrase "reasonable and fair" as allowing considerable latitude in establishing contractual relations.

In this setting, planters, farmers, and laborers began to work out arrangements for the future on their own. The process, out of necessity, moved rapidly. Projected high prices for cotton in the early summer had stimulated a major rush by farmers and planters to bring in a good crop. Prices had dropped to fifty cents per pound from even higher levels during the war, but this still looked very promising relative to the eleven cents a pound averaged in 1860. Planters made profits at the latter figure; the higher one promised an enormous return. As a result, they had to ensure the cultivation of the cotton planted that spring. Some even hoped to plant a late crop. The expected return on their investments even encouraged many army officers to rent land on which to make a crop. Only the rapidly developing concern of many whites about the freedmen as laborers constrained this optimism.

Given their conclusions based upon military guidelines regarding labor relations, many planters tried to get their workers to sign agreements that seriously restricted their freedom. Typical contracts offered the freedmen a wage for their labor, then set the terms of that employment. Usually they provided for a work schedule of ten hours a day, five and a half days a week. They often allowed the landowner to deduct wages for any time taken off or as punishment for what might be considered negligence. Most wage workers usually continued to perform their tasks in gangs, supervised by a foreman who took over the role of the overseer and driver of slavery days. They often lived in the old slave quarters, receiving housing, clothing, and what had been slave rations, with the employer deducting the cost of these from wages. Some contracts included clauses that required workers to remain on the plantation unless given permission by their employer to leave. At least some planters even hoped to incorporate provisions allowing them to use physical punishment to ensure hard work from their employees.

While trying to create a system that allowed them to exercise considerable control over their workers, planters found that they also had to offer very high wages. They confronted a major problem when it became clear that the state did not have enough laborers to ensure the full success of the 1865 harvest. This shortage resulted from several changes in the labor pool. Competition from small farmers, who might not have been able to buy slaves but could afford to hire a freedman, spread existing workers among a larger number of landowners. In some cases the efforts of the freedmen to establish family life caused many women to leave the fields so that they might work in the household instead. Other former slaves, including those who had been brought into Texas during the war, may have simply left the state. Federal officials later reported only 200,000 freedmen in Texas, an unexplained drop from the 275,000 reported to have been there at the war's end. In December, 1865, one federal official estimated that the Texas economy needed between twenty and fifty thousand additional workers. As a result, cotton growers had to bid against each other to secure laborers, usually offering lucrative contracts to their hands. Officials reported what they considered to be very high labor prices, with some planters offering wages that ranged from $96 to $180 per year, estimated to be the highest ever offered in the state.

Despite the money, many planters could not get workers to sign contracts landowner's considered necessary to ensure the type of labor necessary to bring in a harvest. From the beginning, the freedmen made it clear that their own view of a desirable labor system differed from that of their former masters. Freedmen realized that they had to work, but they did not wish to work under the arrangements sought by many of the planters. By July many former slaves in the plantation areas along the coast had refused to sign contracts, holding out for better conditions. Rumors that the government intended to break up the landholdings of the old masters and redistribute them among their workers circulated that summer and may also have encouraged the freedmen to even greater resistance. They may also have known of the overall labor shortage and realized that it gave them some ability to force employers to change the character of the terms they offered.

Federal officials early observed that most freedmen desired an alternative system to that wanted by landowners. The preferred arrangement, usually called sharecropping, offered the worker an opportunity to cultivate a particular piece of land in return for a share of the crop. Typically, the landowner furnished the land, a house, farm equipment and draft animals, seed, and possibly advances of cash for supplies; the worker, in turn, provided the labor. At the end of the year, the worker received anywhere from a quarter to a half of the crop for that labor. The landowner received the rest in payment for the use of the land and other materials supplied. Most of the freedmen favored sharecropping to the wage system, with its memory of slavery. Given the shortage of labor, many planters bent to the wishes of the freedmen and shifted to sharecropping, though most did not believe they could get the same effort from their workers. By the end of the summer of 1865, it had become the pervasive system for working most of the old cotton lands of the state.

Despite the difficult adjustments made in the labor system during the summer of 1865, those who acquired workers remained very optimistic about the prospects of a good yield. Federal officials from around the state predicted that the upcoming harvest might find that farmers had produced a bumper crop. They estimated that the state's farmers not only had planted as much cotton as they had in past years but also had large amounts of land planted with corn and wheat. If the weather remained good and pests stayed out of the fields, farmers would get a good return on their investment, the state would be on its way to recovery, and the experiment with free labor would have worked.

When Governor Hamilton arrived in Galveston on July 21, he discovered that despite the optimistic outlook, concern with free labor remained a dominant issue among the landowning interests of the state. While planters admitted that their former slaves had gone back to the fields, they now worried whether or not they would be as productive as before emancipation. Many continued to believe that the freedmen would never succeed as free laborers, and Hamilton found that a month of dealing with free workers and the military had encouraged some to believe that they still might be allowed to impose greater restrictions on their former slaves and increase control over labor. Such hopes received additional encouragement by political news from the North, where Democratic politicians and journalists speculated on the inevitability of a split between the president and Congress over Reconstruction policy. Most believed that a victory by President Johnson in such a confrontation would make it easier to impose controls over the former slaves. This complicated the governor's already difficult task of restoring civil government because it led many whites to believe that the North would accept the hoped-for labor restrictions. At least in Texas, delay encouraged hope among whites that full freedom for black workers might be prevented.

Hamilton soon received word that many planters apparently willing to accept almost any demands made by the federal government at the time of the surrender now showed an increasing resistance to Reconstruction policies aiding the freedmen. But the governor was certain of a congressional triumph in a confrontation with Johnson and convinced that the North required full recognition of the freedom of the former slaves. These views placed him on a course toward inevitable conflict with the cotton-growing interests. But Hamilton would find that he had few resources available to ensure his own victory in such a struggle.

The provisional governor quickly set about implementing a plan for restoring civil government, but the spreading belief that Texans did not have to

Andrew J. Hamilton, provisional governor, 1865–66.
PICB-0353 Austin History Center, Austin Public Library

recognize the full freedom of blacks complicated his task. From the beginning he believed that he had to further postpone the restoration of the state to the Union. In a series of public address, in his official proclamations, and particularly in his correspondence with President Johnson, Hamilton presented a clear picture of the course that he had determined. He set about preparing for a convention to rewrite the state constitution, but his actions indicated that he had decided that to be successful, the convention must take measures to placate not just President Johnson but also members of Congress. The basis for Hamilton's conclusion is not clear, but during the war, he had developed a close relationship with many Republican congressmen. When he left Washington for Texas, he may have been aware of the fast developing concern in Congress that the majority of southerners remained disloyal and that the president's Reconstruction policy did not demand enough from the defeated South. Certainly, his behavior represented an appropriate response to the concerns being expressed among both Radical and Moderate Republicans in Congress and among a broad spectrum of northern newspapers.[3]

Delay proved to be Hamilton's solution. President Johnson had offered his appointees little guidance on precisely how they should set about securing loyal governments. The proclamation for Texas had only required that Hamilton arrange an election among loyal citizens for a constitutional convention, which would write a constitution that put the laws of Texas in line with those of the national government and assured the creation of republican government. Hamilton's program insisted that Texans show their loyalty with more than an oath of allegiance, demanding that they show the nation they had accepted the results of the war. He emphasized action on three major issues.

First, Hamilton concluded that the convention must create a constitution that would ensure the freedmen's basic personal rights and guaranteeing them equal treatment under the law. Basically, this involved an assurance that the rights of life, liberty, and property would be protected, but Hamilton wanted an expansion on these basic rights. He particularly urged the extension to freedmen of the right to testify in trials and at one point even believed an extension of suffrage might be warranted. Hamilton did not, however, believe in racial equality. He simply believed that securing these rights for the freedmen would be necessary for Congress to accept Texas' restoration to the Union.

The governor also believed that quieting northern concerns required Texans to take formal steps recognizing the end of slavery. He acknowledged that many whites remained unconvinced of the finality of abolition, having heard of the rumors flying across the state about the federal government's reversal of policy. From the countryside he received word that some slaveowners still held blacks in bondage. If nothing else, these white Texans believed that some other plan could be adopted that would maintain their control over the freedmen. Hamilton concluded, however, that refusing to accept the end of slavery did little to encourage a rapid reconstruction since it encouraged those in Congress who saw the president's policies as a failure to attempt to place further demands on the South. He indicated that Texans had to demonstrate that they had no desire to maintain slavery or to hedge on the idea, hoping it could be resurrected at some point in the future. The governor suggested that the state's representatives should ratify the Thirteenth Amendment, which would place Texans on record not only as accepting emancipation but also as opposing any future restoration of the institution.

Finally, Hamilton concluded that Texans needed to take actions that would assure the North that a restoration to the Union would place the state government in the hands of loyal citizens. Concern in the North that southerners remained rebellious and that the president's policies would allow former Confederates to return to power led to an even closer examination of events in the South beyond issues connected with emancipation or the future of the freedmen. To show their loyalty, Hamilton advised Texans to declare their ordinance of secession null and void from the beginning, thus proclaiming their acceptance of the idea that no legal or constitutional right existed to disrupt the Union. In addition, he thought they must repudiate the debt created to support the war. Hamilton, in a letter to President Johnson, summed up the reasoning that led him to these conclusions. "[S]omething like this," he wrote, "in my judgment, will be expected and demanded by the American people, through their representatives in Congress."[4]

Hamilton realized that implementing this program would be difficult. The governor saw important interests arrayed against him, and he possessed a clear-cut and probably realistic view of the elements of this opposition. The most vocal antagonism he anticipated as coming from those who had led the state into secession and then made war on the Union. This group included many of the men who had controlled the antebellum Democratic party, including the majority of the state's newspaper editors, most of whom usually were closely tied to the Democrats. Hamilton believed that these political leaders would resist an effective reconstruction in part because of their wounded pride and their refusal to accept responsibility for the ruin that their actions had brought on the state. In addition, he believed that such men would not willing give up political power, especially not to those Texans who had opposed them in both secession and war and had emerged as the victors.

While many in the state opposed such measures, Hamilton believed that behind the increasingly vocal opposition to his proposals lay the considerable power of those landowners and merchants whose economic world had been tied to slavery. These men had too much at stake to abandon all hope of retaining some control over their former laborers. They demonstrated open hostility to all efforts at assuring African Americans equal protection under the law of basic rights of life, liberty, and property and looked to the creation of an alternative system of coercive labor. Hamilton thought such feelings prevailed especially among the richest planters, those excluded from the general amnesty because their financial worth was greater than twenty thousand dollars, which led him to adopt a policy of recommending few members of this class to President Johnson for personal pardons.

The governor also recognized a third barrier to his program, the pervasive lawlessness that infected the state and resisted all efforts at restoring order. He saw this as complex problem. Much of it represented a continuation of the local violence that erupted during the war; part of it reflected the frustration of those disappointed in the results of the war and who aimed their anger at the freedmen since they could not safely direct it against the victorious Union. Increasingly, some of it grew from conscious efforts to intimidate freedmen into signing labor contracts. Violence aimed at Unionists returning to the state was yet another part of the disorder. Hamilton feared such conditions did little to encourage the election of a loyal convention. Unfortunately, the absence of either military or civil authority in many counties made it possible for lawless elements to flourish with no fear of punishment.

One of Hamilton's first actions at Galveston was to meet with many local Unionists to determine the current political situation. As a result, he concluded that he existing conditions did not favor his broader agenda. Even some of the prewar Unionists whom he needed to support him balked at the governor's insistence that the freedmen be given equal personal rights. In addition, they insisted that Unionists could not carry an election and advised the governor to delay calling one. Hamilton seemed convinced, and his first priority focused on developing support for his plan and weakening the opposition rather than pushing for an immediate election. His decision to delay became clear on July 25, when he issued a proclamation outlining the process of Reconstruction. He declared that there would be a constitutional convention and that all those who could take the president's Oath of Amnesty would be allowed to vote for delegates. The governor also announced that, as a prelude to an election, there would be a registration of voters. This potentially allowed anyone who did not fall within an excepted category to participate in the process. But none of this would happen immediately. Hamilton simply noted that at a future time he would appoint officials to administer the loyalty oath and register voters, signaling that the reconstruction process in Texas would move at a snail's pace compared with that in the other southern states.

Hamilton, given local conditions, determined that readmission to the Union required him to reorganize local government and place his appointees in positions of authority before calling the election. In other southern states provisional governors had not taken such steps, but in his July 25 proclamation, Hamilton announced that he would appoint all indispensable state, district, and county officials. The definition of "indispensable" ultimately expanded to include virtually every public position. The governor defended his decision on the grounds that conditions in Texas required such action. Given the lawlessness plaguing the state, he argued that a fair administration of the amnesty oath and a fair election required the restoration of order first. Further, the process could not be hurried. When Hamilton arrived at Austin, office seekers inundated him, but he had to solicit information from around the state concerning the loyalty of each applicant. Not until the end of September did newspaper reports indicate he had filled the positions in 103 of approximately 120 counties; only frontier communities virtually abandoned during the war remained without local government.[5]

Hamilton's proclamations and correspondence give a clear picture of the opposition that he believed he faced, and his appointments provide considerable insight into the people he considered his allies. Unionists often asserted that they wanted only loyal men in government positions. The editor of *Flake's Bulletin* at Galveston, the leading Unionist newspaper of the time, stated in one editorial on prospective elections that Unionists wanted to see in office only those who had sympathized with the U.S. government during the war.[6] Such statements may have been intended for northern consumption, however. This definition allowed considerable room for latitude in accommodating prospective allies since sympathy did not mean that the individual had to have shown open support for the Union. Indeed, the governor's appointments indicate that he tried to build a coalition based largely on those opposed to the antebellum Democratic leadership rather than those who had publicly avowed Unionism. He willingly brought even the openly disloyal into the fold when it strengthened his efforts. In short, Hamilton hoped to reconstruct the old Houston party.

The men he named to the principal state offices reflected the governor's broad view of loyalty and his effort at party building. His attorney general was William Alexander, who had practiced law at Galveston prior to secession, then fled to the North with the war's outbreak. Alexander had, in fact, opposed Hamilton's appointment as governor prior to their return to Texas, writing to Francis P. Blair that Unionists other than refugees needed to be consulted on reorganization. Hamilton named Albert H. Latimer comptroller. Latimer, from Red River County, had been a signer of the Texas Declaration of Independence and a member of the Constitutional Convention of 1845. In the secession crisis he had been a Unionist leader in northeastern Texas but remained in the state during the war while his sons served in the Confederate Army. James H. Bell, a lawyer, prewar judge, and planter from Brazoria County, received the appointment of secretary of state. Bell was another Unionist, but he also had remained in Texas during the war and even served as an associate justice on the state supreme court. These three men shared only one major characteristic: they had been part of the antebellum Union party. Hamilton appeared ready to recreate that alliance, no matter what course an individual may have pursued during the war.

The governor carried out his basic ideas about appointments even further in his reorganization of district courts and county governments. The twenty-four district judges that he named shared little in common other than their antebellum politics. They had not pursued similar courses from 1861 to 1865: eight had served in the state or Confederate military during the war, three had been in the state legislature, five had been district judges, and another a district attorney. County appointees followed this trend. The governor filled nearly all county positions with whites who had been in Texas prior to the war's end. Of these, 53 percent had been slaveholders, and 49 percent had previously held elected office. This group also consisted of men who had taken a variety of positions during the war. Some had resigned their office rather than serve under a secessionist government and demonstrated unquestionably loyalty, while others had fought for the Confederacy. None had played a prominent role in the prewar Democratic establishment, however.[7]

Unfortunately for Hamilton, his appointments did not foster the party he wished to create and often created more problems than they solved. Forced to act hastily to restore order, the governor made serious mistakes. In East Texas, one of his appointees to a district judgeship refused to administer the oath of office to Hamilton's appointee to be sheriff of Harrison County, questioning the sheriff-designate's loyalty. The judge charged that the latter had served as sheriff during the war and had used dogs to help Confederate authorities capture escaped Union prisoners being transported through the county. Often appointments set off fights between rival political factions. Local politicians who failed to receive office from the governor were dissatisfied. Some even complained to President Johnson, usually hoping to secure intervention by asserting that Hamilton had appointed rebels to office rather than true Union men.

Despite these problems, as the governor's Reconstruction policies evolved, the importance of his decision to reorganize local governments and place them into hands of men loyal to him became clearer. On August 19 he issued a proclamation outlining the procedure for registering loyal citizens to vote for a constitutional convention. County judges would administer the required oath of loyalty and supervise the registration of voters, assisted by the district and county clerks. The county judge received extensive powers, including the right to interrogate applicants concerning their wartime service and their political views.[8] The directive had important consequences. Observers noted that as the registration progressed large numbers of men eligible to take the oath refused to do so. They speculated that those who refused saw the process as potentially humiliating and consequently did not bother to go through it. Given the attitudes on Reconstruction held by many prospective voters at the time, this potentially worked in Hamilton's favor by securing the representation in the convention that he desired.

The difficulties of restoring civil government, the subsequent slowness of the registration process, and the concerns over the political prospects caused the governor to put off calling a constitutional convention. He faced increasing pressure from people at home and also from the president, but he did not issue an election proclamation until November 15. In it he delayed further, setting the date of the election for two months later, January 8, 1866. The proposed convention would not assemble until February 7.

As Hamilton extended the existence of the provisional state and local governments with the election delays, these entities had to carry out the normal functions of civil authority in addition to those associated with the preparations for a constitutional convention. Given the problem of lawlessness and the considerable concern about the freedmen, opening the court systems represented the most pressing need. In order to do that, however, provisions for financing government operations had to be made. As to the state government, Hamilton had acted almost immediately upon reaching Austin to determine the condition of the state treasury, appointing a commission to examine its records. The commission reported the treasury contained no money and that the state had outstanding debts of nearly $9,000,000. This forced Hamilton to use some of the U.S. bonds given to Texas in exchange for the surrender of claims to the former republic's western territory in 1850 and led the governor into efforts at securing the return of about $130,000 in bonds given up during the war.

During the war, Gov. Pendleton Murrah contracted with George W. White and John Chiles to use these government bonds in order to purchase medicines, hospital stores, and other supplies. Hamilton contended that White had never delivered these materials and demanded restitution, sending Secretary of State James Bell to Washington to negotiate the return of the bonds. Governor Hamilton had complicated Bell's efforts, however, since Hamilton had issued a statement during the war certifying the validity of the bonds to the parties purchasing them from the Confederate state government. In the end the question of the bonds would not be resolved until the Supreme Court heard the case of *Texas v. White*.[9]

Hamilton failed to secure the bonds, which forced him to turn to county taxes. Here lay the importance of why the governor had included among his appointments the naming of local officials to assess and collect taxes. On September 5 Hamilton authorized the assessment for state purposes of an ad valorem tax of 12.5 cents upon each hundred dollars in property except for property exempted by law in 1861. In addition, he authorized a one-dollar poll tax for each male person twenty-one years or older, with the exception of the mentally handicapped and freedmen. He also ordered the collection of occupation taxes that had been in force in March, 1861.

As the provisional government moved forward with the restoration of civil authority and preparations for the constitutional convention, the agency Congress had created to overlook the affairs of the freedmen and the development of a new system of free labor arrived in Texas. Gen. Edgar M. Gregory, assigned to head the Bureau of Refugees, Freedmen, and Abandoned Lands in Texas (commonly called the Freedmen's Bureau), landed in Galveston on September 5. Once he arrived, however, Gregory found extending the bureau's operations into the interior difficult. His lack of manpower necessary to carry out his duty constituted a major problem. The general recruited most of his subagents from the army units stationed in Texas, but many of these men mustered out shortly after the war ended. This meant a short tenure in office for many local bureau agents. Historian Randolph Campbell indicates that by January, 1866, the bureau had managed to hire only twenty-one sub–assistant commissioners. Of these, Gregory assigned them primarily to the towns and villages in the center of the plantation districts along the Gulf Coast.

Gregory reinforced the direction freedmen's affairs had taken under the army. He believed that the bureau had to get blacks to work so they could support themselves, even if this meant restricting their freedom to some degree. On his arrival he made a tour of the counties in eastern Texas to determine what progress had been made toward securing economic independence for the freedmen. He also spoke with the freedmen and urged them to contract their labor to the planters where they resided. Just as his military predecessors, the commissioner offered no suggestions on the details of the new agreements, though he did provide the first statewide outline of mandatory provisions. His few requirements seriously challenged the hopes of those most reluctant to accept black freedom. Gregory stipulated that planters provide contracts ensuring humane treatment of workers and fair compensation and also encouraged them to extend educational opportunities to workers. He also insisted that the terms be written and assured the freedmen that the bureau would enforce their observance.

In addition, the bureau worked to obtain the recognition of the equal rights of blacks in the courts. The successful operation of the contract system of labor required that blacks receive such access. Unless their contractual rights could be ensured legally, little stood in the way of employer exploitation of hired laborers. By the time Gregory arrived in Texas, many employers already had made it clear that they did not take the contracts seriously. As the bureau expanded operations, its agents found that they spent much of their time hearing complaints by workers about employers who did not honor contracts and the lack of any help in enforcing the contracts from the local civil courts.

The bureau had other tasks as well. National administrators had always envisioned the agency as more than an employment office. As the bureau organized in Texas, its mission expanded, particularly as it attempted to establish schools among the freedmen. The agency hired a superintendent of education

Gen. Edgar M. Gregory, Freedmen's Bureau commissioner for Texas, 1865–66.
Courtesy U.S. Army Military History Institute

in the autumn of 1865, Edwin M. Wheelock, a Congregationalist minister who had served as a chaplain to a Union regiment and participated in the U.S. Army's efforts to organize schools in Louisiana during the war. Wheelock opened the bureau's first school at Galveston in September, but he discovered that he could not secure the teachers and supplies necessary to expand the schools to meet the needs of the freedmen. The superintendent did manage to obtained some support from the American Missionary Association, a northern group that sent teachers to work in the bureau schools, but this proved inadequate to meet the overwhelming educational needs of the freedmen. Such problems initially limited the schools' progress. By the end of 1865, the bureau reported only twelve schools and nine teachers active in the entire state. The 615 students enrolled represented only a small portion of those freedmen who needed to develop basic reading and arithmetic skills.

Hamilton's government had been in place a little over a month and the Freedmen's Bureau only some weeks when both confronted a wave of violence that seriously undercut their efforts for the former slaves and helped push Texas Reconstruction along a different path. Through the summer of 1865, observers had commented on the general lawlessness and violence that existed across the state, and frequently directed against the freedmen. Military officials received numerous reports of unoffending blacks shot down or beaten by men simply because of their race. Young white men were often the perpetrators of this brutality, and officials speculated that, at least in part, they acted out of their hatred against the victorious North. Unable to release their frustration safely against northerners or occupying soldiers, criminals directed their anger at the people who could not resist—freedmen and Unionist civilians. But economic reasons may have underlay a large portion of the increased violence as individual landlords and whole communities tried to gain greater control over the freedmen and their labor. In at least one case, when a farmer in Navarro County hired a group of blacks and then started to take them to a plantation in Arkansas, citizens from the surrounding country intercepted the party and returned the laborers to their homes. The mob then surrounded the house of the white farmer and demanded that he leave, threatening to kill him if he ever returned. More frequently this intimidation focused on the workers themselves. Bureau officials also received word that former slaveowners in some parts of the state continued to hold their laborers in bondage.[10]

Violence in the autumn of 1865 had a clearer meaning. As cotton began to be harvested in September, problems for the freedmen intensified. Blacks had faced the hostile outbursts of individual Texans since the war had ended, but the drastic changes in the state's economic prospects that autumn encouraged greater levels of violence. A simple, yet catastrophic, problem set off the outbreak. As has been seen, throughout the summer high cotton prices had encouraged landowners to borrow heavily to get back into cotton cultivation and encouraged them to sign lucrative contracts with the freedmen in order to secure their labor. When the crop went to market, however, buyers offered only half of what they had just months before. In Galveston, prices started at 20–21 cents for middling cotton in September, 1865, rose to 30.5–31.5 cents by November, then peaked at 32 cents in February, 1866. Most farmers had planned their operations based on the 50-cent price that held in the summer of 1865. With the drop the wages promised to workers when they signed contracts looked onerous. Landowners faced a difficult problem—they had to pay not only for the money they had borrowed but also for the wages of their workers.

As the harvest progressed, civil and military officials received increasing numbers of complaints from freedmen. These reports indicated that many landlords tried to cheat their workers out of their share of the harvest. In the eastern counties, planters who had immigrated to Texas during the war harvested their crop, sold it, and then left the state without having paid their workers. In areas away from occupying forces, officials estimated that nine out of ten employers had refused to make a cash settlement with their workers. In a common ploy used by many, landowners drove their workers away from their farms and then claimed the freedmen had broken their contracts and did not have to be paid. Some may even have used local gangs to raid their own plantations, where they beat workers and threatened even-more-dire violence to secure the planter's goal. Any worker who resisted intimidation might well end up dead. In the first year of freedom, bureau officials catalogued the murder of some thirty-eight freedmen.

The provisional government recognized this violence as a threat to restoring loyal government. Military and bureau officials also condemned it. Neither the Hamilton government nor the federal government, however, proved capable of stopping the attacks. One of Hamilton's major priorities had been putting the state's judiciary system back into operation to restore order prior to a general election. Law officers and the courts might have been able to handle individual cases of violence, but the system failed to deal with the general upheaval of that fall. In September the governor had warned military authorities that he did not believe civil authorities would be able to protect the freedmen without the help of the army.

Not only did Hamilton lack the manpower to protect the freedmen against the actions of the larger white community, but also some of his supporters lacked the will. The absence of a clear concern with the problem may be seen in the divisions among Hamilton's judiciary appointees on one issue critical to protecting the rights of blacks, the place of the freedmen in the courts. As the courts reopened, some justices allowed the freedmen complete equality in their courts to initiate proceedings, testify against whites, and serve on juries. Most, however, seriously restricted the rights of African Americans. Hamilton had directed the judges to operate according to the laws in force in 1861, but at that time blacks had no rights in the justice system. The refusal to allow something as fundamental as testimony in cases produced judgments that embarrassed the administration. In one such instance, in Harrison County, whites had whipped and then beaten to death an African American woman named Lucy Grimes. The chief justice of the county refused to issue an arrest warrant because the only evidence came from a black person, the son of the murdered woman.[11] Given such ambivalence on the part of some judges, the courts offered little protection for black rights, even under Hamilton's government.

The military had the will to act against violence but lacked the manpower. Hamilton looked to the army to restore order and requested the continued presence of the state of a sizeable military force. Unfortunately for the governor, this hope ran counter to the broader national desire to demobilize the army as quickly as possible. This downsizing already had hamstrung the operations of the Freedmen's Bureau, and now it also made it impossible for the army to protect the freedmen. The state still had a large military force of 45,424 men in it as late as September, 1865. The army posted most of these soldiers to the Mexican border to demonstrate U.S. opposition to French intervention in that country; the rest went to the western frontier to fight Indians. This left few troops to police the interior counties. These numbers declined even further when the French adventure in Mexico ended and the army withdrew most of its units along the border. By February, 1866, fewer than 5,000 troops remained in the state, most of them assigned to the frontier. Quite simply, the army never had the resources necessary to sustain the efforts of either the Hamilton administration or the Freedmen's Bureau.[12]

As the first year of freedom ended and the election of delegates to a constitutional convention approached, the plan of Reconstruction initiated by Governor Hamilton already had encountered serious problems. His government had supported the idea of protecting the freedmen in their rights, and that decision had placed it in opposition to the mainstream of thought held by most Texans. This allowed the governor's opponents to charge the provisional government with being an instrument of the congressional Radicals, interested in imposing social equality on Texas society. This setting, flavored by issues of national politics and race hostility, did not favor an election that promised to produce results acceptable to those northerners who looked for some acceptance from the South of the military defeat visited on it hardly six months earlier.

Chapter 3

CONSERVATIVE RESURGENCE

Governor Hamilton had set Texas on a course that could have produced significant changes. Along with the army and the Freedmen's Bureau, his administration hoped to secure minimum civil rights for the freedmen and supported efforts to that end. He had considered the protection of these rights as essential to ensuring their economic freedom, and success might have changed the economic lives of many African Americans in future years. At the same time, the governor worked at building a new political party. Its success would have challenged the political power of the interests that had dominated Texas in the antebellum years, even though the new party's own interests were not yet fully shaped. Events in 1866 would determine whether or not the state could move along the course set out by the provisional governor. In January the people of Texas would go to the polls for the first time since the war to elect delegates to a constitutional convention, which would convene in February. Afterward voters would have the chance to elect state officials and establish a new government. Rather than seeing the implementation of Hamilton's goals, 1866 evidenced the rapidly shifting foundations of postwar Texas politics, showed the tenacity in the face of those who had held power in the antebellum years, and placed Texas on a course considerably different from that espoused by the provisional governor.

While Hamilton worked to build the Union party in preparation for the upcoming struggles, opposition to his efforts quickly took shape. In the months prior to the election of delegates, this opposition failed to coalesce into a formal party, but various different political leaders and interests worked together against the provisional government. The broader individual goals of these various opponents often contradicted each other; the future produced serious disagreements on policy. Still, antagonism toward Governor Hamilton's political and racial policies united them, and this hostility proved a strong bond. They embraced the name Conservative Unionists to avoid a party label that might have made it more difficult for individuals from a wide variety of political persuasions to participate. It also kept northerners from raising questions their loyalty. From the beginning this opposition represented a formidable barrier to the fulfillment of Hamilton's plans.

By the autumn of 1865, newspaper editorials and private correspondence had begun to mark the lines of future political battles and to distinguish the important elements. The position of James W. Throckmorton, a prewar Unionist and an important leader from the northeastern counties along Red River, posed a particular threat to efforts because it seriously weakened the Union party. His opposition to Hamilton emerged to a considerable degree from personal hostility. Throckmorton had been one of the delegates who voted against secession in the convention of 1861, but he went with Texas upon the outbreak of war and ultimately served as a Confederate officer on the frontier. He clearly believed that those men who had not supported their state had no claim on leadership, even though they had gone with the victorious side. He also found himself at odds with Hamilton's insistence that the freedmen receive basic civil rights, and though willing to accept emancipation, he could go no further. Throckmorton's refusal to support the new Union party deprived it of an important leader. His desertion seriously undermined the party's hopes of securing support in the antebellum Unionist counties in the northeast.

The refusal of another prominent Unionist to join with Hamilton created further problems. John Hancock, an attorney and politician, had been ejected from the state legislature in 1861 after he would not take the oath of allegiance to the Confederacy. Unlike Throckmorton, Hancock refused to support the rebels. He remained in Texas and practiced law in the state courts until 1864, when he left and traveled to the North. He became involved in Democratic party politics there and supported George B. McClellan for the presidency in the 1864 election. In the summer and autumn of 1865, national Democratic leaders decided to support President Johnson in his growing dispute with Congress. Hancock also concluded that Johnson would win this battle and that, because of this, Texas did not need to go as far as Hamilton desired regarding the freedmen in order to reestablish normal relations within the Union. He subsequently played a major role in encouraging opponents of the governor's program to believe that they could resist it successfully and in bringing them together as a political group.

It is not clear that Hancock attracted any significant antiwar supporters from the Union party, but he played a considerable role in the development of postwar politics. When the war ended, many who had led or supported the Democrats accepted defeat and emancipation but still waited to see what chance they had to influence government policy. Hancock's opposition to Governor Hamilton and his insistence that the president would win his conflict with Congress encouraged these men, usually referred to as moderate Democrats because of their willingness to accept the war's results, to believe that they would be allowed to reconstruct the state with a minimum of change in race and labor relations or with any dislocation of prewar political relations. Antebellum Democratic political leaders who embraced this view included stalwarts such as Ashbel Smith of Galveston. These men maintained a low profile, but Willard Richardson, the editor of the *Galveston News,* became the voice of the "moderates."

The moderate Democrats viewed regaining control of the state government as critical. While willing to accept emancipation, they still saw much at stake in exercising power. The problems of free labor and the freedmen provided their central concern. Moderate Democrats also generally supported what one public meeting at Fort Bend County described as an equitable policy toward the blacks, "one calculated to elevate them as a class." But their racial views and their early experience with free labor during the summer of 1865 had led them to conclude that African Americans required some sort of restraints upon their independence. They looked particularly to the creation of some system of coercion, sanctioned by the state, so that the freedmen's labor would be secured. To do that, the state had to be restored to the Union, and those who understood the "problem" had to control the government. The editor of the *Galveston News* concluded that an effort in Texas might even become the first step toward developing a national policy that would work to this end. "The government is strong enough to keep four millions of negroes in order," he wrote, "provided it can receive the right influences and obtain the proper representations." [1]

Other issues, less obvious than the general concern with labor, also motivated some moderates to seek a rapid return to power. Hamilton had made it clear that his government would treat some of the wartime actions of the Texas governors and legislature in support of the Confederacy to be illegal. In addition, he had indicated his desire to prosecute as criminals some men who had acted in behalf of the Confederacy. Only the refusal of Gen. Philip Sheridan, the U.S. military commander in Texas, kept Hamilton from forming a military commission to try such cases in the autumn of 1865. If the governor's supporters gained control over the restored government, they had the potential of damaging some of the state's most important economic interests if they pursued such prosecutions in the state courts. For example, many considered the legislation allowing railroads to pay their debts to the state in Confederate notes rather than in specie supportive of the Confederate war effort and believed those companies should be made to repay this obligation. A Unionist government might also proceed with efforts at prosecuting prominent Texans who had acted in behalf of the Confederacy, particularly those who had acted as receivers of confiscated property or as military officers who had persecuted Union men. Unionist courts might look favorably on civil suits against the same men for the payment of damages suffered by Unionists for property lost. For companies and individuals facing potential court action, securing a government that might look more favorably on their situation proved a major goal.

Finally, at least a few diehard Confederates joined this opposition to Hamilton's administration. In the campaign for seats in the constitutional convention, some made their pro-Confederate positions clear, though most tended not to blatantly express such views. John Burke of Harrison County, who had served as a colonel in Hood's Texas Brigade, typified the more-radical Confederate politicians. In his campaign Burke stated that he accepted the fact that slavery had ended, but he opposed ratification of the Thirteenth Amendment. Furthermore, he stood against repudiating the state's war debt. He also voiced his opposition to declaring the ordinance of secession null and void or renouncing the right of secession. What motivated men like Burke to believe that they could avoid these consequences of defeat is unclear, but they clearly believed that by regaining control over Reconstruction, they could undo the military results of the war and avoid the personal humiliation of submission. Such men would have opposed Governor Hamilton no matter what his policy.

Emerging out of varying concerns and needs, advocating a wide variety of positions, and espousing hostility to Governor Hamilton, the political opposition that developed in Texas throughout the fall of 1865 tied itself to President Johnson on the national scene and placed itself in opposition to congressional Radicals. The national Democratic party generated much of the rhetoric used by this group and provided it with arguments for its position less confrontational, more justifiable, and more congenial to many northerners. The state's Conservative Unionists increasingly returned to their antebellum political rhetoric, asserting that their opposition to Hamilton and Congress derived not from their racial hostility, but rather from their support of the idea of states' rights. They insisted that they simply sought a return of power to the states, including that over questions of civil and political rights, for constitutional reasons, not to block the changes inherent in Reconstruction. They cloaked their interests in constitutional arguments.

By the summer of 1865, Texas newspapers had speculated on the split between Congress and Johnson and its implications for Texas. On the one hand, most Texans perceived the Radical Republicans as bent upon continuing the centralizing tendencies of government begun during the war. This would mean that they also intended to limit states' rights. To accomplish this, Texans believed the Radicals intended to extend the franchise to the freedmen. On the other hand, Texans perceived the president as supporting a return to limited government and opposing black suffrage. Both issues had implications for the state, and most old leaders saw taking a position as a political necessity. By the time Hamilton called the constitutional convention, Conservative Unionists had come to believe that preventing the Republican party from achieving its goal of greater centralization and returning power to the states required blocking the imposition of black suffrage on the southern states. "Against the new and radical measures which the dominant party in Congress will strive to enforce upon us," the editor of the Conservative *Galveston News* wrote, "there is, among our people, union of opinion and feeling, and a spirit of uncompromising hostility."[2]

All of these issues played a role in the canvass leading up to the January election of delegates. Differences still existed among the Conservatives, but three major themes emerged in the electioneering. The first emphasized their opposition to a further extension of civil rights for freedmen. In their speeches and in newspaper editorials, opposition candidates asked voters to support them because they would fight even the most modest extension of civil rights. Their explanations invariably rested on racial fears. Surrendering on any issue would be tantamount to opening the flood gates. Allowing blacks to testify in courts would lead to blacks sitting on juries, then to suffrage, and finally to total social and political equality.

The second theme stressed Conservative support for President Johnson in his growing dispute with Congress. An army officer reported that in the Houston area, the politically active viewed the national government as divided into two parties, that of the president and that of Congress, generally referred to by most Texans as the "Radicals." He believed most felt particularly bitter toward the latter.[3] They hated the Radicals particularly because some, though not a majority, now proposed to extend suffrage to freedmen, a step even more threatening than the offer of basic civil rights that already had created such concern. Candidates urged voters to support them as a sign of support for the president, who they indicated stood between the South and a Radical Reconstruction at the hands of Congress.

Conservatives also embraced a third campaign tactic, claiming their right to public support because of their war records. In speeches they insisted that Unionists had been traitors to the people of the state—Conservatives had stood by Texas and the Confederacy, even if some of them had not supported secession—and often recounted their own war service. Texans confronted another crisis now, and they assured voters that the Conservatives could be counted on to uphold local interests in the face of a renewed attack on states' rights and individual freedoms by the national government.

The men who supported the governor in the canvass called themselves Unionists, although their opponents labeled them "Radical Unionists" because of their alleged sympathy with the Radical Republicans in Congress. Like the governor, they campaigned for votes by claiming that they represented the only party that could bring about a successful end to Reconstruction. They had come to believe that most northerners now believed that the southern states must ensure basic civil rights for the freedmen, including allowing them to testify in trials and sit on juries. These Unionists interpreted the flow of events in the North correctly and had concluded that only the protection of these rights could prevent further intervention. Their opponents charged that the Radicals had accepted black suffrage, but no Radical Unionist candidate for the constitutional convention ran on such a platform. Nonetheless, their opponents argued that even if the individual candidate opposed suffrage, their position on Reconstruction made possible a national victory for the Radicals and opened the way for that ultimate end.

Given the interests at stake, the January 8 election of delegates passed quietly. More surprisingly, few voters turned out. While 127 of 134 organized counties held elections, fewer than twenty-eight thousand voters went to the polls. This represented only 44 percent of the number who had voted in the 1861 election on the question of secession. The turnout confounded contemporary politicians, who searched for explanations. Some believed that a lack of eminent candidates and the absence of unanimity among the population on the issues fostered the disappointing numbers. Others blamed bad weather on election day. James Throckmorton believed that most Texans did not vote because they thought if they expressed their true feelings, they would be overridden anyway. Federal policy, however, had not excluded most residents from voting.[4]

Although the precise results of the election would not be fully known until the assembly of the convention, most observers concluded that Hamilton's opponents had won the day. Military officers who had observed the elections reported that successful candidates had usually campaigned on their war records as Confederate soldiers or on their opposition to Reconstruction. The governor reported to President Johnson that virtually no Unionist had been chosen. Hamilton clearly had failed disastrously in his efforts at developing a majority party based upon prewar loyalty. The task of completing the president's Reconstruction program would be in the hands of men who Hamilton considered his enemies, and he feared they would do little to adopt policies ultimately acceptable to the North.

When delegates assembled at Austin on February 7, the character of the convention clearly justified Hamilton's concerns. A correspondent of the *New York Times* reported from Austin that the convention contained men from all political parties, including those he described as Radical Unionists, Conservative Unionists, and secessionists. Hamilton's supporters composed the first group. Men such as Throckmorton and Hancock figured prominently among the Conservative Unionist. Secessionists included men like Oran M. Roberts, the president of the secession convention in 1861, colonel of the Eleventh Texas Infantry, and chief justice of the state's wartime supreme court. Initially, it appeared that the secessionist faction held a majority. Service to the Confederacy constituted the one thing that most of the ninety delegates who appeared at Austin had in common. More than a third of them had held commissions as officers in the Confederate Army, and perhaps another third had served as enlisted men.[5]

Many who had served in the Confederate Army or supported secession did not prove to be among the diehards, however. As has been seen, some who had supported the Confederacy had originally been Unionists. Others, including some who had backed secession, had decided to accept the outcome of the war. Hamilton realized that the election had spelled the doom of the coalition he sought to forge in the last half of 1865, but he continued to be confident that the convention would produce results acceptable to the North. Five days after the convention assembled, he optimistically telegraphed President Johnson that, despite the presence of "violent & impractical men" in the hall, he still hoped that the convention would act favorably. In telegrams sent on February 20 and 27, he retained this optimism, and in the latter he noted a daily improvement in the "temper" of the delegates.[6]

The election of the president of the convention turned into a test of the relative power and identity of the various factions. Radical Unionists and Conservative Unionists quickly showed their presence, but the so-called secessionists actually turned out to be those Democrats who refused to surrender their party identity to fusion with Throckmorton. Even they divided between groups referred to as radicals and moderates. In the election of the president, all groups put forward their candidates. The Radical Unionists nominated Albert H. Latimer, the Conservative Unionists James W. Throckmorton, the radical secessionists former governor Hardin R. Runnels, and the moderates William Taylor of Houston County. The first ballot clearly indicated that Runnels and Taylor did not have the votes to win, and they withdrew in favor of Throckmorton to block any chance the Radical Unionists had for success. Throckmorton won on the second ballot by a vote of forty-one to twenty-one. The twenty-one who voted against him constituted the core voting strength for the Radical Unionists. Several of the secessionist radicals refrained from voting.

Struggles between the factions continued following Throckmorton's election when a Radical Unionist, Isaiah A. Paschal, introduced a resolution calling for members to swear the oath of allegiance, generally known as the "test oath." Most ex-Confederates found this objectionable because it required them to swear that they had never "voluntarily borne arms" or "voluntarily given aid" to those who had borne arms against the government of the United States. The oath also placed a further restriction on membership since it excluded all who had held any office under the state or Confederate government during the war. Paschal's resolution failed to secure a majority, and an alternative resolution, offered by the Conservative Unionist John Hancock, that required only those who had not taken the amnesty oath to do so, passed by a vote of forty-one to thirty-nine. After a night of lobbying, however, the delegates again took up Paschal's measure the next day and passed it. Eleven men, including future Democratic political leaders DeWitt C. Giddings and John Ireland and former governor Hardin Runnels, showed their diehard attitude by voting against it. In the end the convention excluded none of the elected members for failing to take the oath.

The character of the majority of delegates did not favor the implementation of Hamilton's program, but the divisions among the governor's opponents encouraged him to believe that some might still be carried through, that is, with careful manipulation. Hamilton delivered his message to the convention on the day following the oath debate. He outlined the steps he believed essential to the state's readmission to the Union: the delegates needed to renounce the right of secession; ratify the Thirteenth Amendment, showing their acceptance of abolition; repudiate the state's war debt; and grant freedmen the civil rights and privileges to which they were entitled as citizens. Hamilton went so far as to propose that the convention consider measures giving blacks limited suffrage. By the time of the Texas convention, events in other states indicated that northern concern with events in the South had become significant enough that Congress had delayed readmitting any of the other former Confederate states. Hamilton warned the delegates that the same fate awaited Texas unless the convention acted decisively to show their willingness to accept the results of the war.

Over the next two months, the convention took up each of Hamilton's items, though it also considered a wide variety of other matters. The first major debate developed on February 13 over the question of how to deal with the ordinance of secession. Radical Unionists proposed that it be declared null and void from the beginning, a position that became known as *ab initio*. Conservative Unionists and secessionists offered alternatives simply stating that the ordinance was void as a result of the war. The convention did not dispose of this business until March 12, when, by a vote of forty-three to thirty-seven, they authorized a resolution declaring secession null and void and renouncing the right of secession.

The amount of time spent on this single piece of business indicated its critical character in the postwar political scene. It proved to be the one issue that most deeply divided the members of the convention. Historian John Carrier believed that secessionists considered the issue so repugnant because it required them to admit not only that they had been defeated in battle but also that they had acted illegally, even treasonously, in seceding. Yet he also recognized that some feared the legal ramifications of such a declaration, that they recognized how it potentially threatened to invalidate every marriage, contract, and debt made since the ordinance's passage.[7]

The ease with which delegates passed a measure nullifying the state debt suggests that of the two, the implications of *ab initio* upon obligations contracted during the war sparked the greatest amount of concern. Nullification of the state debt should have been equally repugnant to the diehard Confederates in the convention, though some opposition did exist. On March 15, however, only two weeks after a proposal came to the floor, the delegates passed it by a vote of forty- nine to twenty-eight. They declared all of the state debt, except for the unpaid obligations of the Republic, to be null and void. The majority showed none of the same reluctance to nullify Confederate war debt that they showed on the question of *ab initio.*

Some delegates had hoped to confine the convention to consider only Reconstruction issues. The majority, however, agreed on the need to carry out other legislative functions. The issues introduced further suggest the widespread concern with the legal implications of the Confederacy's defeat. The delegates repeatedly acted to assure that defeat did not impair any private contracts made during the war, disturb judicial findings, or open the way for the prosecution of Confederate officials. In one action tantamount to legislation and closely connected to the issues raised by *ab initio,* the convention declared all acts of the courts and their officers and by the executive and his agents that did not conflict with the U.S. Constitution and had not been specifically nullified to be valid. In another measure the delegates banned suits against or the prosecution of officials acting under the authority of the Confederate Congress or the state government. The convention's actions recognized the legitimacy of most of the actions of the state's judiciary and executive and relieved them of future liability.

In a variety of ways, the delegates also moved to clear the way for the state's economic development. They demonstrated their great concern by adding a new section to the article on general provisions in the state constitution that allowed the government to guarantee the bonds of railroad companies. This authorized the state to issue fifteen thousand dollars in bonds for each mile of railway constructed, an action that changed the traditional policy of land grants in effect before the war. Their action on *ab initio* also strengthened the railroads, accepting their payment of state debts in Confederate money and freeing them to borrow more money for future expansion.

On questions concerning the civil rights of freedmen, the convention actually witnessed relatively little debate. The members quickly tabled a proposal by Edmund J. Davis to leave out any references to race or color in the suffrage provision of the constitution. On the issue of the rights of blacks before the state's courts, the convention accepted a provision that allowed their testimony in court only in cases that involved them, though it gave the legislature power to authorize testimony in other cases. The original bill came from the secessionist Oran Roberts, but it brought together the secessionists with the Throckmorton and Hancock Conservative Unionists in one of the most lopsided votes of the convention, passing fifty-six to twenty-six. That the majority agreed to allow any black testimony at all may have indicated an increasing awareness of growing northern concern with southern affairs. The measure clearly indicated the furthest a majority of the delegates would go in their guaranteeing legal rights to the freedmen.

Given the basic unwillingness of the white majority to extend full legal rights to blacks, their other actions regarding the freedmen presented no surprises. Delegates excluded blacks from the various benefits provided by the state. The new constitution specifically refused them any access to the state's general school fund. They also banned marriages between whites and blacks and denied freedmen the right to hold state offices. To avoid any federal interference with state elections, the majority excluded blacks from being counted in the apportionment for representatives.

Before adjourning, the delegates approved the state constitution as it had existed in 1845 with the amendments on secession, the war debt, and the freedmen to be in force but provided for an election on June 25, 1866, to consider ratifying the whole document. Voters would have the choice of accepting the revised constitution with the various acts of the convention as a whole package or voting it down. If it failed to pass, the state would be governed by the Constitution of 1845. The convention also provided for the election of state officials on the same date, the winners to take office on the first Monday in August. After these final steps, the convention adjourned on April 2, 1866.

The political factions that had developed prior to the meeting at Austin had continued to jockey for position for the upcoming election throughout the sitting of the convention. The secessionist delegates, those who had been leaders of the Democratic party before the war, realized that their political future required an abandonment of their prewar issues. Indeed, their performance in the convention had indicated this awareness. While they wished to minimize changes in Texas, they understood that they must show a willingness to accommodate some northern demands. Showing further their understanding of the situation, during the convention they had approached James Throckmorton to suggest that he head a coalition ticket in the first postwar gubernatorial campaign.

Throckmorton had worked well with both the Conservative Unionists and the old Democrats in the convention. The support the latter gave him clearly flattered him. He agreed to head a ticket along with former secessionist George W. Jones and numerous other like-minded candidates. A meeting that styled itself the Conservative Union Caucus put forward this ticket on April 2 at Austin. In addition to adopting a slate of candidates, the caucus announced its support of three principles: opposition to African American political equality, opposition to the racial program of Congressional Reconstruction (referring to the Civil Rights Act then before Congress); and support of

President Johnson. The caucus dubbed their movement the Conservative Union party.

The Unionists had more trouble preparing for the upcoming election. The constitutional convention was dispiriting. From the beginning the Unionists knew they had no chance of controlling the proceedings. But the actions of the convention convinced them that their opponents were successfully avoiding any acceptance of the changes demanded by defeat, those considered essential by the northerners for readmittance. Radical Unionists organized for the general election anyway, even though most believed they had little chance for success. A caucus organized the Union party to challenge the Conservative Unionists. In an address to the people of Texas, they condemned the failures of the convention to declare the secession ordinance null and void *ab initio* or to follow through on the president's plan of Reconstruction. They charged the Conservatives with trying to reverse the results of the war.

The caucus first asked Andrew Hamilton to run as their candidate for governor. Hamilton refused. In a letter to the Republican majority in Congress, he indicated his basic reason, that he could not support any government organized under the proposed constitution. In his place the caucus chose former governor Elisha M. Pease. A prewar Unionist, Pease had managed to remain at home in Austin during the conflict. He possessed pure credentials as a Unionist, yet at the same time his having remained in Texas left him relatively immune to charges of treason, unlike those who had left and fought against the Confederacy. He appeared on the ticket with other antebellum Unionists, showing again the effort being made to reconstruct the 1859 Houston coalition. Along with Pease, the caucus ran men of clear Union lineage such as James Bell, who sought a place on the Texas Supreme Court.

In the canvass Union candidates generally emphasized the same themes. Pease himself criticized the convention for its failure to provide for the education of African Americans and its restrictions on their testimony in the courts. Such actions would ensure congressional intervention in the state and produce the very results the Conservatives said they did not want. Pease and Bell both warned voters that unless they elected men acceptable to Congress, they could guarantee that body would respond ultimately with measures requiring the enfranchisement of blacks. They warned also of the probability that Congress would enact more stringent measures disfranchising disloyal whites.

The party initially tried to retain those Unionist voters who supported Throckmorton. When they announced their candidate for lieutenant governor, they named Benjamin H. Epperson, a friend of Throckmorton from northeastern Texas, which gave the ticket regional balance and some appeal for Unionists of Throckmorton's ilk. Politically ambitious, Epperson had considered running for governor if an election had been held in 1865. He may initially have agreed to run but ultimately withdrew. His reasons remain unclear, but Throckmorton contacted his friend and encouraged him not to run at all, going so far as to promise to support him in a bid for the U.S. Senate if he would withdraw from the Union ticket. With Epperson's withdrawal, Pease lost any possibility that he could gain much strength from northeastern Unionists at Throckmorton's expense, which virtually ensured a defeat.

The Conservative Union party's candidates ran on essentially the same theme that anti-Hamilton candidates had used in their bid for the convention the previous February. Their first position once again insisted that they best represented the policies of President Johnson and that support for them offered support for the president. The second asserted that a vote for the Union party represented a vote for the policies of Congress, and if congressional Radicals were victorious in their fight with Johnson, they would overthrow the work of Reconstruction already undertaken. Indeed, Conservative Unionists recognized that Congress might even impose black suffrage on the South. Furthermore, they argued that a vote for Union party candidates would assure the strengthening of the powers of the central government at the expense of the states' rights. In addition, in both state and local races, Conservative Unionists once again attacked their opponents for their opposition to the Confederacy during the war, charging them as having been disloyal to Texas and its people. In Colorado County the local newspaper included the military record of each candidate in its endorsement of the Conservative ticket.

In part, the focus on Congress and the Union party as proponents of African American equality allowed the Conservative Unionists to avoid issues that may have divided the unnatural alliance of prewar Democrats and Unionists who supported Throckmorton. The convention had in many ways reflected the economic policies of men like Throckmorton, especially in its liberal support of railroad construction. It also had expanded terms of office and increased salaries for officials, actions opposed by many old Democrats who had long insisted on a limited state government. Offering themselves as the only party that stood between the masses of whites and black equality, however, the Conservatives submerged these other issues; no one considered them in the campaign.

The Union party, however, conducted what could at best be called a disheartened campaign. Pease did not believe that he could win but at least put forward a platform calling for reform of the executive and legislative branches, redistribution of the tax burden, and the promotion of immigration and transportation, frontier defense, and education. He actively denied charges that he favored black suffrage, though he did make clear that if Congress imposed this requirement on the state for readmission, he would accept it. Hamilton, who might have campaigned for the party, appeared to reflect the general consensus that defeat was inevitable when he left the state for Washington to lobby for congressional action against Johnson's policies and a new intervention in southern affairs.

Efforts at creating organizations to support Unionist candidates across the state reinforced the sense of doom pervasive among most Radical Unionist leaders. They found few men willing to stand with them and believed that this was the result, in part, of the pervasive fear of secessionists many still felt. They also concluded that the majority of Unionists had accepted Conservative arguments that Johnson would win in his struggle with Congress and that supporting the president was the quickest way to end Reconstruction. With no one willing to put himself in open opposition to those widely believed to be the ultimate winners, the Unionists failed to organize. With no organization, they had no chance at all.

Still, the Conservatives did not take their victory for granted. On May 31 Governor Hamilton had issued a proclamation clarifying the qualifications for voters in the upcoming election. Some politicians had concluded that those stated in the proposed constitution would apply in the election, but Hamilton made it clear that no one could vote who could not show he had subscribed to the amnesty oath or had obtained a special pardon from the president. Conservative leaders feared that this would limit the vote for their candidates. since many who supported them would not cast a ballot rather than take the oath, which required them to support the laws and proclamations related to emancipation, considered by many of them to be illegal. The editor of the *Galveston News* urged them to take the oath anyway. "We are not called upon to adjudicate upon the constitutionality of these laws," he wrote. "We are simply bound to obey them until they are set aside."[8]

Turnout in the June 25 election indicated that efforts to convince voters of the critical nature of the election for the future of the state had worked. The two gubernatorial candidates received a combined total of 61,345 votes, representing an increase in the absolute number of participants over the 1861 referendum on secession. The figure also showed a slightly smaller percentage of adult white males than that voting in 1861, but the election appeared to reflect a recovery of interest in state politics from the convention election. It also indicated that the registration carried out by the provisional government had done little to restrict the number of persons who either legally or illegally voted.

The results confirmed the worst fears of the Unionists. Throckmorton won handily, securing 49,277 ballots to Pease's 12,068. Such a victory assured the success of most Conservative Union candidates for other state and local offices as well and indicated the breadth and strength of the coalition. Throckmorton handily carried traditional Democratic counties as well as all of those in northeastern Texas that had voted against secession in 1861. Pease had managed to win the votes of only hardcore wartime Unionists throughout the state. He succeeded in getting a majority vote in the counties of central Texas with sizeable concentrations of German voters, though they may have opposed Throckmorton as much for his prewar nativist politics as for his wartime positions. Counties along the Mexican border, where white Unionists successfully brought Mexican American voters to the polls for Pease, provided the only other good news for the candidate.

Voters also ratified the new constitution. Roughly 10,000 fewer ballots were cast on the ratification issue than in the gubernatorial canvass. The tally for the constitution was only 28,119 votes to 23,400. At least part of the vote against the constitution came from Unionists, who by defeating it could prevent the new government from taking power. Yet the numbers indicate that many who supported Throckmorton also voted against the constitution or failed to vote on the issue at all. About the only explanation that voting patterns can give for this behavior is that many who remained secessionists at heart preferred to remain outside the Union rather than in and that their votes were designed to defeat the constitution, if possible, but to elect Throckmorton in the event that it was adopted. Certainly, the election indicates the complex character of Throckmorton's support in 1866.

The Conservative Unionist coalition had successfully imposed barriers to the implementation of much of Governor Hamilton's plan in the constitutional convention. At the same time, they had demonstrated a willingness to moderate their own stand on some issues when necessity demanded. It remained to be seen whether or not Throckmorton and the moderate Democrats could carry the state on a course that would produce a successful Reconstruction. Even before the governor-elect took office, however, the Radical Unionists had moved the fight to control the Texas government to Washington, where pressure increased in Congress to intervene against the Johnson-appointed governments elsewhere in the South. The Throckmorton administration faced the difficult task of rebuilding the state while convincing the North that it was indeed the loyal government demanded by Congress.

Chapter 4

The Throckmorton Administration

When Governor Throckmorton and the legislature arrived in Austin in August, 1866, the new government faced not only a wide variety of internal problems but also growing concern in the North with the course of the provisional governments already established in the South. By the spring of 1866, even moderate Republicans in Congress expected these governments to be loyal and willing to protect the basic civil rights of freedmen but found reasons to doubt that they were either. The election of large numbers of ex-Confederates to state and local offices, plus the continued violence against blacks, raised grave concerns. In response Congress had pushed forward further measures to secure the goals of the war, passing them over President Johnson's vetoes. One bill not only extended the life of the Freedmen's Bureau but also gave it legal jurisdiction over cases where blacks were denied basic civil liberties. A second, the Civil Rights Bill, tried to define those rights inherent in American citizenship and empowered federal courts to step in when state officials failed to protect them. Finally, Congress had refused to seat any of the House or Senate members elected from the former Confederate states, thus delaying a real end to Reconstruction.

The new Texas government thus had clear warning of the congressional majority's concerns and its intention to reject state governments it considered disloyal or that refused to protect freedmen. Over the course of the next year, the legislature and the governor pursued policies destined to bring them into conflict with federal authorities and doom any chance that Texas might enjoy early readmission to the Union and avoid the fate of the rest of the South.

The new state legislature convened at Austin on August 6. Three days later, with his election certified by the assembly, James Throckmorton assumed the office of governor. In his inaugural address he set the agenda for the session, urging legislators to attend to a variety of issues. His central concern was that they take no action that would raise questions in the North concerning the government's loyalty, indicating clearly his own awareness of the complex national political picture. Much of his message concerned noncontroversial needs of the state, and he urged lawmakers to consider measures that would promote immigration, foster internal improvements, and encourage development of a system of public education. At the same time, Throckmorton gave advice on issues that other southern states had addressed in a way that had provoked controversy. He suggested that the legislature not act on the Thirteenth Amendment since it was already assured of ratification. The governor also urged them not to ratify the Fourteenth Amendment, which created national citizenship and extended basic civil rights to all citizens. Finally, he supported some sort of system regulating labor; although aware of northern hostility to labor codes elsewhere, he counseled measures that would guarantee the protection of law to all Texans.

The men who had been elected on the Conservative Union ticket, despite their differences, generally followed the governor's advice. Their general consensus did not prevent a struggle between the two factions over the election of U.S. senators, however. The House appeared to have a moderate majority and elected a Unionist to be Speaker, but Conservatives had a majority in the general assembly and did not appear willing to compromise with the Unionists in the selection of these officials. John Hancock and Ben Epperson, both Unionist supporters of Throckmorton, ran against Oran M. Roberts and David G. Burnet, both prominent secessionists. In the polling Roberts and Burnet, neither of whom could take the test oath required of congressmen, carried the day. After this triumph, the Conservatives appeared willing to follow Throckmorton's lead and acted, especially in comparison to other former Confederate states, with moderation.

The general cooperation between Conservative Union factions reappeared after the election of senators. They acted as a unit again when the assembly considered ratification of the Thirteenth and Fourteenth Amendments. Throckmorton's opposition to this found strong support among legislators. They accepted his recommendation on the Thirteenth Amendment and did not bother to act on it while rejecting the Fourteenth Amendment outright, declaring their opposition to a measure they believed was intended to degrade the South. Lawmakers insisted that the amendment's extension of citizenship to the freedmen while disfranchising many former Confederates was nothing more than an effort to raise blacks above whites. The solidarity among Conservative Unionists on this issue could be seen in the vote, seventy to five against ratification. Within days, the Eleventh Legislature had demonstrated the very conservative tendencies of the great majority of its members.

Following action on the amendments, the House and Senate turned to the day-to-day business of lawmaking, which would keep them in session for almost three months. While legislators would act on a wide variety of issues, consideration of a system of labor occupied much of their time and turned

James W. Throckmorton, governor, 1866–67. Courtesy Texas State Library and Archives

out to be the most immediately controversial of the measures they passed. Whites generally agreed that some sort of regulations were required to control the labor of their former slaves. Events in the spring and summer of that year had not only confirmed them in their beliefs but also lent a sense of urgency to considering the matter.

When the legislature met, the planting season was well underway. The success of the crops planted that year remained critical to the state's economic recovery, and despite labor problems in 1865, most farm owners expressed optimism about the cotton crop of 1866. Old landowning planters had been joined by small farmers and what the head of the Freedmen's Bureau called "travelling speculators" in planting cotton. All sought to take advantage of good prices to make their fortunes. By the summer bureau officials found that the farms and plantations along the lower Colorado River, where it had enough agents present to observe trends, showed prospects of producing harvests equal to that of 1860. Such conditions did not prevail everywhere, but within individual counties this promised a rapid recovery from the effects of the war.

By midsummer, however, many farmers expressed growing concerns about the success of their cotton. The immediate concern developed when heavier than usual June rains encouraged the growth of grass in the fields. Workers usually spent June and July hoeing cotton to keep out the grass and weeds that could hinder the growth of the young cotton plants, but water in the fields made that task more difficult. Many farmers complained that the grass had already taken over their fields. If it choked out the cotton, then what had promised to be a bumper crop would quickly be lost. From one of eminent economic recovery, the picture had changed quickly to one of potential disaster.

Planters filled Texas newspapers with their evaluation of the situation, and they usually blamed their workers for the possible disaster, complaining that landowners either could not find enough laborers to clear the fields or that those under contract failed to do as good a job keeping the fields clean as they had as slaves. Letter writers also usually went on to speculate on this new inefficiency, frequently charging that it represented the lazy character of African Americans outside the structure of slavery. Planters maintained that even when the freedmen signed contracts, they could not be counted on to carry out their obligations and willfully allowed crops to be ruined. Even though the Freedmen's Bureau did much to encourage blacks to work, the agency also came in for a share of the blame among local whites. Planters charged that the continued rumors of free land in the future and the intervention of local agents in labor problems only encouraged blacks in what whites considered their natural indolence.

Landowner complaints actually reflected more than just worries about that summer's crop and the labor shortage. They actually revealed a much deeper apprehensiveness about evolving conditions produced by the steadily changing character of both free labor and the freedmen's community. In fact, landowners had real trouble finding enough workers during the 1866 season, but this had nothing to do with the character of their former slaves. The shortage occurred in part because some freedmen left farms in the wake of the problems during the harvest of 1865 and looked for work elsewhere. In some counties railroad and timber companies competed for their labor, something that never would have occurred before. The increase in the number of farm operators also produced a scramble for extra hands. Then, the increasing demand for workers in the field produced by rain in the summer of 1866 compounded the problem of competition and added a new dimension. To save the crops, the search for workers became so intense that employers who needed men often became cutthroat in their efforts to obtain them — recruiters even tried to entice laborers away from employers with whom they already had signed contracts.

The Freedmen's Bureau actually worked hard to secure the men needed by local farmers, even though farmers repeatedly criticized its agents for disrupting the workforce. In March, Gen. Joseph B. Kiddoo replaced General Gregory as assistant commissioner in Texas, and he recognized the critical importance of having enough workers to ensure the success of the year's crop. Kiddoo issued orders intended to break up efforts at enticing workers away from their contracts, imposing fines on anyone who tried to do so and also on employees who did walk away. The general shared native white assumptions that a lack of a proper work ethic among blacks heightened the problem, so he also lectured freedmen on the need to carry out contractual obligations and threatened fines against those who did not. With only twenty-nine agents in the field and more than two-thirds of the state having no agents, the bureau had only a limited effect. Ultimately, Kiddoo realized that a simple shortage of enough hands to fill the needs of farmers had created the problem. He attempted to solve this by encouraging the immigration of freedmen to Texas, even assisting efforts by Texas planters to seek hands outside of the state. Yet neither fines, lectures, nor the promise of more workers in the future did much to solve the immediate problem.

The existence of a much broader revolution in race relations beyond simply the labor issue may help account for why the shortage provoked such great concern that summer. The competitive advantage given the freedmen by the demand for labor constituted only one element of a larger trend that saw blacks attempting to secure a greater degree of economic and social freedom. The power it gave to African Americans offered them perhaps the best means at hand to secure economic independence and then other rights. The freedmen understood this. Those still working as laborers forced farmers to provide increased pay and improved working conditions. Benjamin Truman, the *New*

Gen. Joseph B. Kiddoo, Freedmen's Bureau commissioner for Texas, 1866–67. Courtesy U.S. Army Military History Institute

York Times reporter, noted after his visit to Texas in early 1866 that competition for farm workers had raised wages to a level higher than anywhere else in the South, an observation supported by other contemporaries. Field hands signed contracts ranging from $120 to $180 per year plus rations and quarters; house servants demanded even more, sometimes as much as $300 per year. Whites believed that wages had risen to the point that employers could not make a profit and far beyond the actual value of labor. Such conditions not only heightened concerns but also generated a clear desire among white employers to limit the freedom of their black workers.[1]

Circumstances also gave the freedmen the opportunity to change their working arrangements in a way that many whites feared would make them less productive. As has been seen, when bureau officials first arrived to supervise the new labor system, they noted that most blacks wanted contracts that gave them greater control over their own and their families' lives. This usually translated into a preference for some sort of share-cropping arrangement over working as a farm hand for wages. By the spring of 1866, bureau officials estimated that three-fourths of the labor contracts that had been signed provided for some sort of farm tenantry rather than wages, with the tenant typically acquiring a share of the crop. Landowners had little opportunity to respond to the demands of black laborers because of the shortage, but most remained convinced that these contracts created less productive conditions.

Tenants in Texas, like wage workers, also managed to secure more advantageous arrangements than elsewhere in the South because of local conditions. Generally, the share of the crop that a tenant could get depended on what he brought to the negotiations. Freedmen who brought nothing other than their labor usually settled for a quarter of the crop; the landowner furnished all provisions and supplies. But the prospective tenant who secured his own provisions and perhaps provided his own animals might receive half of the crop.[2] Texas observers believed, however, that local workers secured much more favorable bargains than this. Contemporaries reported that in some cases workers managed to contract for three-fourths of the crop. Again, landowners considered this to their own disadvantage.

The continued efforts by black sharecroppers to exercise greater control over the labor of their own families also inspired fear among many whites. The rise of the black family meant that parents rather than employers controlled what a family's children did. Many freedmen emerged from slavery believing that education offered a means to a better life and preferred that their children be in school rather than the fields. Despite the hostility of southern whites, the Freedmen's Bureau had begun to offer them that opportunity. The bureau's school system had begun slowly after its creation in the autumn of 1865, but that spring Superintendent Edwin M. Wheelock expanded the system significantly, creating schools where students paid $1.50 per month in tuition to help defray costs. He also secured teachers from northern groups, particularly the American Missionary Association. By May, 1866, the bureau supervised ninety-nine schools located primarily in the plantation counties. For the freedmen these represented a path to a better future, and they took advantage of the opportunity. Wheelock reported by the end of that spring that the schools had enrolled 4,796 pupils. For landowners the nearly five thousand black students represented an unused labor force at a critical time, and the fact that freedmen's schools were often the objects of violence probably reflected their annoyance.

The ability of families to determine the type of work that individual members would perform also brought about the continued removal of large numbers of women from the agricultural workforce, a matter of equal consequence for labor conditions. In fact, the bureau had done much to encourage the freedmen to enter into traditional marriages. Marriage and the creation of families witnessed efforts by many African Americans to create a family life modeled on that of whites, whose women usually did not work in the fields. By 1866 freedmen's officials reported that a growing number of black women refused to sign contracts for field labor on the grounds that they preferred to work in their own homes. During the antebellum years women, representing half of the black population, had been a major part of the workforce during periods of peak labor demand, and their withdrawal represented a major problem for landowners and only added to the labor shortage.

Freedom clearly gave African Americans greater control over their own lives and increased power in their relationships with whites. But few whites, planter or otherwise, viewed such trends as anything but detrimental toward their own interests. That whites resisted this process with whatever means they could was a predictable result, and this increasing aggravation with the freedmen resulted in more frequent outbreaks of violence against blacks in the summer of 1866. Most whites believed black freedom threatened their own economic futures. Bureau agents noted that employers had begun to use physical abuse and intimidation to coerce their workers. Some hunted down and dragged back to work freedmen who left their farms, no matter what reason prompted their leaving. Bureau agents noted that workers who displayed any signs of their increasing freedom often faced beatings or worse. Landowners now openly condemned the developing free-labor system and talked more and more about using the government to restrict farm workers. By the time the new state government assumed power in August, 1866, considerable pressure existed to do something that would reverse the trends troubling so many white landowners.

Warned by Throckmorton not to provoke Congress and aware that the passage of laws that limited black freedom, known as black codes, in other southern states had produced a storm of protest in the North, the legislature moved carefully on this matter. Ultimately, they put together a set of laws that drew heavily upon antebellum statutes from both the North and South that had regulated free blacks. They also incorporated many provisions the Freedmen's Bureau had applied to black laborers after the war, perhaps seeing these as more acceptable to the North. Given the precedents that existed for controlling free blacks, few in the legislature believed their own black codes would provoke much criticism.

The legislature attempted to control the freedmen's labor through the use of a variety of laws concerning apprenticeship, contracts, and vagrancy. The apprentice law allowed minors to be placed with a master, either with the consent of parents or by order of the county court, until they reached the age of twenty-one. It gave the master the use of the apprentice's labor, the power to use corporal punishment to secure work, and the right to pursue runaways. The contract law required written agreements for all work to run more than a month. Employers were allowed not only to set requirements for basic work but also establish a code of behavior. They also could deduct the pay of workers who were disobedient, impudent, swore, or absent from a farm without the employers permission. Finally, the vagrancy law authorized local courts to arrest people with no means of support or labor contract, fine them, then place them at work in order to pay that fine if they did not have the money. Taken together, these laws pressured the freedmen to sign annual contracts, even though they might be highly restrictive, or face legal action and court-mandated labor.

The legislature placed enforcement of all of these laws exclusively in the hands of local justice courts. In contract disputes workers could protest to the local court. The justice of the peace then created a panel to hear the case, consisting of himself and a representative chosen by each of the parties to the dispute. This arrangement typically ensured that the panel would return a two-to-one vote for the employer. Although these laws made no mention of race, legislators clearly intended them to be used to place the freedmen back under the control of their white employers. A bureau agent described the contract labor law as "the most oppressive legal instrument yet invented to defraud the laborer of his wages. . . . The wisdom of the men who made such a law would be lauded by a Mexican hidalgo for it is nothing less than a system of peonage." [3]

The legislature also passed measures dealing with issues beyond labor that further restricted the opportunities of blacks. Its "Act to define and declare the rights of persons lately known as Slaves, and Free Persons of Color" defined the basic civil rights of blacks and actually extended much more to them than other southern states. It guaranteed blacks basic property rights, prohibited discrimination in the criminal law, and assured them of personal security and liberty. Nonetheless, it specifically excluded them from voting, banned them from juries, prohibited their testimony in cases involving whites, and forbade marriage to whites. A railroad law required companies to provide separate accommodations for blacks. Other southern states had passed harsher laws, leading many white observers to conclude that the Eleventh Legislature had acted in moderation toward freedmen, even though they had made it clear they did not consider blacks equals. Hoping to avert criticism, they almost immediately found themselves under attack from Republicans in Congress. Local Unionists echoed that censure of the legislature for failing to expand black rights.

Members of the Eleventh Legislature might agree on measures related to African Americans, but its actions in connection with railroads produced serious opposition and ultimately became the focus of many subsequent political struggles. Nevertheless, some legislation raised few complaints. The legislature chartered thirteen new railroad companies during its sessions and passed laws providing grants of lands to any road over twenty-five miles in length. Measures dealing with railroad debts to the school fund and special legislation favorable to the Houston and Texas Central, however, produced widespread protests. Regarding the debt, the legislature passed a bill that stayed the immediate collection of some three hundred thousand dollars in interest owed to the fund and allowed railroads to pay the debt over a four-year period beginning in January, 1867. Lawmakers avoided even more controversy on the debt issue when they failed to take action on the railroads' request to validate the payments that had been made during the war in state scrip rather than specie as required by law. The legislature's confirmation of the charter and land grants of the Houston and Texas Central, despite its failure to meet the construction deadlines provided in the terms of the original land grants, only added to the furor.

Changes in the boundaries of the state's congressional and judicial districts also sparked political recrimination, with Unionists claiming that legislators drew the new lines to limit their chances of electing Unionist congressmen and to eliminate sympathetic district judges. The realigning of congressional districts saw western Texas gerrymandered so that coastal counties balanced out whatever Unionist strength might exist in the interior. The legislature's judicial act reduced the number of district courts from twenty to fifteen. Only five Unionist judges had been elected in the preceding state election, and the redistricting eliminated two of these. Unionists, charging that the action punished them, pointed to this legislation as proof of the basic disloyalty of the new civil government.

Beyond the black codes, railroad legislation, and redistricting, most of the work of the Eleventh Legislature produced few objections. It passed a new homestead law that allowed actual settlers, with the exclusion of blacks, to claim 160 acres of land from the public domain. It also established the existence of a "homestead" of 200 acres that could not be alienated from its owner for debts. Its school law committed the state school fund to the support of a new system of public education, again excluding blacks from receiving any part of that fund, to be administered by the counties. A new tax law imposed an *ad valorem* property tax of fifteen cents per hundred-dollar valuation, providing roughly half of the tax monies raised by the state. A one-dollar poll tax, an occupation tax of 0.5 percent on the salary of those earning more than six hundred dollars annually, and an income tax of 1 percent on incomes over one thousand dollars and up to 3 percent on those earning over five thousand dollars supplemented the property tax. There were additional levies on saloons, billiard parlors, circuses, and similar entertainments. Combined, taxes raised over five hundred thousand dollars in 1867.

Despite its efforts to write freedmen laws that would be acceptable in the North, before the legislature adjourned, its members showed how little their attitudes toward the Union had actually changed. Lawmakers took two actions that could not have done more to inflame northern opinion than a purposeful insult. Members appropriated two thousand dollars for the state funeral and burial in the state cemetery of Confederate general Albert Sidney Johnston, setting up a confrontation between military and state authorities. They also passed a resolution calling for the release from prison of the former president of the Confederacy, Jefferson Davis.

Events in Washington soon after the legislature's adjournment on November 13 clearly showed that many members of Congress did not consider political affairs in Texas acceptable. The two men elected to the Senate by the general assembly and the four representatives selected in a special election that October traveled to Washington to take their seats in Congress. None of the men had demonstrated their Unionism during the war. The two senators had been drawn from the antebellum Democratic leadership and supported secession, though the elderly Burnet did not play an active role. The four congressmen included one Conservative Unionist, Governor Throckmorton's friend and associate in railroad schemes Benjamin H. Epperson. Claiborne C. Herbert and Anthony M. Branch, former Confederate congressmen, and George W. Chilton, a Confederate colonel, could not take the required oath of office. Congress probably had no intention of seating any of the southern congressmen anyway, but the credentials of the men sent from Texas did not help their case. Despite the fact that on August 20, 1866, President Johnson had declared the rebellion to be at an end in Texas and had returned the state to the control of civil authority, Republicans in Congress concluded the time premature to reestablish the state's normal relations, and the congressmen remained officially unrecognized.

The refusal to seat the delegation signaled problems for the state government, but the subsequent course of Governor Throckmorton did little to convince northern observers that the his administration was any more loyal than the congressmen the state had sent to Washington. Throckmorton concluded, following the president's proclamation on August 20, that civil authority had been restored, with the military once again subordinate to civil officials. He insisted that the county and state courts would supervise future contract disputes between laborers and employers and would provide protection and justice for all Texans. In the governor's view, the Freedmen's Bureau no longer had either reason or authority to interfere in such matters. In communications with local federal officials, he urged that military forces be withdrawn from the state's interior. No longer needed to protect the freedmen, the governor argued for their deployment to the frontier for protection against Indian raids.

The bureau's Texas commissioner, General Kiddoo, appeared willing to give civil authorities an opportunity to prove that they would suppress violence and ensure justice for all citizens, black and white, within the state. Neither he nor other federal officials gave any indication that they believed this would be the case, however. Despite the governor's views of the subordination of military authority, bureau officers did not doubt their legal right to intervene in matters that involved freedmen, and they prepared to do so when civil authorities did not secure justice. Gen. O. B. Howard, bureau commissioner at Washington, issued orders in September that instructed local officers to continue to intervene in cases when necessary. Gen. Philip Sheridan, in command of the military district including Texas, also expressed serious doubts about the ability of civil authorities to protect the freedmen and insisted that troops remain in the settled parts of the state to maintain peace.

Through the rest of his administration, Throckmorton's actions placed him on a collision course with federal officials. Rather than responding to the growing list of complaints that landlords cheated the freedmen and subjected them to considerable violence, he repeatedly contended that the reports did not fairly reflect conditions in the state. He ignored cases where the civil government failed to protect the rights of the freedmen. At the same time, he challenged the military's and the Freedmen's Bureau's intervention in any matters. Backed by the Conservative press, the governor pointed to cases where federal officials may have overstepped their legitimate authority or abused it to show the dangers of military government. Throckmorton displayed a manifest willingness to overlook the broader picture of race relations in Texas.

Without question, incidents did occur that gave the governor ammunition in his attack upon the continued presence of troops and Freedmen's Bureau officers. The most highly publicized of these took place at Brenham in August and September. D. L. McGary, editor of the local Democratic newspaper, laid the groundwork for events when he began a vitriolic editorial assault against the troops of the Seventeenth U.S. Infantry garrisoned there in the spring and on the local bureau agent. In August the agent, Capt. Samuel A. Craig, arrested the newspaperman after a particularly impassioned attack on freedmen's education. McGary refused to pay his fine, remained in jail, and continued his campaign against the military from his cell. Craig ultimately released McGary after Throckmorton complained to President Johnson and General Howard's review of the case concluded that the agent had gone beyond his authority in arresting the editor.

Relations between civilians and the military remained uneasy, and on September 7 an altercation took place between soldiers and local whites at a freedmen's dance. During the fight, locals fired at the soldiers, hitting two of them. Later in the evening, troops from the garrison appeared in the town and set fire to a store. The fire soon spread to the rest of the town's business district, which burned to the ground. An investigation of the incident by the army later concluded that the soldiers should have been punished. Nonetheless, despite Throckmorton's demands that they be turned over to civilian authorities for punishment, the army neither gave the men to local officials nor punished them itself.

Throckmorton and his supporters added every such incident to a catalogue of evidence supporting their contentions that the military as a whole refused to recognize legitimate civil law and institutions. At roughly the same time as the Brenham incident, the bureau agent at Victoria, also Captain Craig, took two black soldiers accused of murder from the hands of civil authorities. Craig raised further complaints when, after being reassigned from Brenham to Seguin, he released a soldier charged with gambling from the hands of local authorities. He also became the center of attention when Judge John Ireland had the captain arrested for his actions at Seguin, and military authorities sent cavalry to the town to force his release from jail. Over the next months, civil authorities also raised complaints against the military at Lockhart and in Anderson, Bell, and Grayson Counties.

Conservative newspapers focused on such events to raise public ire against the continued federal presence, yet they and the governor ignored the reasons that gave the military cause to remain. The crisis began at harvest time. Freedmen's Bureau officials indicated that despite problems, most planters dealt well with their freedmen through the summer of 1866. Probably, most intended to pay their workers what they owed them at the end of the year. By the autumn, however, a variety of conditions that had begun to emerge in August and worsened through the harvest season undermined such good intentions and led to wholesale swindling of many freedmen. The situation presented the new civil government with a major test of its ability to protect the rights of these workers. Federal officials watched events closely.

Weather played a major role in setting up that autumn's problems. The cotton crop had been promising through much of the summer, then in late August and throughout September, the state experienced constant and widespread rains. The rains interfered with the development of the cotton bolls and kept workers out of the fields. Farmers around the state also reported their crops infested with the cotton worm. By early October most observers had altered their predictions of a bumper crop and replaced them with gloomier forecasts. General Kiddoo feared that the losses would be so heavy that many of the freedmen who worked as sharecroppers would not make enough money to allow them to survive the winter.

Predictions turned to reality as the harvest proceeded. There are no reliable statistics for the amount of cotton harvested that autumn, but the evidence that exists indicates that the 1866 crop amounted to less than two-thirds of that for 1865. At Galveston *Flake's Bulletin* published weekly summaries of the cotton received at that city through the harvest season each year. Their statistics paint a bleak picture. Between September 1, 1865, and March 1, 1866, Galveston cotton merchants had taken in some 160,686 bales. During the same period the next year, the city's merchants received only 97,574 bales.[4]

A sharp decline in cotton prices at the same time worsened the situation. In September prices had been slightly higher than at the same time in 1865, but they fell rapidly thereafter. By January, 1867, the price for middling cotton fell 20 percent below where it had been the same time the year before. Thirty-cent cotton had dropped to twenty-five cents. By March prices had dropped even lower, some 30 percent below the previous year's figures. Given the reduced crop in 1866, prices should have risen, but few cotton growers had realized the full implications of revolutionary changes in the market during the war years. The development of cotton farms in Egypt and India offered British mills an alternative source, and by 1866 world supply rather than that of the United States alone set these prices. The causes of the decline mattered little to both tenants and landowners, however. With a crop 30 percent less than had been predicted and prices 20–30 percent lower, local farms faced a disaster of monumental proportions.

In this situation landowners attempted to preserve their own profits by depriving their workers of their wages or their share of the crop. Their methods included fraud, economic pressure, and violence. As the harvest proceeded bureau officials began to receive reports of such efforts. In a typical ploy, armed men showed up on farms threatening to kill laborers if they did not leave. When the workers fled the planters claimed that they had forfeited their wages or part of the crop because they had left without permission. Probably, most landowners did not bother to create a legal pretext for their actions; they simply refused to pay their workers the share or wages due them. Jilted laborers could go to the courts or the bureau for redress, but planters often threatened violence against any who protested.

Through the winter of 1866–67, the efforts at depriving the freedmen of their payoffs continued. To make the point that little could protect blacks, whites often attacked those institutions connected to their new status. Schools for the freedmen attracted particular attention. The bureau's efforts at creating schools had come at the same time that tension grew between whites and blacks over labor, and whites generally believed that the schools encouraged the freedmen to increased assertiveness. In a typical incident a mob greeted the first freedmen's teacher to arrive at Marshall in January, 1867. During the melee, the mob broke out the windows of the teacher's home and fired bullets into the house. Papers reported numerous additional cases of such violence throughout this period.

Civil authorities provided little help in protecting the freedmen from this victimization. Most civil officials refused to prosecute landowners. Even if a freedmen could find a willing official to take a case to court, the Eleventh Legislature's laws prohibiting blacks from testifying in a case involving whites or sitting on juries weighed the system almost completely in favor of the landlord. Instead of protecting the freedmen, local bureau agents reported cases in which sympathetic civil courts actually helped planters gain further advantages over their workers. In one such occurrence a planter sued his field hands for property damages for parts of the crop that had been lost, up to the amount of their wages. The verdict favored the planter. Bureau agents found other courts willing to aid in the intimidation of the freedmen, arresting them without warrants and imprisoning them after offering them little opportunity to defend themselves.[5]

The bureau could do little to help. In May General Kiddoo had been notified of General Orders No. 26, issued by the Adjutant General's Office, which prevented the bureau from establishing military tribunals to try civilians where state courts operated. It could act as agent in reconciling contract disputes but had no enforcement authority. Initially, the Texas bureau remained out of the picture amid the problems that fall. In October Kiddoo instructed local agents to arbitrate differences between planters and freedmen, though only to ensure that parties lived up to written contracts and then only in extreme cases. As the harvest progressed, however, bureau officials found themselves besieged with freedmen complaining of just such severe treatment, as planters violently defrauded their workers and the courts refused to act. Some agents responded with actions that did little to quiet the disputes with civil authorities. At Houston Col. Jacob C. DeGress responded to complaints that landowners had refused to pay wages by ordering that no cotton be shipped through the city unless accompanied by a verification by a bureau agent that the men who had grown the cotton had been paid. Kiddoo later forced DeGress to modify his order, but conditions forced bureau officials to conclude that the state's justice system would not protect the freedmen.

The most obvious cases of fraud and violence came to the bureau's attention, but agents realized that the majority of planters did not have to resort to such tactics in their efforts to secure an advantage over their workers. Over the year landowners had developed a variety of means to achieve that end, and the new labor laws strengthened their hand in the matter. In one of these subterfuges, planters used what General Kiddoo called "buzzards" to prey upon the freedmen. These "buzzards" were country storekeepers who set up their businesses in the old plantation areas to sell provisions, typically shoddy clothing and poor animals, to sharecroppers at high prices. They also encouraged the freedmen to buy unnecessary items, particularly cheap jewelry that they sold at high rates, and even offered cash advances. These business practices often meant that blacks owed much of their profits to the storekeeper at the end of the year. These merchants worked to the advantage of local landowners, however, because in many cases they worked in partnership with them. Commonly, the landowner who allowed the merchant to establish a shop on his property and permitted the sale of such goods to his workers shared the profits at the end of the year.

Others used provisions of the state labor laws that allowed them to fine their workers for improper behavior and work. The employer kept the records and determined the impropriety of a worker's actions. They then deducted these fines from a worker's wages on payday or from a sharecropper's profit at the time they sold the harvest. Bureau agents reported workers being fined for legitimate reasons, such as neglect or injuries to property, but they also found planters levying fines for disobedience, loss of time, impertinence, or feigned illness. Employers easily added to the lists of possible fines when necessary, and workers in many cases found that, after deductions for fines as well as for their dealings with the farm merchant, they had no money at the end of the year.

One of the most novel techniques practiced in the plantation counties that the Freedmen's Bureau encountered was for landlords to rent their land to farm managers, leaving the manger to make labor arrangements. These men then paid the owners their rent when they harvested the crop but did not pay the workers; instead, they pocketed the rest of the profits and left the country before authorities could intervene. Since the landlord had not committed the fraud, at least openly, the worker had no recourse against him or his property. Under the law little could be done.

Bureau officials could intervene when planters clearly broke their labor contracts, even though they could not force a settlement, but they watched with even greater frustration as many planters used the new labor laws to take advantage of their workers legally. Landowners fully exploited the new labor laws to implement a variety of practices designed to give them the upper hand in relations with their workers. Their actions convinced most federal observers that state law did not guarantee the rights of the freedmen. Most went further, concluding that the passage of these laws had shown the refusal of Texans to accept the results of the war.

On December 31 General Kiddoo issued orders that required all contracts with freedmen to provide full details of the responsibilities of the laborer and landlord, indicating the general's clear dissatisfaction with the operation of the state's labor laws and its civil courts. Aware that in the past season landlords had taken advantage of the ambiguous character of many contracts, he now demanded that they spell out every detail, including who was to pay for what supplies and precisely how and on what basis crops were to be divided or wages paid. In effect, his order responded to the abuse of the existing labor law's provisions allowing planters to deduct fines and costs from a worker's settlement. While not nullifying the state laws that had been placed on the book, Kiddoo's order limited the possibilities that they could be used by planters to abuse their workers in the upcoming year.

If there had been a chance for the survival of the Throckmorton administration, it would have been to have successfully proven that its actions could guarantee the rights of the freedmen. It did not. The black codes written by the legislature, the application of these laws that took place in the autumn of 1866, and the refusal of the civil courts to protect blacks left the officers of the military and the agents of the Freedmen's Bureau convinced that the existing government could never ensure the freedmen their rights. As a result, these federal officials added their voices to those in Washington calling for a new Reconstruction policy to be imposed by Congress.

For a variety of reasons, discontent with President Johnson's Reconstruction policy across the South had grown. The actions of the Throckmorton government made certain the inclusion of Texas in any new and harsher plan that emerged from Congress.

Chapter 5

Congressional Intervention and the Politics of Violence

Conditions in Texas and elsewhere in the South brought about congressional intervention in Reconstruction in the spring of 1867. This action capped a year-long struggle between President Johnson and Congress that revolved around both Reconstruction policy and national politics. For Texans, this turn of events meant starting anew in their bid for full restoration of their state to the Union. The period known as "Congressional Reconstruction" began that spring and lasted for Texas until 1870, when Congress finally restored civil government and accepted the state's representatives. During this period, Texans witnessed radical changes in the state's political life. All of this began with the passage on March 2 of the first Reconstruction Act and the beginning of army supervision of state affairs. The months that immediately followed witnessed the organization of the Texas Republican party based upon a biracial coalition. It also saw the emergence of political violence that attempted to block the changes made possible by Congress.

With the Reconstruction Act, Congress declared that no legal governments existed in the former Confederate states and that those currently in power were provisional. It also divided the South into five military districts and authorized district commanders to keep order and protect the rights of the people of the states under their authority. These officers were to supervise the elections of delegates to state conventions to write new constitutions, which had to conform to the U.S. Constitution, had to include universal suffrage, and had to be ratified by popular vote. The first state legislature afterward then had to ratify the proposed Fourteenth Amendment as a final step toward reunion.

The act also contained provisions for the elections that included measures that threatened revolutionary change in the political life of Texans and the rest of the South. Congress excluded from voting those individuals who had taken an oath of loyalty to the United States, then supported the Confederacy. This applied primarily to high military, state, or federal officials. The only requirement for registration was that the prospective voter swear loyalty to the U.S.

government and affirm that he was not excluded from registering under any of the acts of Congress. At the same time, the law required that all male citizens twenty-one and older, regardless of race or color, be allowed to vote. It was this change of the electorate that had the most immediate effect, providing a central force shaping politics through the rest of Congressional Reconstruction.

Initially, the actions of Congress did not produce widespread upheaval in local government. Texas became a part of the Fifth Military District. Gen. Philip Sheridan commanded the district, but Gen. Charles C. Griffin, named by Sheridan to head the subdistrict of Texas, actually directed affairs in the state. Civil officials who took office as a result of the election of 1866 continued to hold their offices, though under the Reconstruction Act they did so on the condition that they support the military commander in his duties. A tense relationship between the civil authorities and the military existed from the beginning. Governor Throckmorton, still asserting his belief that the president had restored civil government, contended that as long as state officials supported the process, the civil government, rather than the military, represented legitimate authority in Texas. This led to inevitable conflict since General Griffin believed that the existing governments did not enforce the spirit of the law regarding the freedmen and had shown little loyalty to the nation. Immediately after assuming command, Griffin asked Sheridan whether he could replace local officials, contending that as long as they remained in power, he could not carry out a successful registration or satisfactory convention. His superiors also expressed uncertainty about whether or not he had the power to remove civil officials, so Congressional Reconstruction began with the already elected officers still in place.

The questions regarding the military's powers delayed Griffin's plan to remove state officials, but he did use his powers in an effort to suppress the widespread violence that had plagued Texas since the war's end and to create a climate favorable to the registration of voters and a peaceful election. That April he issued two orders concerning the operations of the state courts and designed to ensure justice for the freedmen and Unionists. On April 5 his Circular No. 10 authorized local military commanders to intervene in court cases if they decided local civil tribunals did not try cases impartially or failed to render decisions based on evidence and the law. Griffin instructed local commanders to arrest offenders in such cases and present the facts to army headquarters. The general might then decide to try the case again in front of a military commission. On April 27 Griffin issued a second order, Circular No. 13, commonly called the "Jury Order." This required all jurors to swear the "Ironclad Oath" formulated by Congress in 1862. The oath was intended for prospective federal officeholders and required a statement that the individual had never voluntarily aided the Confederacy. The April 27 order also extended the privilege of sitting on juries to freedmen.

Gen. Charles Griffin, military commander of Texas, 1866–67.
Courtesy U.S. Army Military History Institute

Although the general's threat to remove cases from state courts to military tribunals produced criticism from Conservative newspapers, Griffin did not use the tribunals in any major case. His subordinates did use the authority, however, to intervene in numerous local proceedings. For example, in Robertson County the Freedmen's Bureau agent had arrested men accused of murdering blacks in an attack on a political meeting. The initial trial had been held in the state courts, and the jury acquitted them. Receiving reports that justice had not been done and the evidence pointed to their guilt, Griffin ordered the accused rearrested and threatened a new trial. In this case the men escaped before being tried, but the general's decision indicated his willingness to intervene if he thought conditions warranted.[1]

The Jury Order produced more public outrage than the threat of military tribunals. Governor Throckmorton not only distributed it to the state's judicial officers but also sent an immediate protest to President Johnson. Throckmorton claimed that if enforced, the order would shut down the state's courts because they would be unable to seat enough jurors to hear trials. He argued, on the one hand, that it made the majority of white men in Texas ineligible to serve on juries. On the other hand, state law imposing property requirements on prospective jurors excluded most blacks. The governor warned that the inability of the courts to meet would encourage further violence and urged the president to intervene.

Some of the state courts did close and judges reported that they could not find jurors. General Griffin did not believe that enough whites could not be found to take the oath. Many white Texans could swear to an oath if they asserted they had not voluntarily served in the Confederate forces. Griffin believed judicial officers simply did not want to enforce the order. State officials did little to encourage men to swear the oath, and in some cases district judges closed their courts without any serious effort at finding qualified jurors. Despite the protests against the order, the president did not intervene in the situation, and Griffin's instructions remained in force until the next autumn.

Amid the controversy produced by his efforts, Griffin proceeded with voter registration. The general outlined the basic procedures on April 17. He would name three men to be registration supervisors in each of the state's fifteen judicial districts. These in turn appointed three-man county registration boards to carry out the actual enrollment of voters. As a critical condition for an appointment to either board, the appointee had to subscribe to the Ironclad Oath. In addition to this congressional requirement, Griffin attempted to place at least one black registrar on the board in counties with African American majorities. The task of finding qualified registrars, coupled with local opposition, delayed the task, and in many counties enrollments did not begin until the end of June or early July. Registration efforts ended in August, but because of delays in implementing the program, Griffin approved another six-day period in September.

As the registration started, political affairs within the state changed rapidly. Of particular significance, Congressional Reconstruction brought about the emergence of the state's Republican party. Postwar Unionists, the men who had supported Andrew Hamilton's administration in 1865 and the candidacy of Elisha Pease in the 1866 election, took the lead in building the new organization. The activities of the Eleventh Legislature and the Throckmorton administration convinced them that the Conservatives had refused to accept not only the results of the war regarding slavery but also the consequences of their treason. Rather than punishing those who had persecuted Unionists during the conflict, the new government actually protected them and in some cases included them in the distribution of charters and other benefits. Hamilton and Pease both had journeyed to Washington to lobby for congressional intervention and had supported Radical Republican plans for a new Reconstruction policy based on black suffrage. They concluded that the plan offered the only way of guaranteeing a loyal government in Texas.

Most of these Unionists returned to Texas shortly after the passage of the congressional acts to participate in the organization of a new state Republican party intended to create a biracial and loyal coalition. In April Unionist leaders in Austin called for a convention at Houston to be attended by all who accepted the congressional plan. They proposed a party platform that would include the elimination of the restrictions placed on blacks by the previous legislature, a free public school system, government encouragement of public transportation, and the restoration of law and order in the state. Unionists across Texas responded with local meetings that endorsed the idea of a convention and announced their new Republican connection.

These Texas Republicans believed black enfranchisement offered the only way to secure loyal government, and they moved quickly to consolidate the support of the freedmen behind their efforts. They often used their public meetings to educate blacks on the political situation and to inform them of their new rights. To further this campaign, they introduced the secret Union or Loyal League. The league had emerged in the Border States during the Civil War as a forum for the expression of Unionist sentiment and as a means for mobilizing pro-Union voters. It had spread into the South after the war, used by Unionists for organizational purposes. The league's organization reflected that of many other contemporary secret fraternal organizations. National Republican leaders came to see its structure as a useful framework for attracting, educating, and mobilizing black voters. In the spring of 1867, Judge James H. Bell, a white Unionist, introduced the league to Texas and became its first state president.

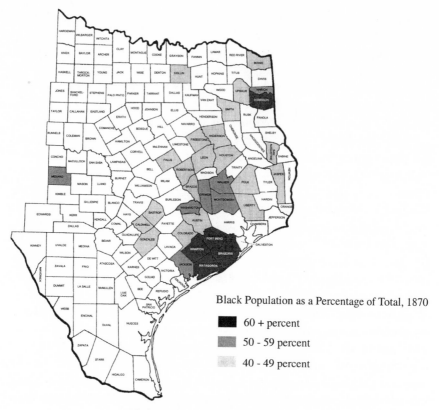

Black Population as a Percentage of Total, 1870

■ 60 + percent

▓ 50 - 59 percent

░ 40 - 49 percent

Black Population of Post–Civil War Texas

Representatives of the state Republican party, often assisted by the local agents of the Freedmen's Bureau, played a major role in forming local league councils. African Americans responded well to the organization, and it spread quickly through local communities. It proved especially strong in those counties with large African American populations and especially in those along the lower Brazos and Colorado Rivers. By their very nature secret, these local councils left little recorded information concerning their operations, but they succeeded in bringing black voters to the Republican party's support.

The Union League not only mobilized black voters but also became the incubator of the state's first African American political leadership. These early leaders included Benjamin F. Williams of Colorado County, a minister of the Methodist Episcopal Church and a former slave. Williams helped form the local league and went on to serve in the 1868 convention and then in the legislature in 1870, 1879, and 1885. Scipio McKee played an active in the league in Washington County and continued political participation as an officer of the constitutional convention and then as a supporter of A. J. Hamilton in the 1869 gubernatorial election. George T. Ruby, an African American agent of the Freedmen's Bureau, used his position as a supervisor of the bureau's schools to play a major role in organizing league chapters around Galveston, then emerged as a prominent member of the Republican leadership through the end of Reconstruction. Stephen Curtis of Brazos County also advanced upward from playing a major role in organizing the local league to a seat in the constitutional convention.

White Unionists and African Americans met at Houston on July 4 to organize their new party. The delegates produced a platform appealing to both groups. For blacks, the convention offered support of a homestead law that would not discriminate against them and a public school system that allowed them equal access. To attract white Unionists, the party offered support for Congressional Reconstruction and demanded that all civil officials who had served the Confederate cause be removed from office. The black vote and the removal of ex-rebels promised Unionists a means of securing political power. Whites remained unclear, however, as to the political agenda they hoped to implement once they gained control.

Following the Houston convention, Republican leaders focused particularly on efforts to remove officials elected in 1866 and place their own men in their stead. They had many reasons for wanting to do this but clearly believed that none of the state officials would protect the newly enfranchised black voters. They also had concluded that few local officeholders would do so either. Unless violence and intimidation could be controlled, even the black vote did not offer a secure path to power. Republicans began placing pressure on Griffin almost immediately after the passage of the First Reconstruction Act to remove state and local officials who were unwilling to enforce equal justice. Fortunately for the Republicans, they found that party interests lay parallel to those of the general.

Griffin had made it clear as early as March that he was dissatisfied with Governor Throckmorton's efforts to protect Union men and freedmen. The violence that accompanied voter registration did little to convince him that he was wrong. The general also believed the governor was dragging his feet on the Jury Order, intentionally assisting in the closure of the district courts and failing to support registration. Only the uncertainty concerning the power of district commanders to remove civil officials stayed his hand. Finally, he secured that power as a result of the passage on July 19, 1867, of the Third Reconstruction Act by Congress, a measure defining more clearly the power of local military commanders. Throckmorton, other state officials, district judges, county officials, and even city officers who had been under

Elisha M. Pease, governor, 1867–69. PICB-06786 Austin History Center, Austin Public Library

the general's scrutiny now held their positions subject to his power to replace them. On July 30 Griffin removed Throckmorton as an impediment to Reconstruction.

In Throckmorton's place the general named former governor Elisha M. Pease, a Unionist who had played a major role in the formation of the Republican party. On August 8, 1867, Pease took control of the executive offices at Austin. Four days later the new governor asked Griffin to remove all officeholders not friendly to the U.S. government, its policies, and its principals. Griffin agreed that loyal men needed to be in power, but even though he believed most currently in place should be removed, he insisted that reason be shown before vacating any office. As a result of Griffin's demand that there be clear reason for a removal, Pease did not get the wholesale replacement of officials that he desired. Griffin did not take any further action until August 15, when he removed three district judges and members of the city government at Galveston. Then on September 6 the general discharged the rest of the executive officers, the supreme court, and three more district judges. Republican hopes apparently received a setback, though, when Griffin died from yellow fever on September 15. But his replacement, Gen. Joseph J. Reynolds, continued the removals until the process ended after Gen. Winfield Hancock replaced Sheridan and ordered that Reynolds cease.

Conservatives charged that Griffin and Reynolds carried out a drastic and successful purge of state and local offices in order to secure the future of the Republican party. Indeed, they removed all of the principal state officers, but at the local level, their reluctance to act without cause limited the revolutionary character of their operations. The state's Republican leaders recognized this. A report by a committee in the constitutional convention later indicated that of the 2,377 elective offices filled in the 1866 general election, the military found acceptable officials to fill only 500. The army found it particularly difficult to find men to fill the county-level offices. Generally, commanders showed a reluctance to replace officials, and civil authorities who showed any willingness to cooperate with the military or local Republicans remained in place. In Colorado and Jefferson Counties, for example, the army removed no county officials, considering all there either loyal or cooperative. In Harrison County orders vacated the county judge's position but left in office the sheriff, who could not take the oath but appeared willing to enforce the law. Thus, even though the military secured local governments that would sustain the Reconstruction process, these officials did not necessarily favor the new Republican party.[2]

This represented a potentially deadly failure for Republicans. As they put together their organization, party leaders soon discovered that the fragility of the coalition they wanted to build and how easily it could be disrupted by their opponents. Texas had a reputation for violence even before the war, and it had been intensified in the war's wake. Freedmen had been the particular object of murder, assault, and intimidation. Such activities worsened once registration began, then exploded in the autumn of 1867. In order to ensure the reliability of black support, Republicans determined to suppress this violence. Achieving this goal required control over those offices charged with administering justice. The survival of Conservative officeholders in many of these positions left the success of Republican goals uncertain.

Most contemporary observers agreed that lawlessness increased in the latter part of 1867. Conservatives charged that the mounting problem was caused by the Jury Order and the disruption of the courts, as Throckmorton had warned. Republicans countered with their own charges that it was part of a Conservative effort at interfering with the registration of black voters and the organization in the Union League. The actual cause of the disorderly acts of individuals can not be known, but the conditions creating a climate favorable for criminality are obvious.[3]

Unquestionably, growing hostility toward the army and the Reconstruction process played a role. Initially, state authorities had believed that they could reach an accommodation with the military and that the new Reconstruction policies might bring a rapid end to federal involvement in the state. Governor Throckmorton wrote to Ashbel Smith in early April expressing his belief that Texans should show no hesitance in conforming to conditions imposed by Congress. Furthermore, he urged them not to stand in the way of the integration of blacks into the political process. While humiliating, Throckmorton believed that such behavior would make it possible for Texas to return to the Union in equality. He suggested that it also positioned the people of the state to aid at some future time in "restoring the government to its original purity."[4]

Throckmorton's April letter indicated, however, that many in Texas did not willingly accept Congress's new plan. He wrote it in an effort to overcome what he believed were the "animosities and prejudices of the popular heart" and the "outraged public sentiment" that had greeted Congress's actions. The subsequent inclusion of blacks on the registration boards, the military's interference with the courts, and then the Jury Order aggravated those feelings. The operations of the registration boards created the greatest hostility. As registration progressed, Conservative newspapers charged the boards with arbitrarily refusing to add eligible white voters. Their attacks intensified when Conservatives discovered that Griffin had ordered the boards to deny enrollment to individuals who had served in any civil office before or during the war and then supported the Confederacy. In fact, the general had given the boards considerable discretion in registering voters, allowing them to refuse to record any person whose loyalty was questionable. At the same time, these newspapers charged the boards with overregistering black voters. Editors complained that registrars were willing to place African Americans on the voting lists regardless of eligibility.[5]

The Conservative press added to the general sense of dissatisfaction and also contributed to a climate of fear when, in midsummer, unofficial reports suggested that large numbers of blacks had registered but only a very small percentage of whites had signed up. Newspaper reports indicated that in a typical situation in Fort Bend County, fewer than one-fourth of potential white voters had bothered to register. Editors made efforts to encourage registration by publishing frightening predictions of what would take place if the Republican party and its black supporters controlled the convention and the state government. The editor of the *Houston Telegraph* offered a picture of the future typical of that portrayed by many others when he contemplated black politicians confiscating the lands of Texans and depriving whites of their livelihood. In a particularly ominous warning, he observed that the state would be in the hands of blacks, just like in Santo Domingo. The reference presented a particularly frightening threat since the slave uprisings on that Caribbean island had led to the slaughter of white slaveowners.

At the same time that political events created growing concern among whites for their future, the economic picture added its own negative dimensions to the problem. As in the previous year, another economic disaster affected the cotton-growing regions and resulted in a widespread outbreak of troubles. Despite the problems of 1866, Texas planters and farmers had gone back into cotton heavily in 1867. Even though cotton prices had fallen, many still believed that, with cotton selling from between eighteen and twenty-two cents per pound, money could be made if costs could be contained. Bureau officials actually believed that more land had been planted in cotton that spring than in 1866. The troubles began with very wet and cool weather in April and May; crops planted in March had to be replanted two months later. A wet summer followed the late spring, then rain continued into the harvest season. As a result of these problems, weeds and grass choked back cotton plants, the cotton worm reappeared in August, then workers could not get into the fields during the harvest, and much of the cotton rotted in the fields. The overall result was a serious blow to the state's farming interests.

Texas newspapers reported in the autumn that the crops in the traditional plantation country near the mouths of the Colorado and Brazos Rivers— Brazoria, Fort Bend, Wharton, and Matagorda—had proven a total failure. A planter along the Brazos informed the editor of the *Houston Telegraph* that he had planted eight hundred acres of cotton, but because of the cotton worms, he had harvested only 6 bales compared to the more than 400 he should have brought in. Farms along the lower Trinity experienced similar losses. In November newspapers predicted that the farms farther upriver might still bring in a partial crop if there was a late frost. No one was optimistic, however, and when the crop came in, their outlook was justified. In 1866 the state's farmers had produced 191,720 bales of cotton, with reports of some 165,000 shipped from Galveston. The harvest in 1867–68 dropped to 122,399 bales, 36 percent below that of the previous year, and the export from Galveston to 101,749 bales.

As in the past, where freedmen worked the land, landowners blamed the losses on their workers, the same criticisms leveled against blacks the previous year. Landowners reasserted their claims that they had not worked hard enough to clean out the weeds and grass during the summer, nor had they done their best to get the crop harvested before it had been lost to the weather. Most continued to assert that, as slaves, blacks could have been forced to give a greater effort and that they would never prove to be good free workers. Refusing to see the variety of problems responsible for the bad harvest, planters found conditions perfect for them to reaffirm their long-held views of blacks as a race.

Anger at military intervention, concern with the efforts to organize blacks into the Republican party, and the agricultural problems in the autumn provided the context for the outburst of lawlessness. Some incidents originated out of purely economic circumstances. As problems with the crops became apparent, landowners in some areas tried to use violence to force their laborers to work harder. In Bowie County, for example, local planters hired the gang of Cullen Baker, an outlaw who led a large band that had plagued northeastern Texas since the end of the war, to serve as enforcers to punish freedmen who shirked their work or complained of their treatment. The use of the Baker gang was the most notorious effort at disciplining African American labor, but such practices became widespread.

The loss of the cotton crop led many planters to attempt once again to cut losses by depriving their workers of their share of the harvest. As in the previous year, these efforts often involved violence. The usual manipulation of records to the advantage of the landowners continued. Employers used violence to punish any freedman who protested. The technique of driving workers from the farms to allow owners to claim that they had broken their contracts and given up their rights to wages or a share of the crop also reappeared. Such incidents appeared to be even more widespread than in the previous year. Bureau officials reported that, particularly in the northeastern counties, the outlaw gangs used to force the freedmen to work reappeared during the harvest to drive them from the farms. While the Baker gang played a particularly important role in this effort, bureau officials also reported the Ben Biggerstaff gang at work in Wood, Hunt, and Van Zandt Counties. Smaller bands of local outlaws worked in Titus County and the Jefferson area.

In other incidents economic factors became intertwined with the political. Planters were never very happy with Republican efforts at organizing African American voters. Often Republican organizers talked about how planters had exploited the slaves and warned that Conservatives would return the freedmen to slavery. Landowners feared that reminding former slaves of their plight before emancipation might make them restless, and the farmers worried that this might lead workers to quit the fields altogether. In addition, they complained that their laborers spent too much time in political activities and the Union League and that these interfered with their work. As a result, Republican organizers became convenient scapegoats, along with blacks themselves, to explain farm problems.

Landowners took action to restrict the Republican effort. Union League organizers reported that, in response to their fears, many planters threatened workers who joined the organization with loss of jobs and assaulted those who took the lead in the party's organizational work. At Brenham one planter, upset that his workers wanted to go to town to register to vote, hired members of the local army garrison to punish them, justifying his action by claiming that they demonstrated bad work habits. The soldiers went to the plantation and tied the workers up by their thumbs. After several hours the freedmen apparently went back to work, their political hopes dashed.

Political concerns clearly motivated other acts of violence and reflected the anger both at the military and the Republican party's efforts to use black enfranchisement to their advantage. A considerable amount of this specifically aimed at disrupting the registration process and dissuading blacks from participating. In some communities opponents of the convention disturbed this process by threatening members of the registration boards with violence. Griffin found many prospective registrars too fearful to serve and received frequent resignations of appointees who initially accepted. Even the assignment of troops as escorts for the boards as they did their business did not blunt these hostile efforts, nor did it keep threats from being carried out. In Panola and Washington Counties, unknown parties not only threatened but actually attempted the assassination of registrars. At Clarksville a white man assaulted the black member of the local board. At Fort Worth the black member of the board received numerous threats that he would be murdered, and later the circulation of rumors that the board members would be attacked caused them to suspend business.

Bureau agents and white Republicans flooded Griffin's headquarters and the governor's office with reports of threats delivered to blacks who were politically active. A Republican informant from Bell County informed Governor Pease that local Conservatives told the freedmen that they would kill any black who tried to vote Republican, though promising there would be no problems if they supported Conservatives. In Navarro County local whites told blacks they would kill any who spoke with Radicals. In Freestone County doctors advertised that they would treat no one who belonged to the Union League. Whites hung around the courthouse in many counties and forced black registrants to walk through crowds that jeered and shouted threats. The intimidation was explicit and widespread.

Ultimately, the source of violence mattered little to the future of the state Republican party and biracial politics. Any violence, and especially that aimed at the freedmen, destabilized the black community. This in turn undermined

Republican efforts to mobilize black voters. Remarkably, intimidation does not appear to have worked in 1867. In November when authorities announced the results of the initial registration, the figures indicated that despite the lawless conditions that had existed, blacks had registered in large numbers. The statistics stunned the state's Conservatives. Even though some 57,368 whites registered, Conservatives saw no clear victory in the future when African American registrants numbered 47,430. An additional drive held in January saw the number of whites increase to 60,445, a total equal to about one-half of eligible voters. Blacks also added voters, reaching 49,550, about 89 percent of those eligible. The registration had clear political implications. While whites outnumbered blacks by almost 11,000 votes, Unionists had secured over 12,000 votes in 1866. If the new Republican party could hold on to those voters, they, combined with the black vote, would ensure that the party could elect enough delegates to control the constitutional convention.[6]

Conservatives charged that local boards purposefully excluded eligible whites, thus accounting for the low white registration. In fact, modern scholarship has shown that the majority of boards were scrupulously honest about adhering to the rules. In most cases low registration did not result from board policy but rather from white hostility to the whole process. In black-majority counties the realization of whites that they could not register enough potential voters to overcome that majority also discouraged registration. Where blacks were not in the majority or where the military and Freedmen's Bureau did not offer protection to black registrants, mainly those counties in northern Texas, whites registered fully and blacks tended to be underrepresented.

The completion of voter registration set the stage for the next step in Reconstruction. On December 18 General Hancock announced that the election on the question of holding a convention and on prospective delegates would be held at county seats between February 10 and 14, 1868. Republicans already had initiated their preparations for an election with the formation of the Union League. They now continued efforts at expanding the league throughout the state to ensure a large turnout of blacks in the election. Conservatives, however, had made no plans for the election and were divided on the best course to pursue. As Republicans continued their efforts to secure a vote in favor of a convention and to elect a majority of delegates, the Democrats were forced to decide what action they would take.

Prior to the release of the official registration figures, Conservatives had debated the proper course their party should take. Throckmorton argued that Conservatives should register but vote against holding a constitutional convention. He insisted that remaining under military rule would be preferable to a civil government in which blacks were enfranchised and whites disfranchised, a situation that would ruin the state's future. The former governor believed that military rule would last for only a short time because, he predicted, the North would soon tire of it, and at that point Texas could return to the Union without suffering the indignity of black rule.

Many of the leading Conservatives at Galveston and Houston agreed with Throckmorton as to the undesirability of a radical constitution, but they disagreed on the means to prevent one from being written. These men believed that if they had enough support registered to prevent the meeting of the convention, a preferable plan would be to vote for the convention and use their strength to elect a majority of Conservative delegates, who could then write a constitution that rejected black suffrage and force Congress to accept or reject it. Like Throckmorton, these men perceived a change in northern public opinion and concluded that it ensured that Congress would not continue to block the state's return.

The results of the registration meant that neither proposal would work. Almost every one of the registered whites would have to oppose the convention to counter the heavy black participation. That was a highly unlikely possibility. As a result many of the old Democratic leaders united to call a Conservative convention at Houston on January 20, 1868. At the same time, white Unionists who had found themselves unable to accept black suffrage issued a call for a Conservative Reconstructionist convention to meet in the same city on the same date.

Their assessment of conditions in the states was not the sole reason these men decided to call the two conventions. Presidential politics also played a role. President Johnson had already decided to run in the next year's election, and a conservative Texas readmitted to the Union on his principles would strengthen his chances to retain office. The president's supporters believed that a Conservative convention writing a constitution based on his principles would allow Johnson to assert himself to an even greater extent as the champion of states' rights. Local supporters, including General Hancock, wanted Texans to follow this course, and their encouragement played a major role in the decision of Conservative leaders to meet.

The Houston conventions attracted widespread attention in the state and produced a turnout of many prominent antebellum leaders. The Conservative Reconstructions met first, and supporters of President Johnson, including John Hancock and Collector of the Customs A. B. Sloanaker, directed affairs. They subsequently adjourned to meet with the Conservatives, where men like John H. Reagan, former postmaster of the Confederacy, and Ashbel Smith played prominent roles. Although some discord plagued the meeting and a few of the Johnson Unionists left, the two groups forged a coalition committed to full registration of white voters, a campaign against the convention, and voting for candidates who opposed black suffrage in an effort to secure a conservative constitution if the convention were called.

While Conservatives struggled over what position to take, Republicans proceeded in their efforts at mobilizing black voters. As in their efforts with voter registration, they continued to encounter widespread violence aimed at blocking them. Much of the intimidation was directed at individual organizers or active Republicans. There were, however, major outbreaks of violence. In Wood County masked parties broke up a Republican rally by firing into the meeting place and wounding and killing several who attended. One of the most violent encounters took place at Marshall in Harrison County on December 30. There, the local police chief broke up a meeting being held at the county courthouse to encourage African Americans to vote in the upcoming election. In the melee that followed, someone shot at Colbert Caldwell, a military appointee to the Texas Supreme Court and a candidate for the convention from the county. Caldwell charged that this had been an effort to assassinate him.[7]

The fact that the violence did not keep blacks from exercising their new political rights proved to be among the significant results of the political strife of 1867–68. In the face of hostile mobs, the organizational efforts had continued. League officers did not falter in their efforts to mobilize black voters. The presence of former Union soldiers as agents of the Freedmen's Bureau and the existence of military garrisons probably played a major role in reinforcing blacks in their resolve to participate. Military officials noted that in some communities African American women also played a significant role in organizing for the election, insisting that men carry out their new duty. An event that reflected the persistence of the effort took place on January 27, 1868, at Marshall, where violence had accompanied organizational efforts less than a month before. There, a thousand freedmen attended a mass rally to hear Republican spokesmen appeal for their support and unity.[8]

This tenacity carried over to the election, in which voting took place at the county seats of the state between February 10 and 14, again in the face of violence. General Reynolds ordered federal troops to some locations to observe the proceedings but instructed them to stay away from the polls. Neither the Freedmen's Bureau nor the army had enough resources to place men in every county, however, opening up opportunities for whites to try to keep blacks from voting. In San Augustine County an armed mob attacked the polling place, shot and wounded one of the voters, and threatened others. At Bastrop the gathering of large crowds of whites that harassed black voters caused election officials to suspend voting for a period. Almost everywhere groups of whites continued the practice initiated during the registration drive, standing around where people voted and threatening blacks with future retaliation unless they supported Conservative candidates.

Still, African Americans went to the polls in large numbers despite these conditions. The Union League, wherever organized, turned out the vote. It served another function as well, offering black voters protection. In many communities league members went to the polls together and voted en masse. At Webberville in Travis County, they followed one of their leaders, armed with a saber and carrying an American flag. Whites in Harrison County complained that black voters came to the polls in groups, marching by platoons, and charged that Republicans brought them in this way to control their votes. Unquestionably, the method protected them. Jerry Moore, an African American in Harrison County, later described how the league worked in that place in later elections, possibly describing its effort in 1868: "The Democratic Party had no chance to 'timidate the darkies. The 'publican party had a 'Loyal League' for to protect the cullud folks. First the Negroes went to the league house to get 'structions and ballots and then marched to the courthouse, double file, to vote."[9] The league provided instruction, but even more important, it allowed blacks to act as a group to resist the threats of violence aimed at them by the Conservative opposition.

With the publication of the results, Conservatives found that they had experienced an election disaster. The tally of votes showed that they not only had failed to secure a full registration of white voters but also had not managed to retain the support of those who had registered to vote. Roughly 89 percent of the registered black voters went to the polls, casting 36,932 votes for the convention and 818 against. About 31 percent of registered white voters turned out, and of this number, 7,750 voted in favor of the convention while 10,623 voted against it. For most observers, the outcome of the election resulted from the failure of whites to register and then vote. If even the whites who had registered had gone to the polls and voted against the convention, those seeking to prevent the convention would have carried the election handily.

Conservatives also failed to elect a majority of candidates to the convention. Early reports indicated that they had carried many of the positions in the northeastern part of the state, but Republicans overwhelmed Conservatives in the plantation counties and the west. Republicans had successfully won their first battle in the changed political circumstances created by Congress. Still, some aspects of the election presented a less positive picture. The pro-convention white vote, of which Republicans probably cast the majority, showed that the party had received nearly five thousand ballots less than Pease had received in his 1866 gubernatorial bid. Many Unionists had not accompanied the transition from Unionism to Republicanism.

The results showed that the future of Texas Republicans depended on the party achieving two major objectives. First, they had to maintain their base among the state's African American electorate, and that meant protecting them from the violence that had attempted to keep them out of politics. With extensive organization, as well as the continued presence of federal troops, even in modest numbers, blacks had been able to come together and go to the polls. That organization had to be maintained in the future. Some way of protecting voters also had to be secured. Second, Republicans had to attract white voters. These goals were critical, but the party's ability to do either was uncertain as the political struggles within the state moved from the electorate to the constitutional convention.

Chapter 6

REPUBLICAN COMPLEXITIES AND THE
CONSTITUTIONAL CONVENTION OF 1868–69

W hen the constitutional convention assembled on June 1, it became clear that the new Republican party had swept the election. An overwhelming majority of delegates represented the party; scalawags, carpetbaggers, and African Americans dominated the proceedings. Nonetheless, despite being Republican, they did not represent any single interest. Some of the internal problems of the Texas Republican party had become clear before the convention, but the complexity of interests did not become apparent until the actual proceedings began. The convention itself would be the forum within which the various components of the party fought for their particular agendas. This struggle uncovered key weaknesses in the new coalition that doomed it almost from the beginning.

The convention opened at Austin on June 1, 1867. Ninety delegates had been elected, but before the meeting adjourned, ninety-three different individuals would have seats in it. Of that number only eleven voted as Conservatives; the remaining eighty-two were Republicans. Of the latter, sixty-four were "scalawags," the derisive term the Conservative opposition applied to native white Republicans. Nine of the members were African Americans; all but one were from the South and had been slaves prior to emancipation. Nine more delegates were either "carpetbaggers," northern whites who came to Texas during or just after the war, or men whose origin is unknown. The large number of native whites in the convention made Texas unique in the Reconstruction South. Their domination of the proceedings prevented both African Americans and carpetbaggers from exercising the same kinds of influence their counterparts did in other states and ensured a more conservative, homegrown variety of Republicanism.

Traditional scholarship has emphasized the relative lack of political prominence among the men elected to the 1867 convention, insisting that few of them were politically important in the immediate prewar years. One scholar has suggested that they were not economically prominent either, noting how few were on corporate boards of companies chartered by the Eleventh Legislature.

That many antebellum leaders would not be in the convention should not be surprising, given the oath delegates had to take that they had not voluntarily supported the Confederacy. The lack of corporate board members also could be expected, given Conservative control over the legislature in 1866 and the Unionist background of many of the delegates. That does not mean that the credentials of those attending were not substantial. An examination of both Republicans and Conservatives shows that while many of these men may not have been part of the antebellum Democratic elite, many of them had been involved in politics during those years and most of them were, if not among the richest in Texas, men with a financial stake in the state's future.

The southern-born Republican leaders came from a variety of backgrounds. Their occupations included planting, farming, and ranching. Scalawags had served both as Union and Confederate soldiers. At least seven had served at some level in the state judiciary; seven others had served in the state legislature and one in Congress; and two had served in the Constitutional Convention of 1866. They included two veterans of the Texas Revolution and one survivor of the Santa Fe expedition. The two most prominent southern-born Republican delegates were Andrew J. Hamilton and Gen. Edmund J. Davis. Hamilton had done much following his time as provisional governor to bring about Congressional Reconstruction. Davis, a Florida-born Texan who had served in the Union Army and commanded a cavalry brigade, had returned after the war to become one of the party's leaders.

The nine African American delegates would be characterized by their party's political opponents as ignorant men incapable of understanding or working for the best interests of all Texans. Again, the actual situation differed considerably from the Conservative portrait. All but one had been a slave, but three since had acquired land and worked as farmers. Four had been craftsmen, among the elite of the slave community, and had continued to work at their respective trade after the war. Two had been teachers who had worked with the schools of the Freedmen's Bureau. Few details are known about most of the black delegates, but their lives varied considerably from the stereotype created by Conservatives.

Less information exists about the carpetbaggers in the convention than about any other group. Almost all of these men probably came to Texas with either the U.S. Army or the Freedmen's Bureau. While carpetbaggers played vital roles in the constitutional conventions of many of the other southern states, such men remained in the background during the Austin meeting. The best known of them, primarily because he was assassinated during the convention, was George W. Smith. Smith had come to Texas with the federal army and remained at Jefferson as a teacher for the Freedmen's Bureau schools when mustered out. He also opened a store there and became involved in Republican politics. Another man who emerged prominently within the party after the convention was James P. Butler. Butler had served with the army at Brownsville and Huntsville, then worked with the Freedmen's Bureau, and ultimately edited a Republican newspaper in Galveston.

The Conservative delegates also included some prominent citizens, even though none came from the Democratic leadership of the late 1850s. All of them were professional men or landowners. David Muckleroy from Nacogdoches had been in the state senate and was one of the largest planters in his community before the war. Others had served in public office. James T. Armstrong from Jefferson County, who had served in the Congress of the Republic, the Constitutional Convention of 1845, and the state senate, may have been the most experienced and most widely known of the Conservatives. Also prominent in his service had been Lemuel D. Evans, who also had been a delegate to the 1845 convention before going on to serve one term in the U.S. Congress.

Political factors turned the proceedings into the longest constitutional convention in the state's history. Before ending, its seating alone extended through two sessions, the first beginning on June 1 and adjourning on August 31. The second began on December 7 and ended in disarray on February 6, 1869. Much of the trouble that delayed the writing of a new constitution centered around the profound disagreements among Republican delegates over a wide variety of matters. These differences began to create problems on the very first day of the convention, when the party's caucus could not agree on a candidate for the presiding officer. Associates of the Pease administration advanced Colbert Caldwell as their nominee. Apparently, many considered Caldwell to be too radical, and this opposition advanced Edmund J. Davis. Failing to settle on a party candidate, the decision was left to an open vote on the convention floor, which Davis won by a vote of forty-three to thirty-three, with some Conservatives throwing their support to him. The inability of Republicans to agree in this dispute foretold serious future problems for party unity and for the process of writing the constitution.

Governor Pease had been one of the chief organizers of the state Republican party, and he established its priorities for the convention in his message to the delegates on June 4. Ultimately, the proposed constitution would have to be submitted to Congress for its approval, and the governor insisted that it had to show the loyal intentions of the men who drafted it. Given that perspective, Pease devoted most of his message to his ideas on how to make that clear, particularly his views on the actions that should be taken toward the ordinance of secession and the legislation and actions of the civil government during and after the war. He asked the delegates to declare the ordinance null and void, but he requested that only those measures by the state government that directly aided the rebel government be annulled, which would leave intact private laws that had been passed by wartime legislatures. In addition,

Pease asked that the convention void all laws that discriminated against persons on account of their race, color, or previous condition and that the constitution provide for equal civil and political rights for all Texans.

The governor also offered suggestions that ran beyond convincing Congress of the state's loyalty but did reflect his party's political agenda. He urged that the constitution provide the basis for a system of free public schools. He also urged that it include provisions allowing the state to aid internal improvements and to foster immigration; one particular recommendation regarding the latter issue was a constitutional provision for free homesteads on the state's public lands to actual settlers. On questions of suffrage, Pease indicated that some sort of temporary disfranchisement of former Confederate leaders might be necessary to ensure the success of Reconstruction. On an issue that had been part of the state's politics from the prewar years, dividing the state, the governor encouraged the delegates to take no action. He argued that the area and population of Texas could not successfully support two governments, and he warned that, since the Reconstruction Acts applied only to one state, division might actually delay a return to normal relations within the Union.

The question of nullifying the wartime actions of the state government early on became the central issue in the initial stages of the convention. This issue had emerged during the 1866 convention, with Unionists urging that the ordinance of secession plus subsequent actions of the state government should be null and void from the beginning, that is, *ab initio*. In the 1868–69 convention the question evolved to include not only the actions of the Confederate government but also those of the convention of 1866 and the subsequent Eleventh Legislature. United in 1866, old Unionists now in the Republican party split. Factions within the party and the Pease administration on this issue first had become apparent in the autumn of 1867, when Comptroller Morgan Hamilton, brother of former governor Andrew Hamilton, refused to pay the salaries of some state officials because their offices and the pay for them had been created by the Eleventh Legislature. Hamilton refused to accept its legal existence, and he was sustained by Attorney General William Alexander. Hamilton subsequently became the leader of the Republican faction known as *ab initioists*.

Governor Pease opposed Morgan Hamilton's position and received the strongest support from Andrew Hamilton. On October 25 Pease responded to the comptroller's action by declaring not only the acts of the Confederate state government not invalidated by the federal government but also the Constitution of 1866 and the laws of the Eleventh Legislature valid. Morgan Hamilton and Attorney General Alexander refused to accept Pease's declaration. Both of them continued to agitate the issue, and Hamilton ran for the constitutional convention arguing that it needed to take action to settle the question of legitimacy and declare all governmental actions after 1861 as illegal from the start. The supporters of this position precipitated debate in the convention on February 5, when one of the delegates introduced a measure declaring the ordinance of secession, the acts of the Confederate legislature, and the actions of the Eleventh Legislature null and void from the beginning.

Traditional scholarship has emphasized the theoretical nature of the *ab initio* debate, but the issue actually involved matters of much more substance, which made the factions involved so unwilling to compromise. The question touched on a wide variety of topics. Were court actions taken against "loyal men," especially seizures of land, during the war legal or not? Further, could these loyalists secure some sort of restitution for their losses? Did taxpayers such as Morgan Hamilton, who had extensive landholdings across Texas, owe back taxes to the state government for the war years? Was legislation legal that allowed the state's railroads to pay off their debts to the state school fund in Confederate money, and at full value (which had left the fund practically bankrupt), rather than in specie as required by law? Were the charters issued by the Eleventh Legislature to numerous railroad companies, particularly the Houston and Great Northern, and other corporations legitimate? Could freedmen demand compensation from their former masters for work done following secession? Obviously, important and powerful economic interests had a stake in resolving the question of *ab initio* in their favor, and the struggle was a bitter one that saw no compromise.

Rancorous discussion of the ordinance exploded after its introduction on June 5, 1868. A major split between the delegates appeared, mirroring that of the leadership. On the floor much of the debate centered around the 1864 law allowing railroads to pay their debts to the school fund in state and Confederate warrants. Obviously, this was not the only issue touched by *ab initio,* but it was an emotional one and an obvious example of how the Confederate legislature had acted in a way that hurt many Texans. Morgan Hamilton charged the railroads with conspiracy, alleging that they had colluded with the legislature to defraud the school fund. Andrew Hamilton responded that *ab initio* was too radical and that nullifying all law and civil action since 1861 would produce chaos. The former governor introduced his own emotional appeal, countering his brother's charge that those who opposed *ab initio* represented the interests of the corporations against the people with his own assertion that only impractical radicals supported the measure.

As the debate proceeded, the character of the division within the party became apparent. Those Republicans who strongly supported the state's railroads tended to oppose the measure. In the convention this included A. J. Hamilton, who had interest in the Memphis, El Paso, and Pacific and the Houston and Texas Central, both of which benefited from wartime legislation and the subsequent recognition of the legality of this legislation by the convention of 1866. A group of delegates from eastern Texas, who generally followed the lead of James W. Flanagan of Rusk County, another railroad developer associated with the Memphis and El Paso, also opposed *ab initio*. Supporters of the measure came primarily from delegates out of western Texas. Their motives for backing it are less clear, though many of them appear to have supported it in order to set aside a wide variety of other measures that appeared to unjustly effect loyalists, as in the case of Morgan Hamilton's concern with wartime taxation. Other Texans from the western counties may have been interested in breaking the monopoly the railroads of Houston and Galveston had over the state's largess. These advocates of *ab initio* found strong support among the convention's African Americans, possibly because they saw its support as a means of restoring the assets of the school fund.

A vote on the *ab initio* question did not take place until June 29, when A. J. Hamilton introduced a substitute to the original motion that would have recognized not only the nullity of the secession ordinance and those laws designed to aid the rebellion but also the legality of those laws and government actions not in violation of the laws of the United States. This obviously did not satisfy those supporting *ab initio* nor did its declaration of the nullity of secession find acceptance with most Conservatives. When the proposal received a favorable vote, supporters of *ab initio* moved to table the substitute and received Conservative support in doing so. The motion to table passed, though only by a margin of forty-six to forty-three, with Conservatives supporting Morgan Hamilton and western Republicans; supporters of Andrew Hamilton and Republicans from eastern Texas constituted the majority. The question continued to simmer until a final vote accepting the legality of wartime legislation took place on August 20, but the vote on June 29 indicated to *ab initio* supporters that they did not have enough support to carry their point in the convention. They refused to give in, however, and their lack of strength forced them to move the struggle beyond the convention and into the Republican party itself.

The second major issue occupying much of the time during the first session was the question of dividing the state, even though the governor had urged the delegates not to consider the question. For political and economic reasons, there was strong support for division. West Texans believed that Galveston and Houston dominated the state's politics and its government and that only division would relieve them from that control. Unionists from that section also worried about whether or not a pro-Union government could be maintained in a unified Texas. African American voters backed the westerners, possibly in return for their support of broader civil rights legislation. East Texas Republicans also expressed concern for the power of Galveston and Houston. Even Conservatives like Lemuel D. Evans, primarily an advocate of economic development of eastern Texas, supported division. Ultimately, this unlikely coalition introduced a resolution endorsing an effort underway in

Congress at that time to divide the state into two or more new states. Administration supporters opposed the resolution and secured some Conservative backing, though only the skillful parliamentary manipulation of Andrew Hamilton prevented action in support of division early in the convention. On July 16 the delegates voted not to consider division again unless Congress authorized the creation of a new state.

Almost the only items directly related to writing the new constitution that came up for debate in the first session were provisions concerning civil rights. Once again voting patterns shifted. Morgan Hamilton controlled the Committee on General Provisions, created at the beginning of the session, and, whether on the basis of principle or political expediency, sought to forge an alliance with African American delegates. In the draft of a "Bill of Rights" that came from his committee, one section attempted to broaden the concept of civil rights by declaring unconstitutional any discrimination on the basis of race by any operator of a business open to the public or subject to state licensing. Traditionally, civil rights guaranteed equal access to the law and protection of life, liberty, and property. The new measure ensured not only these rights but also the right of equal access to public institutions, particularly to schools.

On this measure Morgan Hamilton and the western Texans combined with African American delegates in what would become a permanent bloc for the rest of the convention. This raises questions about Hamilton's motives and whether or not he was actually committed to this view of civil rights or only trying to gather support for his positions on *ab initio* and division. In this case, however, he was among the minority, for the majority of white delegates wanted nothing to do with the measure. Republicans from the eastern part of the state, with the westerners on division and opposed to them on railroads, went with the administration on this question. With Conservative support, all efforts at producing an expanded view of civil rights died an early death on the floor.

If they could not agree on the need of *ab initio,* the desirability of division, or the necessity for a broader definition of civil rights, Republicans did unite in their concern for widespread violence in the state and the importance of doing something about it. The question of whether the mayhem most persons believed afflicted Texas resulted simply from the activities of a lawless element or had been spawned by their Conservative political opponents mattered little to Republicans—any violence served to suppress the freedom of African Americans and to undermine the party. One of the first committees created was one to study lawlessness and violence. Drawing on reports from county officials and information gathered by the Freedmen's Bureau and the army, the committee reported that nearly a thousand individuals, 509 whites and 468 blacks, had been murdered between the end of the war and the summer of 1868. Members attributed most of these murders to politics and pointed specifically to the rise of crime following the appointment of Gen. Winfield S. Hancock, a Democrat and an officer hostile to Congressional Reconstruction, as commander of the Fifth Military District the previous November. Conservatives denied the political character of the violence, arguing instead that it simply reflected the unsettled condition of the state.[1]

Unquestionably, much of the violence that took place during Presidential Reconstruction was of this type and reflected a combination of personal and economic motives. With the beginning of Congressional Reconstruction, and particularly after the Republican party started its efforts to organize blacks as voters, politics was the issue. Republicans had every reason to fear the consequences of violence. The Democrats' national campaign to regain the presidency in 1868 had led to the reorganization of a party organization in Texas in January, and its leaders' efforts to deliver the state's electoral votes to a Democratic candidate the next fall produced disturbing tactics. Party leadership faced several major problems in reorganizing, though. First, they had to mobilize their traditional voters. This was a pressing difficulty since many whites had shown little concern with politics up to this point. Second, they believed that they had to control African American voters in order to ensure that the pro-Republican results of the election for the constitutional convention were not repeated.

The Democratic campaign to attract both white and black voters ultimately centered on the freedmen and issues of race. In their efforts at gaining control over African Americans, the Democrats first offered the freedmen a carrot, promising them that they would be protected if they would join with Democrats in driving the Republicans from power. Proclaiming themselves the freedmen's best friends, Democrats offered jobs and protection of property and lives for those who joined Democratic clubs. They also held barbecues for black farmhands. Prominent Democrats, including John H. Reagan, spoke to those attending and encouraged their joining local clubs. At a meeting in Trinity County, white leaders asked blacks to sign a pledge of fidelity to the Democratic party, in turn, any who did received a written certificate that was supposed to protect the individual from violence.[2]

If black voters did not accept the carrot, Democrats offered a stick, the very intimidation, threats to property, and violence from which they had promised relief. At Jefferson, Democrats resolved not to hire any Republicans or to patronize their businesses. There and at Marshall, planters acted on these promises and dismissed workers who joined the Union League or otherwise participated in politics. In Bowie County former governor Hardin R. Runnels took the lead in carrying out the same policies. The editor of the leading Democratic paper of the time, the *Galveston News,* encouraged others to adopt such practices. "No one can be more opposed to mere proscription of every kind than we are," he wrote, "but we agree with the [*Harrison*] *Flag* that 'our all is at stake,' and, as old Hickory said of the Union, 'it must be preserved.'"[3]

Economic threats made up only part of the effort at intimidation, however, and as the campaign continued, brutal attacks upon the freedmen broke out. Ultimately, Democratic campaign rhetoric provided an atmosphere that encouraged this violence and made it practically inevitable. In Texas, Conservative politicians had embraced the message of the national Democratic party when it decided to make Reconstruction and black suffrage the central issues in the election. Democratic politicians in Texas added their own volatile rhetoric. At the party's convention in Houston in January, 1868, John H. Reagan had declared that the Conservative coalition had organized "to save the State from negro supremacy."[4] Local meetings of Democrats declared their refusal to accept black suffrage. The party press charged that black voting meant the Africanization of Texas society and had to be opposed at all costs. Democratic leaders painted a picture of crisis that threatened the very existence of white society.

The relationship of Democrats to the outbreak of violence may have been more, however, than simply providing a favorable atmosphere for it. As preparations for the elections progressed, the appearance of local Democratic clubs saw the parallel development of the Ku Klux Klan within the state. This organization had originally developed elsewhere and had been used effectively in southern politics. Now it arrived in Texas. The connection between Democratic clubs and the Klan cannot be known with certainty, but the fact that both organized at about the same time strongly suggests a relationship. At least one Democratic correspondent to the *Galveston News* gave tacit approval to the Klan when he argued that he wanted to see secret organizations created to counter the Union League and to make possible "a purer social atmosphere and as the last hope for the maintenance of the supremacy of the white race in this Republic."[5] Later apologists for the Klan would suggest that its goal was to punish African Americans who acted criminally, but its actions in the spring and summer of 1868 aimed principally at discouraging blacks from participating in politics or at least from voting Republican.

Amid a summer of bloodshed, one of the most violent of these political encounters took place at Millican in Brazos County. On July 15, armed whites calling themselves the Ku Klux Klan paraded through the Freedmen's Town, intending to intimidate blacks who had begun political organization. But the freedmen attacked them and drove them out. The whites returned, however. This time they assaulted the blacks and killed as many as twenty-five men, including local political leaders. Among the casualties was George E. Brooks, a Methodist minister who had organized the local Union League. The Millican encounter was not alone in its brutality. In Marion County whites planned a Fourth of July barbecue to encourage blacks to join Democratic clubs, and when most failed to attend, a mob of three hundred whites drove all blacks and white Unionists from the town of Jefferson. Republican activists were attacked, and in some cases killed, in Fort Bend, Gillespie, Nacogdoches, and Washington Counties. Freedmen's schools, where teachers often encouraged political activity, were singled out. Groups calling themselves the Klan attacked schools run by the Freedmen's Bureau in Anderson, Fort Bend, Harrison, and Red River Counties, driving the teachers out of the neighborhoods. The degree to which those committing these attacks would go became clear in October, when assassins killed George W. Smith, a member of the convention. A Democratic newspaper justified the violence, its editor writing, "the sanctity of home, the peace and safety of society, the prosperity of the country, and the security of life itself demanded the removal of so base a villain."[6] Across the state African Americans and their white allies faced a virtual war.

Republicans in the constitutional convention correctly saw that, if they were to succeed, they needed to stop the violence that undermined the political activities of freedmen and Unionists. As a result, they agreed to send a commission to Congress to make known the extent of crime in the state. In addition, they were to ask that Governor Pease be given power to continue removing uncooperative civilian authorities and replace them with persons who would enforce the law. The convention authorized the commission to ask for permission to organize an armed state militia to deal with the threats. The delegates' requests demonstrated not only the concern among Republicans about the growing violence but also a total lack of faith that the U.S. Army would provide the protection they needed if they were going to be successful in the upcoming political battles.

Delegates accomplished little in the first months of the convention, finally adjourning in August. The Radicals took the lead in the move for adjournment. Andrew Hamilton did not want to delay the convention's work and, with the cooperation of the Conservatives, managed to stall the Radicals for a time. Ultimately, he was forced to concede to the Radicals, however, when all of the money originally appropriated for the meeting ran out. General Reynolds refused to authorize further funds because not enough money was coming into the treasury to pay for the session's extension. Delegates voted to levy a convention tax of twenty cents on each hundred dollars of property, which had to be paid by December 1. They then adjourned to reassemble on December 4 after the new tax had generated sufficient funds.

On the whole, the first three months of the convention saw little substantive action taken toward the writing of a new constitution. The reasons for this are not clear. Given the overall state of things in Texas and on the national scene, the most likely explanation for this lack of progress was that the Republicans were delaying, trying to keep the state from seeking readmission before the national elections that autumn. A victory by Gen. Ulysses S. Grant appeared certain, but given the rapid resurgence of the Democratic party in other southern states, that victory would be even more certain if Texas remained out of the Union. Indeed, Republican leaders were uncertain that, if allowed to participate in the presidential election, they could deliver the vote to Grant. President Johnson's and General Hancock's interference with the military's replacement of Conservative local officeholders had limited Republican efforts at building local parties. At the same time, the Radicals hoped for a new Congress more favorable to their plans for division, and being able to show that no government had yet been organized would make their efforts easier.

Whatever the reason for the delay and adjournment, the interim between the sessions did nothing to heal the wide divisions within the party and made the establishment of a broad-based opposition to the Conservatives less likely. On August 12, at the Republican state convention at Austin, the differences turned into a party schism that resulted in the creation of two separate party organizations. One, the Administration or Moderate Republicans, included the men in the convention who had supported Governor Pease's program and followed the leadership of A. J. Hamilton. The other, the Radicals, included the supporters of *ab initio,* many western Republicans, and most blacks.

The division in Austin was preceded a month and a half earlier by George Ruby's takeover of the Union League from administration supporters. Criticizing the Pease government for its failure to use force against white terrorists, its waffling on civil rights in the convention, and its refusal to give blacks greater opportunities for political offices, Ruby had defeated the administration's candidate for president of the league. His victory was critical to subsequent events, for it meant that the black vote was no longer controlled by administration forces but open to other leadership. Now, opponents of the administration no longer needed to compromise but could run for office on their own with some chance of success. If they could gain league support, then they could even defeat their opponents.

In the state Republican convention, Morgan Hamilton and Edmund Davis courted Ruby, and the new head of the league threw his support to them. They could not control the party convention, however. It proceeded peacefully enough until Davis introduced two resolutions that broached the topic of *ab initio.* These resolutions, in fact designed to produce some sort of agreement, became the clearest statement of what made this issue so divisive. Davis wanted two resolutions added to the platform. One would have supported nullification of all laws passed during the war except for grants to persons in actual residence. The other would have backed the nullification of the laws that had allowed the railroads to repay the school funds in state warrants rather than specie. The Moderate majority refused to endorse either, and Davis and his supporters left the convention.

On August 15 Davis met with anti-administration Republicans and formed a new organization. The basic differences between the two groups was made clear in a platform that looked largely like that passed in the regular convention except that it embraced the two resolutions he had offered in the regular convention. In addition, it called for the collection of all money owed to the school fund and stated its hope that the use of such monies would create a public school system that would take precedence over support for railroads. Responding to the blacks who had moved to the breakaway organization's support, the delegates also called for an end to residence restrictions for office holding aimed at blacks and for strict enforcement of the law. With the issues that had divided the convention now in the open political arena, little chance existed that a compromise would be reached when the constitutional convention reconvened.

While the Republicans squabbled, the Democrats continued their efforts at organizing and mobilizing voters for the autumn elections. On July 10 they had held a state convention at Bryan. The delegates gave their strong support to the candidates and platform of the national Democratic party. On Reconstruction issues their position appeared moderate, though a threat to the entire process was embedded within their statements. The convention passed resolutions acquiescing in the abolition of slavery and embracing the Union. Other resolutions declared the party's intention to protect the civil rights of African Americans. But the delegates asserted that the right of suffrage ultimately should be determined by the states. Throughout the campaign, Democrats made it clear that only those African Americans who might vote with them, if any, should have the suffrage.

The Democrats' organizational effort took place despite the fact that on July 20 Congress had passed a resolution to exclude from the electoral college the votes of states that had not yet been reorganized. As a result, Republicans had not nominated candidates to the electoral college at their convention. National Democratic leaders, however, encouraged local Democrats to organize and hold an election anyway. In late September the chairman of the party's state committee, William Walton, asked General Reynolds to order an election under the authority given him by the First Reconstruction Act. When it was clear that Reynolds would not do so, Walton recommended that the people meet in each county on November 3, name election officers, cast votes for president, and deliver the results to the state executive committee. On October 1 Reynolds brought the discussion to an end by stating that he intended to abide by the congressional resolution and forbade the holding of an election.

When the national election finally occurred, Grant handily defeated the Democratic nominee, Horatio Seymour. The Republican victory ensured that Reconstruction would not only proceed but also be implemented now by an executive who was in agreement with the policies of Congress. Texas

Democrats realized there was no chance for an early end to Reconstruction, and their efforts at organization abated. The new national political situation would help change the dynamics of local politics, and in the months that followed, the resurgent Democracy would seek new means for recapturing control of the state government.

When the constitutional convention reassembled at Austin on December 7 the *ab initio* question had disappeared and been moved to the public arena, where the two Republican factions hoped to achieve their goals. The question of division, however, would not die and continued to occupy the attention of the delegates. All the economic reasons for it remained, but the growing violence had convinced many Republicans that it also was the only means for securing a loyal state. James P. Newcomb of San Antonio once again brought the question to the floor. Once again Andrew Hamilton used his parliamentary skills to stymie the divisionists. Ultimately, however, in January, 1869, the divisionists managed to brush aside Hamilton's efforts and pass a resolution that called for the convention to send a delegation to Washington to lobby Congress for the splitting up of Texas.

Despite the continued struggle between factions, delegates spent much more time on the actual task of writing a constitution. Here another issue emerged that reinforced the split within the Republican organization, the franchise. Led by A. J. Hamilton, Moderates in the convention moved to include most adult males in the franchise, restricting voting only to those excluded by the Fourteenth Amendment. This represented a reversal of policy from that outlined by Pease the previous June, when he advised that some sort of limits on suffrage might be necessary. This shift is best seen in the changing political landscape, for the Moderate loss of league support the previous summer required that faction to secure greater support from among whites if it were to succeed. This could only be achieved by attempting some sort of reconciliation with former Confederates. In the convention Conservative delegates and the East Texas Republicans who had supported division joined with Hamilton and his supporters to achieve a clear majority, and ultimately the new constitution's provisions excluded no one from the franchise or from office other than those already prohibited by Congress.

Ultimately, the struggle over the franchise broke up the convention. The Radicals now were convinced that Republican government was impossible. The Andrew Hamilton faction continued to move forward and on February 5, with Conservative support, secured the passage of an ordinance that provided for an election submitting the constitution to the people during the first week of July. Radicals entered a protest on the convention record, recommending that the constitution be rejected because of its position on *ab initio* and its suffrage provisions. The ordinance passed that morning should have brought the convention to an end, but an evening session degenerated into a struggle between the Davis and Hamilton factions over adjournment, with the Hamilton group attempting to keep the convention in session. The departure of two Radical members broke the quorum, providing the means for Davis to adjourn the session. Despite the efforts of the Hamilton group, Davis walked out, leaving his opponents to carry on in a rump session that had no real authority.

Hamilton Republicans and Conservatives reconvened the convention then next day, but the Radicals and Davis were not present. A committee sent to discuss the situation with Gen. E. R. S. Canby received word to complete the body's bookkeeping and adjourn. The Davis faction met that evening, at Canby's suggestion, but only a few delegates attended. Fearing all of the work of the convention would be lost, the general set about collecting the records from the various secretaries and clerks of the convention. Canby then put those men and part of his own staff to work putting together a constitution based upon the minutes of the convention and earlier drafts. He had a delegate from each of the factions present to make sure that the completed document was accurate.

The state constitution pieced together by the clerks and observers ultimately would go before the voters. Even though the Republican majority had been divided on many issues, the document ultimately produced was the result of considerable agreement among them. Governor Pease and his backers sponsored some of the more significant changes from the older constitution. The Radicals generally supported their efforts. Overall, many of the changes reflected the belief among most Republicans that Texans were not yet ready to establish a loyal government and that some sort of controls had to be maintained in order to secure the long-term goal. The resulting document significantly changed the character of the state government.

From the very first section of Article 1, the Bill of Rights, the concern with the white majority was apparent. That section declared the Constitution of the United States and the laws passed by the federal government to be "the supreme law"; the authors considered the new state constitution to be "in subordination thereto." Gone was any recognition of states' rights. Instead, the delegates had attempted to ensure that Texas could not take any action to undo the Reconstruction measures implemented by Congress. A further indication of the lack of trust implicit in the new constitution was a change in the power to suspend the writ of habeas corpus. Previous constitutions had allowed this only in time of war or rebellion; the new constitution allowed the legislature to act "when the public safety may require it." Clearly, Republicans sensed that they still were in a war with the former rebels.[7]

The proposed constitution also carried out a major restructuring of the state government that gave greater power to the executive branch and to the government as a whole. These were not novel ideas but reflected antebellum beliefs that the size of Texas made administration difficult and required more leadership from Austin. The governor was given considerable appointive powers, authorized to name with the advice and consent of the state senate the secretary of state and attorney general. The elected judiciary was eliminated, and the governor given the power to name district-court judges as well as those of the supreme court (whose numbers were decreased from five to three), though provisions were made that the state could return to an elected system at some future time. Given the violence that had beset Texas up to this point, Republicans were reluctant to place the justice system in local hands. A remarkable action counter to this centralizing trend was the constitution's placing of the power to assess property value for tax purposes in the hands of local justices of the peace, thus leaving this in the hands of the county courts.

Its provisions for a public school system also reflected the new document's tendency toward the centralization of authority. These created an office of state superintendent of public instruction to supervise the operations of the state schools and gave the governor the power to appoint him. While previous state constitutions had given general support for the idea of education and dedicated some of the public lands for its support, the new one directly charged the legislature with establishing "a uniform system of public free schools throughout the State." To accomplish this, the legislature was empowered to raises taxes to support the system and even allowed to make attendance at schools compulsory.

The new constitution was not all about Republican concern for creating a loyal state, however. It also reflected a general belief that the state needed to sponsor and support economic development, authorizing the creation of a "Bureau of Immigration" to draw new residents to Texas. The constitution also provided for state support to internal improvements, though it embraced a major change in how this would be done. Prior to the war, the state had underwritten railroad construction using the permanent school fund and, in some cases, actual land grants, all of which the new constitution prohibited. Instead, railroads could secure the support of the legislature or local authorities, who were permitted to issue bonds to encourage internal improvements. Other measures indicating the strong belief that the state should promote economic development included an end to restrictions on the creation of state banks and a prohibition of the legislature's ability to limit interest rates.

The convention's course toward the freedmen reflected the overall tendency of white Republicans to accept them as political allies but not as social equals. The radical report from Morgan Hamilton's committee that had called for a guarantee that African Americans would have access to any establishments open to the public on an equal basis had been voted down. Instead, the new constitution recognized only the "equality of all persons before the law." Yet some aspects were a direct response to the concerns of freedmen. Section 22 of the new Bill of Rights prohibited the adoption of "any system of peonage, whereby the helpless and unfortunate may be reduced to practical bondage." The residency requirements for all state offices were reduced, making it easier for blacks to run for office. In addition, the new constitution removed the restrictions placed on African Americans by the 1866 document. Finally, it declared those former slaves who had established unions before emancipation or up to the time of the new constitution to be legitimately married.

In the end the section with the greatest future political importance would be that dealing with the right of suffrage. Hamilton's supporters, who had desired that no restrictions be placed on former Confederates, won the convention battle. The new constitution declared that all male citizens twenty-one years of age and older who did not remain disqualified under federal law or who suffered under some other disability named in the state constitution would be able to vote. This section paved the way for a greater participation in the electoral process by whites. Its adoption meant that Republicans faced an even greater necessity of winning support from that constituency.

With the adjournment of the convention, the course of Reconstruction in Texas once again was placed in the hands of the state's voters. As president of the convention, E. J. Davis issued an election declaration naming the first Monday in July, 1869, as the date for Texans to vote for or against the constitution. At the same time, citizens would chose members of the legislature and fill all state, district, and county offices. The struggles over the constitution and the election of constitutional officers would be the next step in the state's course through Reconstruction.

Chapter 7

The Election of 1869 and the Question of Legitimacy

Following the adjournment of the convention, Texans prepared for the critical election to either ratify or defeat the proposed constitution. In the event they ratified it, they also had to vote for state and local officials, who would serve if the constitution was approved and Congress readmitted the state to its place in the Union. Much was at stake in this election, the first since 1866. Even in times of stability, elections serve more than one function in a democratic society. They decide who exercises political power and holds offices, but an equally critical role is that of legitimizing the government that comes into power. In theory, victory affirms that the government in power represents the people's will, at least the will of a majority of citizens. Because of this, the loser must accept the opposition's hold on power until the next vote. That the 1869 election fulfill this legitimizing function was essential if stability in Texas was to be restored and the justification of political violence, which had grown to considerable proportions, ended. Its character would be critical to the future stability of whatever government took office afterward.

A very complex political situation provided the context for the election. The Republican party emerged from the constitutional convention with its two factions unable to heal the breach that had developed. The Radicals clearly believed that little chance existed to establish a loyal government. Edmund Davis, Morgan Hamilton, and James W. Flanagan, the most prominent members of the commission to make the case for state division before Congress, had left for Washington shortly after adjournment. They submitted a memorial that proposed a division of Texas, admission of the area west of the Colorado to statehood, and keeping the eastern parts of the state under military rule. It stated their belief that division was the only way of guaranteeing a loyal government in any part of Texas and of protecting loyal men. The commissioners portrayed the proposed constitution as a product of disloyalty, for its recognition of the acts of the Confederate and Throckmorton governments rewarded treason and its franchise provisions opened the way for the rapid return of the ex-Confederates to power. In discussions with President Grant and congressmen, the commissioners urged that no election be held until Congress could consider the question of division. If an election had to be held first, they insisted that it be delayed until after Congress reconvened.

The divisionists had been followed east by A. J. Hamilton and others calling themselves the "people's commissioners." Hamilton and his associates also met with the president and members of Congress and offered a different point of view. They argued that Texas was again at peace, that the proposed constitution represented the work of loyalists, and that it would produce a loyal government. They strongly opposed division, arguing that it was impractical, and charged the divisionists with being nothing more than disappointed office seekers. The immediate goal of the "people's commissioners" was to get Congress to provide for an election as soon as possible and bring an end to the squabbles that had broken out within the Texas Republican party.

Hamilton's group found a powerful ally at Washington in Gen. Joseph J. Reynolds, who had gone to the capital following his replacement as commander of the Fifth Military District in November by General Canby. Reynolds, a classmate and friend of President-elect Grant, had been supportive of the Moderate Republicans during the convention and opposed division. Three days before the inauguration, he introduced the antidivisionist commissioners to Grant so that they could make their case. Reynolds apparently stated his own opposition to plans for division at that meeting, though avoiding any endorsement of the Hamilton faction. Hamilton's arguments and Reynolds's support appeared to sway Grant against division. The antidivisionists believed they had won the day, and the president's reappointment of Reynolds to command the Fifth District shortly after the inauguration seemed to confirm their conclusions.

Reynolds also arranged a meeting of the divisionists, though not until after the inauguration. By then the new president clearly had determined his opposition to dividing Texas. The divisionists did not give up, however. On March 11 they submitted their memorial to Congress. Five days later a sympathetic congressman from Michigan introduced a bill in the House of Representatives providing for the division of Texas into three states. Another bill introduced at the same time would have divided the state into three territories. A bill introduced on March 22 that more closely reflected the ideas of the convention's commissioners proposed the creation of the State of Lincoln from territory to the west of the Colorado River while keeping the rest of Texas under military rule. Hamilton and his commissioners responded to the first bills with a memorial stating the reasons why they should not pass. The divisionists carried out their own public-relations campaign in pamphlets, northern newspapers, and before local Republican groups, trying to pressure Congress to act.

Gen. Joseph J. Reynolds, military commander of Texas, 1867–69.
Courtesy U.S. Army Military History Institute

Congress took up the entire Texas matter on March 30, when the Committee on Reconstruction opened hearings. The committee heard the testimony of both contending parties not only on the matter of division but also on what action should be taken regarding the new state constitution. The testimony was contentious, with opposing commissioners posing hostile questions. With the president desiring action on Texas and opposed to division, and with no overwhelming support for the latter in Congress, the Committee on Reconstruction refused to intervene. Instead, it endorsed a bill that passed quickly through Congress allowing the president to call an election in Texas. Hamilton and his supporters appeared to have defeated division and to have paved the way for their own electoral victory. The only problem with what had taken place was that Grant did not appear ready to call an early election.

With the election inevitable, the Texas politicians in Washington returned home to prepare. Neither side in the factional split appeared ready to make peace. On March 18, weeks before Congress had authorized an election, A. J. Hamilton announced from nation's capital that he was a candidate for governor. Subsequently, the executive committee of the regular Republican organization endorsed his candidacy. While still in Washington, Hamilton lobbied to secure the federal patronage in the state for his supporters in preparation for the canvass. The president accepted the Hamilton faction as representatives of the legitimate Republican party in the state and strengthened that group by naming their candidates to the major federal jobs in Texas. The Galveston postmastership, the collector of customs, and the jobs of assessor and collector of internal revenue all went to Hamilton supporters. The return of General Reynolds to Texas was seen as one of the president's most supportive actions, though the general remained on the fence and tried to remain balanced in naming local officials.

Congress's refusal to act on division had brought an end to that issue. *Ab initio* was dealt an equally mortal blow on April 15, when the U.S. Supreme Court recognized the continued and legitimate existence of state government through the war in the case of *Texas v. White*. The Republican factions refused to make their peace, however. This continued schism raised serious concerns, not only among national leaders but also among many party members within the state. Both factions experienced increasing criticism from Republicans urging compromise. Locally, men such as James Tracy, editor of the *Houston Union*, and Edwin M. Wheelock, superintendent of public instruction under Governor Pease and now editor of the *San Antonio Express*, supported compromise. They found that the opposing groups' positions on issues were too extreme and expressed particular concern with Andrew Hamilton's overtures to the Conservatives. By this time it was clear that the two favorite issues of the Radicals were dead, and critics charged that the continued struggle reflected only the personal ambitions of rival leaders.

In April Morgan Hamilton of the Radical's executive committee had called for a Radical convention to be held at Galveston on May 10 to make nominations for the gubernatorial race. General Reynolds encouraged all Republicans to attend this meeting and discuss putting an end to the division. Andrew Hamilton's backers stayed away from the Galveston convention, but others were there who urged the delegates to refrain from making nominations and come together in early June at a Houston convention proposed to reconcile the factions. The delegates adjourned without making a nomination, accepting the proposals to reassemble again at another date.

James Tracy called the reconciliation convention for June 7. The centrists asked for a compromise and the selection of a single candidate that both factions could accept. Party leaders undertook considerable negotiations behind the scenes and apparently made headway. Rumors spread prior to the convention that an end of the party schism was in the making. The basis for that agreement was that Jack Hamilton would be nominated for governor and E. J. Davis for lieutenant governor. Following the organization of the government, Hamilton would be elected to the U.S. Senate and Davis would become governor. Hamilton and prominent supporters appeared at the Houston convention, suggesting that the rumors might have some validity. The former governor refused to become an official member, however. Observers speculated that he looked at the delegate attendance and concluded that he did not have enough support to secure the gubernatorial nomination no matter what agreement had been made. General Reynolds believed that Hamilton refused because he still desired to bring former Democrats to his support and that he could not running as a Republican. Whatever the reason, Hamilton had seriously misread concern among party members about the split as well as the former governor's course toward the Democrats.

The men who attended the Houston meeting showed that Tracy and Wheelock had attracted a broad spectrum of Republican leaders. Like them, those who believed it was time for party reconciliation were prominent. Many of the delegates represented the western interests that had pushed *ab initio* and division. At the same time, politicians associated with James Flanagan from eastern Texas were there; this group had cooperated with the westerners on division but had not supported *ab initio* and were among the most conservative of all Republicans on race issues. Delegates also included representatives of the Union League, now headed by George Ruby, convinced that Hamilton had sold them out to the Conservatives and now committed to E. J. Davis. The fact that these dissimilar factions remained together and agreed to a slate of state officials indicates the considerable pressure for compromise within the convention, selecting a ticket that represented the effort at restoring party unity. Davis received the nomination as governor and Flanagan was chosen as the nominee for lieutenant governor.[1]

The atmosphere of compromise also produced a more moderate platform that abandoned many of the positions advocated by the Radicals. As noted, the questions of state division and *ab initio* no longer were viable. The compromise convention also dropped Radical opposition to the constitution, instead calling for its passage. Further, the delegates invited former Confederates who accepted Reconstruction on the basis of impartial justice and equal rights to join with them in restoring the state to the Union. Davis appeared caught up in the spirit of the convention. In accepting the nomination, he proposed "to be the candidate of the whole Republican party, without regard to faction or clique."[2]

General Reynolds's assessment of Hamilton's refusal to join the convention may have been the correct one, for the former governor had made it clear at the convention and then in the following months that he believed the future of the Republican party in Texas required bringing prominent whites into the party. His campaign clearly aimed at that goal. In February, 1869, prior to going to Washington, Hamilton gave a speech at Brenham in Washington County that included overtures to whites. Claiming that he and his supporters had protected them from the radical racial policies of his opponents, Hamilton called upon conservative men to support him in the upcoming canvass and help him continue his policy of moderation. His approach was received well by Conservative political leaders such as Ashbel Smith and John H. Reagan; both prominent Democrats endorsed his candidacy, though not going so far as to suggest that this was the start of a permanent alliance. Nonetheless, their support indicated to Hamilton that his policy was potentially successful and that he could forge a new Republican entity out of the moderate elements of both parties.

With Hamilton determination to attract larger numbers of white voters, the compromises made at the Republican convention at Houston failed to end the schism. In fact, the convention not only failed to bring Hamilton back into the party fold but also incensed some of the party's more radical members, Morgan Hamilton in particular. He had been one of the most strident supporters of *ab initio* and division and was convinced that the Republicans' willingness to support the new constitution and to run candidates on that basis doomed the party's future. He could see no way that the acceptance of the constitution and its liberal provisions for suffrage would produce anything but the rapid return of the Democrats to power. Hamilton did not believe that former Confederates could be attracted to the party in any numbers or that a biracial coalition could be created. To him, the party's new position assured that Unionists would never secure justice. In the future Morgan Hamilton's disillusionment with the party denied it a power ally, especially after he went to Washington as one of the state's senators.

The convention did not heal breaches within the party, but it played a critical role in determining the outcome of the upcoming election and had a significant influence on the national Republican organization's view of the situation in Texas. Tracy, named head of the state executive committee appointed at Houston, lobbied national party leaders to recognize his newly created committee as the legitimate representative of the Republican party in Texas. Gaining the support of the national committee offered several potentially important results. First, it opened the way for the state party to receive some financial assistance from the national organization. Second, and possibly more critically, it would give the Davis group support in their efforts at winning recognition from President Grant and then obtaining the removal of political appointees in Texas who were loyal to Andrew Hamilton. If the Davis Republicans could put their own men in place, they would be able to reward those faithful to Davis with offices as well as attract those who wanted patronage. Tracy argued that Davis was the only Republican candidate to be nominated by a convention, which indicated that his candidacy was the only one to represent the will of the majority of Texas Republicans. The appeal got a favorable hearing. On July 7, despite efforts by Hamilton's supporters to block a decision, the Republican National Executive Committee recognized the Davis faction as the regular party organization.

Hamilton was now in a difficult situation. He had lost the support of the national Republican party and its endorsement. The national Union League went with the party and ensured that the state league would be in the hands of Davis's allies. This reduced Hamilton's possibilities of receiving Republican votes and created a situation in which he had to rely on support from the Conservatives to be victorious. They, however, were difficult allies. Former Democratic leaders may have endorsed Hamilton's candidacy, but they did not do this because they supported the former governor's efforts at forging a new party—they simply viewed Hamilton's election and the ratification of the proposed constitution as the best way to bring a quick end to Congressional Reconstruction. At the same time that they offered their support to Hamilton, Conservatives encouraged their local supporters to reorganize the Democratic party and run Democratic candidates for Congress and the state legislature. While still claiming for themselves the title "Conservative," by 1869 this group no longer represented a coalition of Democrats and Conservative Unionists; the Conservative party was now practically synonymous with the old Democracy. In a letter to one of his political associates, Ashbel Smith assured his correspondent that the sole goal of the old Democratic leadership in supporting Hamilton was the "ultimate control of the state government by the Democratic party."[3]

The activities of Democrats at the local level clearly demonstrated the fundamental goal of their party. The state leadership had moved away from fusion politics to reestablish their party as a straight-out Democratic organization during the anticipated presidential election the previous summer. In this effort secret associations had begun to appear, usually making their presence public shortly after Democratic party rallies had initiated the renewal of political activity. Locals often knew these secret groups by different names, but the one name most commonly associated with them was the Ku Klux Klan. No evidence indicates that they were part of a broader southern organization.

Local Klans continued to operate even though Texans had not been allowed to participate in the presidential election of 1868. They became increasingly active as state politicians prepared for the 1869 elections. Masked Klansmen recruited new members, swearing them on the Bible to support the goals of the organization. Klan members usually claimed that the primary goal of the group was to help reestablish law and order at the local level, but they readily admitted their political agenda as well. A salesman who lived in northern Texas and was a member of the Klan at this time outlined its purposes as being to "protect citizens of that country from military arrests and prosecution, and to defeat the radical party, and to prevent negro suffrage." Its members understood that the groups' objects were to be accomplished, "even at the cost of life."[4]

Given the stated goal of these local Klans, their greatest activity in 1869 ironically occurred in areas with relatively small black populations, the counties of northern Texas. In few of these counties did African Americans compose more than one-third of the total population. This fact suggests that the Klan served a greater purpose for the Democratic party than its role in intimidating black voters—it provided a means for mobilizing and controlling white voters as well. Conservatives and Democrats had used racist appeals to attract political support even before the war; the Klan now gave that appeal an increased sense of urgency, suggesting the much feared war between the races had begun. At the same time, it provided a mechanism for forcing political conformity among whites. Another Klansman viewed the object of his group as being to ensure that none voted for any man except a "democrat of the first water. The organization was in part, so that each man could know his neighbor, and whether or not he was a democrat, and to establish a concert of action among the democratic party."[5]

Most Texans understood the Democratic strategy, and this further helps explain the national Republican leadership's shift to Davis and the drift of many Unionists who had been supporters of Andrew Hamilton into the Radical camp. Growing concern about the Hamilton-Democratic coalition within the Grant administration was also apparent, and the president delayed calling the Texas election. Grant waited until July 15 to issue his proclamation, and then he postponed the time for the election until November. This decision reflected the administration's concerns with conditions elsewhere in the South. The president already had seen a coalition similar to that of Hamilton's win control of the state government in Georgia. The victors had refused to purge the legislature of members who were ineligible to serve under the restrictions of the Fourteenth Amendment but did remove its black members. That summer Moderate Republicans and Conservatives threatened to capture the Virginia government as well. Grant did not want to make another mistake in Texas, and delaying the election gave him an opportunity to be certain of the party loyalty of the two factions vying for power. By the end of July, his sympathies had begun to swing toward Davis.

The delay worked to the advantage of the Radicals. It gave them the time not only to make their case before the voters and to organize the Union League more thoroughly but also to convince the president of the disloyalty of Hamilton. After the Virginia and Georgia elections, Grant's cabinet officers and party leaders once again placed pressure on the two factions in Texas to compromise. Several cabinet officials had become convinced that Hamilton was not the man to support. General Reynolds, long a supporter of the Moderate Republicans and a close friend of Grant, played a major role in the election. Reynolds had grown increasingly concerned with the course of events. In August the various parties began to make nominations for the other state offices that would be chosen. In numerous cases the Hamilton Republicans nominated men who had been disqualified from holding office by the Reconstruction laws. The general concluded that if Hamilton were elected, it would be as a result of Democratic votes and that his victory would simply put Texas back into the hands of former rebels. On September 4 Reynolds informed the president of his concerns about the situation, emphasizing in particular the opposition of Hamilton's supporters to the nomination to Congress of former Union general William T. Clark as an example of their bad faith. He made no recommendations, but clearly Reynolds had become disillusioned with Hamilton.[6]

The general's endorsement ended the debate within the administration on which faction to support. After receiving his letter, the president authorized cabinet officers to shift their patronage to Davis, something they had encouraged since the party executive committee had shifted to Davis in midsummer. With the president's decision, cabinet members began removing Hamilton supporters from key federal patronage posts and replacing them with friends of Davis. These positions, primarily jobs in the Treasury Department's services, were politically critical. They brought prestige to the party that held them, indicating they were favored by the national administration. They also offered financial benefits to their holders and the prospects of rewarding party loyalists with the numerous subordinate positions in customs offices. In addition, the jobs almost overnight gave supporters of Davis the financial resources they needed to travel about the state campaigning for his election.

A. J. Hamilton struggled to portray himself as a Republican politician who could represent the interests of conservative whites while remaining true to Republican principles. He appealed to whites who were not Republican by portraying himself as the candidate of reconciliation, and his campaign proclaimed him to be the leader of the "Moderate Republican" party. He emphasized his role in the constitutional convention of producing suffrage provisions that removed all restrictions limiting the voting rights of former Confederates and now invited these men to support him in creating a loyal government that considered the welfare of all Texans. In appealing to Republican voters, especially blacks, Hamilton labored to prove that he had not made some sort of corrupt bargain. He emphasized his Unionist past, his role in bringing down the Throckmorton administration, and the part he had played in paving the way for a new constitution that included black suffrage.

Ultimately, however, Hamilton offered few explicit ideas about the course he proposed to pursue as governor. Instead, he attacked his opponent. Hamilton had a reputation as a vigorous campaigner, and he vigorously went after Davis with campaign rhetoric that unashamedly contradicted itself. He and other Moderates charged that the Davis party comprised impractical radicals whose ideals would lead the state into turmoil. Even though Davis ran simply on the Republican ticket, Hamilton and his supporters provided the label that has stuck through subsequent history: Davis was a Radical Republican, a supporter of the absurd idea of *ab initio,* which would have bastardized all children, nullified all marriages, and destroyed all contracts that occurred during the war. At the same time, with considerable irony, campaign speeches and writings denounced these Radicals as being without principle, simply political opportunists instead who promised anything to get elected. Hamilton and his associates pointed in particular to the shift that had been made in the Radical platform in the June convention to prove their opponents' duplicity.

Hamilton and his followers also used General Reynolds's shifting position to bolster their campaign. Governor Pease resigned almost immediately after discovering that Reynolds had encouraged the president to recognize the Davis candidacy. He accused federal authorities of meddling in the state's election process in order to secure the election of Radicals. Hamilton's supporters insisted that this confirmed the Radical character of Davis. They went further, however, to suggest that the Texas Radicals were willing to use the military to determine the outcome of the election. Reynolds likely had nothing like this in mind and was shocked at the results of his letter. The strident Hamilton response may have been an effort to neutralize the general's influence both in Texas and in the North; it also may have been meant to mobilize white support for his candidacy. Whatever the reason, the reaction of Hamilton and his supporters had important implications for the state following the election, fostering the idea that the 1869 election might be manipulated by the military to produce a desired result, which might not reflect the true will of Texans. If this turned out to be the case, then a Davis victory would not be legitimate because the people would not have elected him.

While Hamilton and his Republican supporters proclaimed their moderation, Hamilton's Democratic allies showed no such restraint. The election involved more than the ratification of the constitution and a gubernatorial race—Texans would go to the polls to elect four congressmen, the entire state legislature, and a full array of local officials. While Democrats generally agreed to support Hamilton, they ran straight-out Democrats for most of these other offices. Campaigns at the local level saw them use the same rhetoric and techniques they had in 1868. Their candidate for Congress in the Second District proved particularly vitriolic in his attacks upon the Radical Republicans and played upon the racial fears of whites. John C. Conner, a captain with the Union Army during the war, warned listeners at Dallas that his political opponents were poisoning the minds of blacks against whites and "encouraging a war of races, which, once inaugurated, would create unutterable woe in the land, and ultimate in the negroes' extermination."[7]

Davis Republicans responded with efforts at creating a Republican organization and at attracting voters by stating their position in newspapers and on the speakers' platform. They directed much of their campaign effort at strengthening and broadening the organization of the Union League. With George Ruby still at its head, the league was firmly behind Davis. The only problem was to ensure that African American voters turned out. Although limited by funding, the state league sent speakers to critical local chapters to be sure that blacks understood the importance of the election to them. Orators charged Hamilton with having sold out to the Conservatives and insisted that a Hamilton victory would mark the return to power of the men who had enslaved them.

At the same time that organizers worked on strengthening the league, Davis carried on a public campaign as well. The candidate had only two newspapers with statewide circulation supporting him, the *Express* and the *Frei Presse,* both in San Antonio, but they served as a major mechanism for disseminating his message. It was Davis, however, who personally took his party's message to the people of Texas. He began a series of speaking engagements that took him across the countryside with an address on the steps of the U.S. Customs House at Galveston on September 22. In it Davis introduced the arguments that were the focus of his campaign, much of it centering on a defense of his record in the previous years, particularly his stands on *ab initio* and disfranchisement. On the former he denied that he had any particular attachment to the principle, pointing out that he and his supporters had been willing to validate all just laws. Instead, they wanted simply to force the repayment of the school fund and recover those lands unjustly seized during the war. On disfranchisement he maintained that he had been right in his position, pointing to efforts by Democrats in the constitutional convention to include provisions disfranchising blacks as proof that many former Confederates could not be trusted to create a loyal government. He had been defeated in these efforts and now was willing to accept Democrats at their word, that they were ready for Reconstruction. He advised his audience, however, that voting for Republicans would be the best way to leave behind the rebellious past.

In late September the entry of another ticket in the canvass muddied the political picture. On September 29 five newspaper editors plus numerous observers from the Democratic party's leadership met at Brenham. The convention nominated a slate of Democratic candidates, headed by Hamilton Stuart of the *Galveston Civilian*. The purpose of the Brenham convention's activities is unclear. Those who attended said that they could support neither of the Republican candidates and wanted a candidate in the election. A. J. Hamilton's supporters suggested that the convention was put up by Davis to draw Democratic voters away from their man. Certainly, a straight-out Democratic ticket threatened the strategy of those leaders who hoped to encourage support for Hamilton. If Democrats supported Hamilton Stuart, then the vote for Hamilton might be split and Davis's election assured. Stuart himself contended that the primary purpose of a Democratic candidate was to rally support against the proposed constitution and to defeat black enfranchisement. That the state leaders of the Democratic party had nothing to do with the Brenham convention was made clear on September 28, when the party's state executive committee issued a circular that advised its members not to vote for Stuart and to support "conservative" rather than "Democratic" candidates for office.

In November, preparations for the elections by all parties focused on ensuring the largest possible turnout by increasing the registration of potential supporters during a ten-day revision of the voter registration lists ordered by General Reynolds to begin on the sixteenth. On October 8 Reynolds named registrars, many of whom were officers in the army. Despite the presence of soldiers on the boards, both sides charged that the process was marred by irregularities. Davis supporters contended that some local officials assisted potential Hamilton voters by failing to administer the required voter oath. At the same time, they charged that whites maintained their efforts at intimidating blacks from registration. The Hamilton party accused local boards of continuing to exclude people who had the right to vote, adding to their claims that the military was interfering with the legitimate electoral process. The largest number of complaints came from Bexar County. There, Hamilton's backers claimed the board, which included the prominent Radical politician James P. Newcomb, took over one hundred men off the voting rolls who had been fairly registered after the revisions had been finished. Despite these charges, the end result suggested that the Davis party may have had the best reason to complain. The process resulted in an increase in the number of registered whites and probably an increase in support for Moderate and Conservative candidates. The total number of men eligible for participation in the election had grown to 135,553. Fifty-eight percent (78,743) were whites; the remaining 42 percent (56,810) were blacks.[8]

The election shortly followed on November 30. Despite the fact that soldiers served as election managers in many of the counties and that General Reynolds sent ten-man detachments of troops to others where officials feared disruptions, the election saw renewed political intimidation, violence, and fraud. Supporters of Hamilton and local Democratic candidates were usually the perpetrators of outright violence, though Davis's backers may have committed their share of electoral fraud. As to the violence, reports from the polls indicated that the pervasive secret organizations were particularly active in northern and eastern Texas. The usual pattern of interference was present, with intimidation being the preferred way of influencing the electoral outcome. Military and Republican officials received what had become the normal reports from throughout the state of black voters being told that they would be thrown off their farms if they voted the Radical ticket. Davis supporters claimed that in Falls County, planters brought their laborers to the polls, where they were given a Hamilton ticket. Blacks with Davis tickets had ballots ripped from their hands and warned that if they voted for Davis, they would be killed. In Upshur County Hamilton partisans allegedly took mules and horses away from freedmen, returning them only if they voted "right" at the polls. Freedmen across northern Texas reported to Republican officials that the threats had become so numerous that they were afraid to vote.[9]

In some places threats turned to outright violence. At Denton a mob drove two Republican organizers out of the county the day before the election, threatening to kill them if they remained. In Hopkins County a black schoolteacher was pistol whipped after he distributed Republican tickets and told to leave the county or die. One of the most violent confrontations took place in Milam County, where an army officer attempted to escort a party of about one hundred African Americans to the polls at Cameron. A crowd of whites responded by attacking the polls, leading election officials to close down voting before the blacks could cast their ballots. In Navarro County, where no troops had been sent, the head of the board of registration stopped the revisions after receiving threats to the lives of the registrars, then held no election. In Hill County, another place to which no detachment of troops had been made, fear of violence caused one of the election managers to remove the ballots from the county before counting them.

As the votes came in, the Hamilton forces initially claimed to be victorious, despite the fact that Davis showed an early lead with returns from the counties with large black populations. Davis supporters were uncertain what their candidate's early lead meant and feared that heavy Hamilton majorities would come in from counties in northern Texas to offset their advantage. As returns arrived at military headquarters from election managers across the state, however, Davis's lead held. When General Reynolds announced the results, Edmund J. Davis had received 39,838 votes to Andrew Hamilton's 39,055; Hamilton Stuart had received 445, not enough to have influenced the results.

Hamilton's supporters were unbelieving. But an analysis of the returns indicates clearly why their man lost—nearly forty thousand registered whites had not turned out to vote. Probably most of these were Democrats and would have supported Hamilton. If they had voted, Hamilton would have swamped Davis. His backers complained that bad weather during the election had limited the turnout. Political leaders also believed that many whites may have concluded their vote was meaningless in the Reconstruction process, and they determined to sit it out. More probable was the explanation that many Democrats probably could not bring themselves to vote for either Hamilton or Davis nor for the proposed constitution, and they simply decided to stay at home.

Hamilton's failure was all the more frustrating for his supporters because it is clear that their efforts at intimidating black voters had worked. After managing an impressive marshaling of freedmen support in previous elections, the Davis Republicans were less effective in 1869. Only about 66 percent of registered blacks went to the polls, a drop from the 76 percent who had voted in the 1868 convention elections. They failed to vote in the same numbers particularly in the counties in northern Texas that constituted the Second Congressional District and had been the center of Klan activity for over a year. In most of these counties, over 25 percent fewer blacks voted in 1869; Collin County showed the greatest reduction (70 percent) in black votes. Davis failed to produce the same turnout, even in some of the black-belt counties.[10]

The result also showed that Davis had been unable to attract significant numbers of white voters. As historian Dale Baum has estimated, probably no more than five thousand whites cast ballots for him. The Davis vote came primarily from the same men who had supported Pease in 1866 and the constitutional convention in 1868. The sources of his greatest strength remained the Republican strongholds in the counties to the south of San Antonio and in the German communities of central and western Texas. While some Republicans who had supported Hamilton may have drifted over to Davis, he still was unable to attract even half of the white voters who had supported Pease in 1866. This posed a major problem for the Republican party, for it added to the credibility of Democratic charges that it was a black man's party.

At the same time, the inability of the Radicals to turn out the black vote in 1869 had significant implications for their party's future. William T. Clark, the Republican candidate, handily carried the Third Congressional District, which included the old plantation counties around Houston and Galveston.

Another Republican, George W. Whitmore, won the First District in Eastern Texas. In the Fourth District, including many of the counties that had supported Davis, Republican Edward Degener won; he won by only seventy-two votes. Over seven hundred fewer blacks had voted in the district, helping produce a close vote out of what should have been a decisive victory. In the Second District the Democrat John C. Conner won. There, over a thousand fewer voters turned out than in 1868. The disappearance of black voters probably was not the only factor in this congressional race, but it helped add to the decisiveness of Conner's victory. One seat had been lost, another faced future problems if black participation declined further.

The electorate also selected state senators and representatives, and the turnout also created problems in those races. With representative districts based on population, Davis Republicans easily won a majority in the House. Counties in the First Congressional District were the center of population. Davis's party was in control there, and these representatives would give the governor-elect his strength in the House. The Senate posed a problem, however. Eleven of the thirty men elected clearly were Democrats, and the party loyalty of the nineteen Republicans was uncertain. Davis Republicans missed a chance to control the Senate when low black-voter turnout proved decisive in two districts. In the Eleventh District, consisting of Fannin and Lamar Counties, a turnout 418 voters lower than in 1868 allowed E. L. Dohoney a narrow victory over his opponent, 618 to 563. In the Nineteenth District, including Falls, Limestone, and McLennan Counties, a reduction of the black vote by 267 gave the seat to A. J. Evans, 1,498 to 1,330. These Democratic victories would create problems for Davis's legislative agenda in the upcoming months.

Of all the races, that for governor proved the most controversial. A. J. Hamilton refused to accept the results and determined to appeal the election to Congress. The basis for his intended appeal was that General Reynolds had interfered in the election and counted in Davis. He focused on events that had taken place in Milam and Navarro Counties. Hamilton's backers complained that both counties would have gone for their man had an election been held there, and they demanded at least the remedy of a new election in each county. Recent scholarship suggests that the complaint may have been simply a ploy to overturn the election results, for the racial character of those communities suggests that, had a fair vote been held in them, they likely would have added to Davis's majority.[11] For Hamilton and his Democratic supporters, however, Reynolds's decision not to order a new election was proof of their charge and the basis for their assertion that the Davis government did not legitimately represent the people of Texas.

Despite the refusal of Hamilton and others to accept the results of the election, events moved rapidly toward the end of Congressional Reconstruction. On January 8, 1870, Reynolds took steps to restore a measure of civil government by appointing Davis, Flanagan, Albert Bledsoe, George W. Honey, and Jacob Keuchler to the offices they had won in the general election. On January 13 he appropriated money to pay the salaries of the provisional officials until the state was restored officially to the Union. Reynolds also called upon the newly elected Twelfth Legislature to meet at Austin and take the steps necessary for Congress to readmit Texas to the Union.

When the legislature organized on February 4, its members took up the various measures required for readmission. Two major issues occupied the group. First, they ratified the Thirteenth, Fourteenth, and Fifteenth Amendments, and they acted on these with little discussion. The second, the selection of U.S. senators, produced considerable debate, however. In the vote, Morgan Hamilton won the longer term by a vote of seventy-one to thirty-nine, and James W. Flanagan won the shorter term by a vote of seventy-four to thirty-two.

These actions paved the way for the state's readmission. On March 30, 1870, Congress voted to seat the Texas delegation and thus to accept the results of the Reconstruction process in the state. Even though Congressional Reconstruction was on the verge of ending, the election of 1869 had left much unsettled. As those elected to the new government took office, their opponents continued to proclaim that Davis and the Republican-dominated legislature held power only as the result of military fiat. The opposition asserted that the new government was illegitimate and did not represent the people. This claim would play a major role in subsequent political struggles. Overcoming this stigma was a major problem that had to be solved if the new government was to govern successfully and if the Republican party was to establish itself in Texas.

One of the most ominous observations on the election's results came from one of the Democrats who had supported Hamilton in the race. Galveston lawyer William P. Ballinger wrote to the state's wartime lieutenant governor, counseling him not to worry about the results. He observed that the Republican party possessed a great flaw in its efforts at building a majority in Texas, one that would ultimately keep many away who might otherwise join it. The alliance they had effected with blacks, he believed, would never be accepted by most whites. He wrote: "the Radicals will never be able to establish themselves here without military force. Their manipulation & control of the Negro will turn the people against them. It will only be a matter of time before the people will rise up and turn them out." [12]

Chapter 8

THE DAVIS ADMINISTRATION,
THE TWELFTH LEGISLATURE, AND POLITICS

On April 28, 1870, military government in Texas came to an official end with the formal inauguration of Edmund J. Davis as governor. Two days earlier, the Twelfth Legislature gathered in response to a call for a special session by Davis, then acting as provisional governor, and organized. On the twenty-eighth, amid the traditional pomp of such occasions, Davis rode in a procession up Congress Avenue to the capitol, a battery of U.S. artillery fired a salute of welcome, for the swearing-in ceremony. Many members of his old unit, the First Texas Cavalry (U.S.) joined in the parade.

After he took the oath of office, Davis made a short inaugural speech. He began with a call on all Texans to put aside the differences that had divided them in the war. From those who had supported the Confederacy, he asked that they "now agree to accept the situation as they find it" and join in a "fresh departure in political affairs." While discussing the past, he looked to the state's future. "We are the advanced guard of this mighty host," he said, adding that the leaders of Texas could ensure that Texans would find it "industrious, prosperous, intelligent, law-abiding, [and] temperate." [1] After Davis finished, those in attendance adjourned to a barbeque sponsored by the First Texas veterans. The address was well received, even by his political enemies, who believed that the address had indicated the governor would pursue a very conservative course as the state's chief executive.

The following day Davis outlined the specific programs desired by his administration in a message to the legislature, one received with less enthusiasm among his political opponents than the inaugural speech. He restated many of the same themes but now outlined the specific legislative program he wanted implemented. The moment was a critical one for the development of Texas, for the new governor offered its citizens a road to the future that veered distinctly from that they had long traveled. For the new administration, these first days were ones of optimism. The struggles that would take place over Davis's proposals in the Twelfth Legislature, however, would ultimately move

Edmund J. Davis, first Republican governor of Texas, 1869–74.
Courtesy U.S. Army Military History Institute

the state along completely different lines than he intended. This fight became central to the future of the Texas and its people.

Overall, the governor's legislative package aimed at achieving three goals. Two of these were explicit in the measures he proposed; the third was never stated nor perhaps even fully understood by the members of the administration but implicit in what they were doing. The first objective was to secure law and order across the state. Davis wrote, "I esteem the matter of first importance, because, having peace and security for life and property, everything else will follow of course." The second was to promote the state's economic development. The last, a purpose contingent on the other two, was the establishment of the legitimacy of the new government, to gain the acceptance of a majority of the citizens of Texas. Davis had taken office amid charges that he had not been fairly elected. His only chance to gain general acceptance of the representative character of his government and his party was if he could bring peace to the people and produce the promised prosperity.[2]

Peace for the governor and his associates meant more than the suppression of outlaws or acting against Native Americans on the frontier. Davis clearly believed that one of the most serious threats to stability was the political and racial violence that had been pervasive since the war's end. The different motives that might be behind attacks upon African Americans made little difference. Whether attacked for racial or economic reasons, the violence denied black Texans the basic civil rights guaranteed to them under the new constitution and helped promote a continued spirit of lawlessness. Of course, it also served to intimidate the Republican party's core of support. Davis believed decisive action was necessary, and he urged the legislature to create new agencies that would promote peace across the state.

His recommendations included provisions for a state militia to sustain the laws in extreme emergencies. To suppress individual outlaws acting in counties where authorities were too weak or too indisposed to take action, he proposed a state-police force. He also suggested modifying the criminal code to punish "mobs of lawless men, assembling and operating in disguise," whose operations generally affected the "recently enfranchised," and making provisions for declaring martial law where local authorities were in sympathy with the mob. In addition, he asked lawmakers to consider having the state build adequate jails in the various counties. Davis pointed out that the new constitution provided the legislature the power to restrict firearms and asked that they ban carrying firearms anywhere other than on the frontier. Finally, he urged new stock laws to end the lawlessness that had developed on the Texas range.

The governor also saw the difficulties with American Indian tribes on the frontier as part of the state's overall problem of violence. Davis stated this clearly when he observed that "peace seems absolutely hopeless as long as one of them [Indians] lives or roams at large." He believed that it was the federal government's responsibility to protect the frontier but concluded that this would be delayed by national politics. As a result, the state should provide for the arming of minute companies to be used against the Indians.

In a novel argument, Davis recommended that civil order also could be ensured if the legislature moved to create a system of public education authorized by the constitution. He believed education helped abate crimes and argued that the success of republican institutions and universal suffrage depended on universal education. In fact, schools offered a means to two goals, the governor pointing out that they would be economically important as well.

Indeed, much of his message dealt with matters of economic growth. Davis recognized the desire of Texans for internal improvements and particularly a system of railroads that would promote "intercommunication" within the state and a connection with the East. Pointing to the liberal gifts of the antebellum years that had produced little, he urged caution in subsidizing railroads. In fact, the governor was not convinced that, in the populated counties of the state, railroads needed any more encouragement than a liberal charter and a grant of right of way. He recognized, however, that the legislature might wish to provide subsidies. He warned lawmakers in such cases to avoid imposing a heavy tax burden by supporting only one road. Davis recommended establishing a line from the Red River to the Rio Grande, for a road across that country would do the most good for the state's people. Another component of his plan was his advocacy of actions to provide some railroads' relief from the threat of forfeiture for not having paid the debt they owed to the school fund, though he promised he would sell their charters if no relief passed. Strongly in favor of railroads, Davis nonetheless believed that they represented only a part of what had to be done for the state's advancement and urged caution in the legislature's support of such companies.

An additional part of the governor's economic plan was to create the Bureau of Immigration authorized by the new constitution. Its purpose was to attract the continuing westward migration of Americans toward Texas. The agency he envisioned would collect and publish the descriptions of the character of the state's land, the prices of land, cost of transportation, and the known natural resources. To facilitate this bureau's work, Davis asked funding for a state geological survey under the commissioner of the General Land Office to collect and catalogue the state's mineral resources.

These new laws and agencies provided the core of Davis's plans, though the governor was forced to remind legislators of many other needs too. His catalogue of matters needing attention showed how little had been done to maintain state institutions since the outbreak of war as well as the costs of restoring basic governmental institutions. Most of the state's eleemosynary facilities needed to be refurbished. Asylums for the blind, the deaf and dumb, and lunatics were inadequate and had suffered from neglect during the war. The penitentiary needed attention. Davis described the capitol grounds as a "waste." The legislature also needed to organize the boards of voter registry, judges of election, and a variety of other laws concerning local affairs.

Davis made it clear that his new programs and the needs of existing institutions would drastically increase the state's expenses. He thought that the expenditures for starting up the schools, building schoolhouses, and buying books and equipment would be particularly high. State aid to any internal improvements would add a further burden. Providing just for the schools, the Immigration Bureau, the militia, and the police would cost, Davis predicted, at least $1.5 million. He saw no solution but to raise taxes. Nonetheless, throughout his message, Davis pointed out the importance of these programs to the state's long-term future and suggested that the increasing wealth that would be produced for Texas would justify the investment. The Immigration Bureau alone, he observed, would bring in about fifteen hundred dollars for each immigrant that it attracted.

The overall character of the governor's legislative program not only indicated his specific social and economic goals but also exposed something of his overall political strategy. By suppressing both civil and political violence, he secured his existing political base. Through economic recovery, he could appeal to the whites who might not have supported his party previously. The latter was particularly important, both to establish his government's legitimacy and to obtain the future success of the Republican party. Although many whites had not gone to the polls in 1869, aiding the Republican victory, that would not be true in the future, and the party's success depended on its ability to attract some of these white voters when they returned to the polls. The need to develop a larger base of support was made greater by the fact that postwar immigration of hundreds of white families from other southern states made the African American population a smaller part of the overall electorate. The party had to bring about peace and prosperity in the hopes of encouraging these whites to consider economic issues over race and history in making their political choices.

From the beginning, the Republicans faced a difficult challenge from an opposition group that wanted white voters not to forget the issues of race and the immediate Reconstruction past. Through the course of the each legislative session during Davis's administration, these men devoted an extraordinary effort to that end. Given the bitter attacks that would take place over the next months, it is important to recognize that at the time of his inauguration, even the opposition press agreed with Davis about the character of the state's problems and even endorsed, with some reservations about the state police and the militia, his programs. The Conservative *Galveston News* and the pro-Hamilton *Flake's Bulletin* and *Austin Republican* concluded that the new governor had shown himself to be a statesman. They also evaluated him initially as a conservative man who would neither pursue radical policy or methods nor seek to exercise tyrannical rule. All believed that Davis intended a full return of the control of government to the people of Texas. Whether these sources honestly believed all this to be true or whether they were encouraging the governor to believe that he could count on their support if he agreed with their policies is unclear. When Davis proved unmanageable, the Democratic and Hamilton press quickly changed their views.[3]

The governor's success in implementing his program depended on the Twelfth Legislature, which assembled at Austin for a special session on April 26, 1870, that would last until August 15. When the lawmakers assembled, Davis's ability to secure passage of the legislation he desired was by no means clear. Early reports indicated that Republicans dominated both houses. In the lower house sixty-nine members had been elected as Republicans compared to twenty-one as Democrats. Twenty senators claimed to be Republicans, but the number who actually supported Davis as opposed to running as Conservatives and supporting A. J. Hamilton remained unclear. Most observers believed that at least ten of the men who had run as Conservatives had Democratic ties, and by the time the session convened, they had proclaimed their Democratic connection. With the Republican majorities tentatively bringing the divisions that had divided the party during the election into the legislature, the governor had no guarantee of success. Even if Republicans did not split along old lines, they also gave evidence of disagreement among themselves on a variety of other issues. These divisions challenged the cohesiveness of Republican legislators as a bloc. Davis had to bring them together from all political camps and sometimes conflicting interests to succeed. Given the character of his party, that would be difficult.

The Republican coalition from its beginnings had consisted of a variety of interests whose goals were not easily reconciled, and its membership in the Twelfth Legislature reflected this great diversity. As in the just-adjourned constitutional convention, African American members made this assembly different from all that had come before. These members would work to secure measures favorable to blacks, especially education and basic protection of their rights. But they hardly dominated the legislature or even the Radical caucus. In the senate two members were black: George T. Ruby, who had served in the constitutional convention and now represented Galveston, and Matthew Gaines of Washington County. In the house blacks were proportionally stronger. Still, the twelve African American members there represented only a little over 20 percent of Davis Republicans, a bit more than 10 percent of the total membership. Nonetheless, the fact that blacks represented a majority of the party's voters guaranteed that the concerns of these lawmakers had to be addressed.

George T. Ruby, Republican senator from Galveston, 1869–74,
president of the Union League, 1869–70. Courtesy Texas State Library and Archives

Matthew Gaines, Republican senator from Brenham,
1869–74. Courtesy Texas State Library and Archives

The majority of Republicans in the legislature were scalawags. These men had joined the Republican party for many different reasons. Factions and individuals often strongly advocated their particular interest, but they sometimes proved willing to compromise on aspects of the governor's overall program they considered less important. Gen. William H. Parsons from Montgomery County represented one type of white Republican, typical of those who had joined the party believing that its basic economic philosophy was better for Texas than that of the Democrats. Parsons had been a leading secessionist and a Confederate cavalry commander, but he had emerged from the war convinced that the Democratic party offered no hope for the successful reconstruction of the state and particularly for its future development. Generally a strong supporter of Davis, Republicans like Parsons did not buy into his caution for restraint when the legislature considered measures supporting industrial growth or railroad construction.

Belief that the party offered the best chance of securing state support for a pet project, usually the construction of a railroad, probably accounts for the Republicanism of a few legislators. Webster Flanagan, son of the U.S. senator and advocate of the proposed Southern Pacific Railroad, was typical. A former Confederate from a well-known antebellum family, Flanagan and other railroad men proved particularly troublesome for the governor since their party loyalty had little ideological basis and no broader goals beyond their single individual interest. They not only ignored Davis's cautions regarding railroad construction but also often actually opposed or were willing to compromise on other aspects of the governor's program.

Another group of scalawags became Republicans because they supported a part of the governor's basic social agenda, particularly the creation of a public school system, but opposed most measures providing support for railroads or other economic developments. Elisha Pettit of Palestine was representative of this type of legislator. An educator associated with Marshall University before the war, Pettit saw the Republican party as an instrument of reform that would establish an educational base for the state's progress.

A final group of Republicans have been called "agrarians" by contemporaries and subsequent historians. These men in many cases were drawn to the party because of their past Unionism, but they did not share the ideas of government activism espoused by other members. They looked with considerable suspicion on many of Davis's programs, which they feared would increase government expenses and force an increase in taxes. These men shared the view of Sen. Morgan Hamilton, who clandestinely encouraged them. Securing the cooperation of men like Parsons, Flanagan, and Pettit presented a daunting challenge.

Noticeably absent among Texas Republicans was the unique carpetbagger interest found in other southern states. There had been few carpetbaggers in the constitutional convention;. Virtually none were elected to the legislature, only two men in the senate. One was George Ruby, whose public interests were indistinguishable from his black constituents. The other was Albert J. Fountain, a soldier of fortune from New York who wound up in El Paso during the war and settled there to practice law. Like Ruby, Fountain's actions in the legislature identified him with the interests of his constituents in El Paso rather than any peculiar ideological position. The number of carpetbaggers in the house is not known, but indications are that their numbers were few.

Democrats evidenced their own divisions. About the only thing that the ten Democrats initially in the Twelfth Legislature shared in common was service to the Confederacy (at least seven of them had served in the military) and hostility to the Republican administration, especially its policies on race. On other issues they showed the same sorts of divisions apparent among their Republican colleagues. James P. Douglas from Smith County, for example, was a strident proponent of railroad construction and played a role in pushing such projects through the legislature over the governor's vetoes. Edward Pickett tied himself to Republican agrarians and actually voted to sustain Davis's veto of the Southern Pacific bill. The potential existed to exploit these divisions, but the governor somehow had to shift emphasis away from the divisions on race that Democratic leaders used to encourage solidarity within the party and court voters from outside.

Two episodes at the very start of the session convening in April, 1870, demonstrated the internal problems within the Republican party. The first of these was the struggle over leadership in the state senate. Governor Davis supported the election of former Confederate general William Parsons of Galveston as president of the senate. Webster Flanagan, who wanted someone who would push more aggressively for his railroad scheme, offered Donald Campbell of Marion County, a friend of his father. Campbell, however, faced opposition by a faction, led from Washington, D.C., by Sen. Morgan Hamilton, that stood against an overly ambitious program supporting railroad construction. Davis ultimately settled the matter when he agreed to support Campbell, paving the way for his election. The struggle over senate leadership uncovered clear divisions between strident prorailroad Republicans (led by Flanagan) and more fiscally conservative, almost antirailroad Republicans (led by Senator Hamilton). It also produced the first step toward a break between Davis and Hamilton. The latter called Campbell's election a victory for the railroads, concluded that the increase in taxes necessary to support them doomed the administration, and criticized the governor's compromise. The U.S. senator began to separate himself from affairs at Austin and the administration.

The second event was the fight over the governor's appointment of Joseph W. Talbot, a rancher from Williamson County, as his superintendent of public instruction. Talbot was a logical choice for Davis since he had been a member of the 1869 convention and played a leading role in the development of the new constitution's education provisions. But Talbot had been a major advocate of *ab initio* and of disallowing all railroad payments made in state warrants to the school fund during the war. Further, he was chair of a committee that proposed to seize and sell those railroads indebted to the fund. In the state senate, Republican railroad activists lined up with Democrats, spurred on possibly by party interests, to block Talbot's appointment.

The Talbot affair illuminated a major dilemma faced by the Davis administration. Even though *Flake's Bulletin,* an Andrew Hamilton paper often sympathetic with Morgan Hamilton's agrarian views, pointed up the obvious railroad opposition, most of the Democratic press asserted that the real reason for opposition to Talbot was that he supported integrated schools. The charge was a complete misstatement of the facts. The nominee did not support integrated schools, but he did oppose including legal restrictions on integrated classrooms in a school law. His reasons are unclear, though such a provision would have run counter to federal law. Politically, however, the fact that the charge was a lie was unimportant. Most people accepted it as the truth and refused to believe evidence to the contrary. This sort of political rhetoric, already used extensively in previous political campaigns, allowed Davis's enemies to tar his administration as radical on race issues. It discouraged whites from becoming Republican and in fact encouraged them to unify in the Democratic party by diverting attention from economic or class differences that might prove divisive. Even more darkly for the future of Texas Republicanism, such charges also helped underpin the later successful development of the notion that the Davis government was not legitimate by not representing the interests of the white majority on questions of race.

The contest for president of the senate and the nomination of a superintendent of public instruction proved only a prelude to an endless round of fights over the Davis agenda, disputes that became increasingly bitter as the session continued. The most acrimonious of these struggles emerged as the legislature took up the first major component of the governor's law-and-order program, creating a state militia. Possibly, Davis could have built up goodwill in the legislature by moving forward the rest of his proposals first, but he believed that the lawmakers would deal positively with his police measures only if he possessed some leverage. The governor held several tools that he could use. His supporters could block consideration of the large number of private bills, especially those sponsored by the railroads, that were before the legislature. He also could hold up the numerous appointments at his disposal in which many legislators had an interest. Knowing the militia bill to be one that would produce the most controversy, he put it forward first, in his words, "on the principle of coming butt-end foremost."[4]

This bill reflected the governor's ideas about how the militia should be organized. Much of it was unexceptionable, modeled after the state's earlier laws. But it did contain several new elements. One was the creation of two classes of militia, one called the State Guard and the other the Reserve Militia. The first would be composed of volunteers, the second, with some exceptions, would consist of all able-bodied men between the ages of eighteen and forty-five. This force would draw its members from among both blacks and whites. The State Guard was intended to be placed at a level of readiness beyond that of the Reserve Militia. The potential for its use could be seen in the bill's provisions that empowered the governor to declare martial law in counties where lawlessness overwhelmed civil authorities, call up and send in state forces, provide for the trial and punishment of offenders by courts-martial, and pay for the troops with an assessment upon the people of the county where they were used.

The militia bill produced rancorous public debate. Events happening elsewhere in the South, where Republican regimes already were developing their own police measures, fueled the bitterness of the fight. In neighboring Arkansas the Republican governor, Powell Clayton, who like Davis was a former Union general, had been given powers similar to those in the Texas bill and had declared martial law in ten southwestern counties late in 1868. His state militia, composed of both whites and blacks, violently suppressed Ku Klux bands that had unleashed a reign of terror against blacks and Republican politicians. Clayton's stiff measures included arrests and executions. He crushed the Arkansas Klan. Democrats across the South had proclaimed Clayton's efforts unconstitutional and an attack upon the white race. Of course, the Arkansas militia also suppressed the intimidation of whites and blacks that had served the political purposes of the Democratic party and, as a consequence, might be seen as a police measure aimed at that organization too. Since Davis already had made clear his belief that some of the violence within the state was political, many of his opponents concluded that the governor intended to use what they called his "nigger" militia to deal with his political foes in Texas.[5]

As soon as the militia bill went to the house floor, Democrats attacked the proposal and a lengthy debate began. The opposition focused on three specific parts of the bill in their criticism, arguing its constitutionality. The first point was that the section giving the governor the power to declare martial law took away a prerogative given in the state constitution to the legislature. The second charged that the provision placing the trials of offenders in areas under martial law in the hands of military tribunals rather than in the civil courts went against the Bill of Rights. Finally, they criticized the provision for the State Guard as creating a standing army, a power denied by the U.S. Constitution. Republicans responded that the legislature could delegate its authorities to the governor and that the State Guard was not a standing army. They pointed out that the Democratic legislature in 1866 had created a militia, giving the governor even greater power then. Neither side convinced the other. While refraining from charging that Davis wanted tyrannical powers himself, opposition politicians and press insisted that the militia bill opened the way to tyranny and despotism. Republicans argued that the bill was essential to protect Texans from violence, especially that of the Klan.[6]

Despite the outcry among Conservatives, the Republican majority in the house held together and passed the militia bill on May 21. In the state senate passage of the bill was not guaranteed, however. A problem for the administration developed immediately when, in addition to the Democrats, at least seven Republican senators expressed reservations similar to those raised by the Democrats.[7] The administration began immediately to whip Republican senators into line, and Davis wielded his appointment power to considerable advantage. The father of Sen. John Mills received the post of superintendent of the blind asylum. Sen. Mijamin Priest was nominated to a district judgeship. Thomas Baker and John Bell moved back into the party fold when railroad lobbyists began to support the militia bill after the governor announced that he intended to veto any private legislation that he received before the militia measure passed. At the time, railroad interests had drafted two critical bills to place before the legislature. One provided relief to the Houston and Texas Central from its debt to the state school fund, and the other reorganized the Southern Pacific line and gave it the rights to the land grants of the Memphis, El Paso, and Pacific. Both would have been dead if vetoed by Davis. To move forward, the railroads came down in support of the militia.

The full details of the log rolling in the senate will never be known, but deals clearly were made, and most of the Republican senators who initially expressed reservations wound up voting for the bill. Yet Web Flanagan, E. L. Alford, H. R. Latimer, and Boliver J. Pridgen remained divorced from the administration and voted with the Democrats in a critical test vote on June 16, which the governor's forces won with a razor-thin majority, fifteen to fourteen. Davis appeared to have the upper hand, and the vote moved the bill toward final passage. Then, the Democrats and their allies attempted to block it in one of the most interesting moves in the state's legislative history.

The opposition, not having the votes to block passage of the measure, decided to use a parliamentary tactic to try to stop it. Under senate rules, a quorum, in this case twenty members, had to be present to carry on business. If all eleven senators who opposed the measures withdrew, they could break the quorum. On June 21, to obstruct a vote that would have engrossed the bill, the ten Democratic members along with Republican senators Alford, Flanagan, and Latimer left the chamber. After a roll call showed them absent, the president of the senate ordered the sergeant-at-arms to arrest them for contempt and return them to the chamber. When arrested, their spokesman, Marmion H. Bowers, argued that they had not intended to break the quorum but had simply withdrawn for a consultation. The senate president did not accept the excuse. Instead, he named a committee to investigate the event, then excused four of the bolters to restore the quorum and left the others under arrest.

Administration forces took advantage of the arrests to push forward the militia bill and the rest of their agenda. With eight members still under arrest and another sick, the militia bill passed, fifteen to five, on June 22. Six days later the senate also passed another controversial part of the Davis program, that creating the state police. The police law had followed the militia bill through the house and would have spurred an equal debate except that it was buried in the uproar over the militia. Davis's police bill created a force of approximately 270 officers and men under the state's adjutant general, who would serve as chief of police in addition to commanding the militia. As in the case of the militia bill, the police law gave the state actual police authority and the ability to act in the place of local officials in certain circumstances. District judges received the legal power to call in the police when they believed local authorities could not or would not sustain law and order.

Other controversial legislation followed. One law restricted the carrying of firearms away from the frontier. Another provided for voter registration by boards of registrars and managers appointed by the governor. The Enabling Act authorized the governor to designate many officials to fill vacant positions until the next general election. In addition, the legislature approved a bill delaying that election from 1871 to 1872, thus extending their own session for another year and giving Republicans the possibility of better securing their position. Finally, a public-printing act authorized the designation of a newspaper in each judicial district to publish the state's official business. With the passage of this legislation, the senate released bolting members from arrest in mid-July.

Amid the strife over the militia bill, the legislature attended to other matters that produced less contention. A bill creating a frontier force was supported almost universally. That law, passed prior to the crisis in the senate, gave the governor the power to call up to twelve hundred men into state service from twenty ranging companies to campaign against Indians. Legislators also organized the Immigration Bureau and established the geological survey. They also delivered a public school bill. The latter created a state board of education, consisting of a state superintendent, the governor, and the attorney general. It empowered the superintendent to appoint thirty-five district supervisors and district boards of directors. These in turn hired teachers, levied and collected school taxes, and otherwise enforced the provisions of the school law.

The school measures did produce some discussion. The possibility that the system's classrooms might be integrated raised considerable concern. Democrats introduced a bill that would have required, by state law, separate schools for the races. Most Republicans opposed this provision and succeeded in tabling the measure. Yet no evidence exists that white Republicans wanted integrated schools. Probably, they were more concerned with the constitutionality of a law that specifically applied a race test to the schools. For whatever reason, they decided to leave the issue of the racial integration to local officials.

Contention had not run its full course, though. With the governor's basic programs implemented, the legislature turned to railroad measures, and new controversies quickly developed. Among Republicans, the debates sharpened divisions that had emerged in the fight over the militia bill. Democrats also split, indicating that, at least on the railroad issue, they were not as unified as their stand on the police measures made it seem. Two types of bills appeared that became the center of contention. The first were those introduced to relieve existing railroads that had received state subsidies before the war from the threat of immediate sale for not having kept up their payments to the state and to provide for the payment of their debts. The second involved the chartering of new railroads, with the debate focusing on what type of support, if any, the state would provide these companies. With much at stake, lobbyists had poured into the city with money to distribute liberally to secure support for their particular concern. Inevitably, charges and countercharges of bribery and corruption emerged from the fight.

The most intense political struggle took place over railroad charters. Two major trunk lines with strong local support asked for charters and requested support from the state in the form of subsidies. One of these was popularly known as the International, which proposed to build a line from the Fulton on Red River to Laredo on the Rio Grande. A second was a road known as the Southern Pacific, already in operation before the war, that intended to build a line from Marshall in eastern Texas to the Dallas area, proposing ultimately to move on to El Paso. U.S. Senator Flanagan and his son supported the Southern Pacific, along with many prominent politicians such as Governor Throckmorton. Bills chartering each of these roads ultimately reached the floor of the house.

Davis had warned that the state had limited resources for subsidies and encouraged caution in appropriations. But with bipartisan support, both houses of the legislature gave the railroads what they wanted. The problem was that in most cases they stepped beyond constitutional bounds when they did so and faced vetoes from the governor. The Southern Pacific bill not only gave that road a subsidy of sixteen thousand dollars per mile of track already built and to be built (the three hundred miles proposed would have cost approximately five million dollars) but also provided a grant of land under the old

Memphis and El Paso charter it had assumed. The new constitution forbade land grants. Railroad-relief bills contained similar problems. Those passed relieving the Houston and Texas Central of its debt to the school fund provided for additional school funds to be placed in the hands of the company. Again, such action was specifically forbidden by the new constitution.

Davis vetoed the Southern Pacific bill and all of the railroad-relief measures. His actions had immediate repercussions within his own party. On July 29, 1870, Sen. J. W. Flanagan wrote to the governor explaining that he could no longer support the administration, specifically the taxes passed by the legislature and the police measures, which he considered unnecessary. He also condemned the legislature's refusal to mandate segregated schools. Most of his anger, however, was addressed at Davis's interpretation of the constitution and his veto of railroad measures in which Flanagan had a major financial interest. The senator's abandonment of the administration had little practical effect in either Washington, D.C., or Austin, for he had never provided much support to the efforts of Davis to carry out his broader legislative program. Flanagan's protest underscored the fact, however, that many white Republicans had come into the party to achieve financial goals and had little interest in any other concerns.[8]

The railroad lobby mounted heavy pressure to override the governor's veto, and in the senate they were successful. In the house, however, the Davis Republican majority was large enough that the lobbyists were unable to gain enough votes. Reportedly, they then attempted to blackmail the governor, attempting to organize enough legislators to block the appropriation of funds for the numerous programs that already had been passed until he let railroad legislation go through. It appears that they succeeded. The backing they could muster forced an apparent compromise. The legislature passed the appropriations bills, though only after a charter for the International Railroad and a general railroad-relief measure moved successfully across the governor's desk.

Davis's vetoes had offended Senator Flanagan, but Flanagan had never been a warm supporter of the administration. But the charter for the International and the relief provided for existing railroads turned the state's other U.S. senator, Morgan Hamilton, against the administration. Hamilton had been concerned with the party's adherence to principle in the 1869 election, when Davis had offered to compromise with A. J. Hamilton and dropped his insistence that *ab initio* remain a part of the party's platform. Senator Hamilton now concluded that, following the International charter, the governor had opened up the way for other railroads to demand equal favors, and Davis would not be able to stop lawmakers from providing them. In his view this would either bankrupt the state or force the party to support higher taxes.

When the legislature adjourned in August, it had done much of the work that the governor had requested. Yet some remained to be done. The school law would prove ineffective, and when the legislature met in its regular session in January, 1871, a new bill would be passed that would create a working school system. The next session also saw further aid offered to the railroads. Other measures also waited until the next year for passage, but the basic program was in place by the end of the summer of 1870.

The actions of the legislature, however, had provided the governor's political opponents with plenty of ammunition. Beginning with the fight over the militia bill, a coalition of Conservative Republicans (A. J. Hamilton's supporters) and Moderate Democrats began to develop. Providing a continuing thorn in the administration's side was ex-governor Hamilton himself and his various political associates. In July, following the legislature's approval of the police measures, Hamilton and others met in Austin to discuss a course of action. At this meeting he delivered an address in which he condemned the activities of the legislature. With considerable sophistication, Hamilton leveled two basic charges. The first was that the police measures infringed upon the civil liberties of Texans. The second, however, was that its programs were too expensive for the state.[9] The conference went on to draft the "Petition of the People of Texas to Congress to Guarantee to the People a Republican Form of Government," which pointed to the militia law, the police law, the Enabling Act, the Voter Registration Act, and the Election Regulation Act as measures designed to deprive citizens of any say in government. Whether or not the majority of white Texans believed this to be true is immaterial, for Hamilton built on the charge leveled during the gubernatorial campaign. He now argued that the administration's behavior further indicated that it did not represent the will of the people. Davis's adversaries even went so far as to accuse the governor's wife, Anne Britton Davis, of actively lobbying for administration measures on the floor of the legislature. Such behavior, they inferred, only sustained claims that Republican efforts represented a dangerous and radical threat to traditional social order. The opposition continued to attack the very legitimacy of the Davis government and its programs.

Such an attack was dangerous to the administration. Opposition leaders were almost suggesting that Texans did not have to obey the laws passed by such a government, especially those raising taxes. They did urge white Texans to join the militia and to give no pretext to the governor for a declaration of martial law, but with their overall attack upon the government, they provided an environment where violence might be expected. Hamilton's attacks potentially legitimized any form of action that the opponents of the government might take.

In the face of this threat, Republicans had shown a tendency to fragment, and that inclination did not bode well for the party's future or for the long-term success of its various programs, ranging from the protection of African American civil rights to education. It suggests that few white leaders within

Mrs. Edmund J. (Ann Britton) Davis. Courtesy W. B. Teagarden Collection Center for American History, University of Texas at Austin, CN-11607

the party had much faith in its long-term future. Many whites would abandon the organization whenever they achieved their specific individual political goals. Ultimately, however, the test of the programs would be in their implementation. On the success of these rested the long-term future of the Davis administration and the state Republican party. When the legislature adjourned after its first session, two major questions remained. Would the adopted programs produce the stability and progress intended? And if so, would these accomplishments give the Davis government legitimacy and attract the broader base of political support that was essential for it and the Republican party's survival?

Chapter 9

Implementation of Republican Programs

The Davis administration implemented its various programs quickly. Within a year the government had created the state police and organized a force for the protection of the frontier. The state militia was established. Texas was ready to support the rebuilding and expansion of railroads by providing state bonds, and aid of a variety of types was available for new industries. A school program was in place by 1870, though it proved unworkable; however, additional legislation in the spring of 1871 created a viable system that opened the next autumn. By the end of 1871, the administration had put into effect most of its agenda. Almost from the beginning, however, problems appeared. Political pressures shaped, then reshaped, what was taking place. In some cases they seriously shifted development away from the direction the governor intended. To make matters worse for Davis, almost the entire program became the focus of criticism from his political opponents, who pointed to each item as evidence of the administration's corruption and its tendencies toward tyranny. The facts indicate that the story of Republican efforts to change the future of Texas was much more complex and the results more fruitful than their political opponents ever admitted.

The speed at which the administration moved forward to establish the various agencies designed to restore law and order across the state indicated the particular importance placed on this by Davis and his advisers. On the same day that he signed the police law, the governor named a former U.S. Army officer, James Davidson, adjutant general. Davidson came to the job with a reputation for dealing decisively with lawbreakers while serving as commander of an army force in northeastern Texas. His task now was to command the various state police forces and the militia authorized by the legislature.[1]

Davidson placed a high priority on recruiting men to the state police. The initial police law created a uniformed force that consisted of four captains, eight lieutenants, twenty sergeants, and 225 privates. An amendment passed in May, 1871, changed the structure of the organization, though not its size, so that the personnel included six captains, twelve lieutenants, and thirty-four sergeants. The increased number of officers and noncommissioned officers was made possible by decreasing the number of privates to 210. The exact reason for doing this is unclear, but possibly it was to create a cadre capable of commanding an additional force authorized at the same time. The special police law empowered the governor to enroll as many as twenty special policemen within a county as needed. Theoretically, they would be commanded by a member of the regular police. They would be paid only when on actual duty and could be called into action if the governor felt local law enforcement officials were incapable of ensuring justice. Through the years, their primary role would be enforcing order during elections.

Davidson encountered difficulty recruiting qualified men almost from the start. The police offered good pay, with officers receiving between $125 and $100 per month; noncommissioned officers and privates received between $70 and $60. There were hidden costs to being a policeman, however. Each man had to provide his own horse for service; he also had to buy his own badge. By August of that year, Davidson reported that he had made progress in filling the regular police positions authorized by the legislature, but at the end of that month, he had appointed only about one-third of the force. By the end of the year, his official report listed 172 privates on the payroll. Davidson was never able to bring his force up to its full authorized strength.

Critics of the police charged that Davidson signed on the worst sort of men, often criminals themselves, who would use their authority to commit further crimes against Texans. Generally speaking, the appointments to the regular organization gave little reason for such criticism. The men came from many different backgrounds, but these were little different from the rest of the people of the state. The force included not only strident Unionists but also ex-Confederates. At the very most, about 40 percent of the appointments were black. Some recent scholarship has suggested that the number of African Americans on the force was even smaller. Regardless, the force was hardly the "Negro Police" condemned by many Democrats. Little is known about the special police, however. There the number of blacks appointed may have been larger.

Unfortunately for the reputation of the police, a few of the recruits were not fit for their duties. Some were drunks. Others were unfit for the job. A small number may have had criminal backgrounds. Several incidents occurred in the first months of the existence of the force that reinforced the prejudices of its opponents. In August, 1870, officers in the company of Capt. Jack Helms shot two men they had arrested. In the investigation of the shooting, officials learned that Helms had been accused of murder earlier. Other shootings took place at Waco, Caldwell, and Tyler. Given the problems of quickly organizing the state police, mistakes in naming personnel might be expected. The real test of the force was the response to such incidents by its commander.

Davidson proved beyond criticism. He waited until he had full information, but when convinced of the wrongdoing of his officers, he removed them.

Even before the force had been fully organized, Davidson set his police to pursuing criminals aggressively. Shortly after being appointed, he requested that county sheriffs forward lists of criminals in their locality who remained on the loose. The resulting roll indicated the enormity of the problem—Davidson had received the names of 2,790 men subject to arrest. Much of the work of the state police involved run-of-the mill law-enforcement activity. Lists of men arrested and the crimes they had been accused of committing were periodically published by the *State Journal,* and these reflect the routine character of the state police's job. One, appearing on July 2, 1871, named fifty-seven men who had been arrested in the preceding two weeks by officers. Of the total, only ten involved charges of murder or attempted murder. Five charges of assault and battery rounded out the total number of crimes against people. The remaining forty-two arrests involved offenses such as horse theft and theft (separated in the accounting and suggesting a different seriousness), swindling, gambling, disturbing the peace, carrying deadly weapons, and "miscellaneous." Nonetheless, the policeman's job was dangerous, and in the organization's history, fourteen men died in the line of duty.

The success of the state police in tracking down criminals was remarkable. By the end of the first year, they had arrested 978 men. In 1871 Davidson's officers brought in 3,602 men charged with crime. The following year the chief reported that another 1,204 had been arrested. Unfortunately, this less dramatic part of the police story remains untold, the good forgotten in the face of a few incidents of police abuse used effectively by Governor Davis's opponents for political purposes. Many contemporaries, however, even when they did not support the administration, welcomed the police and its efforts at suppressing the disorder that had been pervasive in parts of the state since the war's end.

This restoration of law and order was supported by the Davis administration's expansion of the state's judicial system. The legislature had authorized thirty-five judicial districts. The judges were elected, but initially the governor had the power to appoint district attorneys. Davis quickly filled these positions, an action essential to handling the increased burden placed upon the court by the efforts of the police. The state's prison population suggests that they effectively bolstered efforts at suppressing crime through successful prosecutions. In 1860 only 182 prisoners had been incarcerated. By 1871 the prison population had increased to 520. Two years later it had reached 937.

The state militia complimented the efforts of the state police. When dealing with the type of violence that had beset Texas since the war's end, and particularly that associated with Reconstruction politics, regular police agencies were inadequate. The militia was seen by the administration as a force that could step in and help law enforcement in such situations. Under the law, the militia consisted of two different elements. Most Texans would be registered in the Reserve Militia. Its function was that usually associated with the American militia, to organize to provide a trained force that the nation could use in the event of a foreign invasion. The law also provided for a State Guard to consist of men equipped for immediate service when needed. These were the only units to receive weapons from the state and would be the ones readily available if the state government needed to support local law-enforcement officials or the state police.

Davidson proceeded with the militia's organization, signing up men at the same time that he began to hire members of the state police. By the end of the year, he announced that some 90,000 men had enrolled in the reserve, though he also reported that opposition had developed in some parts of the state. As a result of this, the adjutant general had been unable to form units in nearly half of the counties. In his same report, however, Davidson indicated that he had brought the State Guard up to its anticipated strength with the enrollment of some 3,500 men.

Given the problems of lawlessness and the relative lack of power by local authorities across Texas, the use of the State Guard was inevitable. In January, 1871, the governor used the State Guard for the first time when he declared martial law in Hill County. Davis and his political opponents subsequently provided different interpretations of events, but the basic story appears to justify the governor's actions. As early as September, 1870, the sheriff had requested the assistance of state police in arresting a band of outlaws led by Kench West and others that had the protection of some local citizens. Policemen were sent but were unable to arrest the parties or to prevent an attack on the county jail on September 21. Additional policemen arrived in early October under the command of Lt. W. T. Pritchett. At this time Davis threatened to declare martial law unless local citizens willingly turned out to help enforce the law and arrest the outlaws. The governor received assurances of cooperation and named a new sheriff to pursue a more active policy toward the gang.

Conditions continued to deteriorate, however. The new sheriff, assisted by several state policemen, began making arrests, but he found himself unable to go against the West gang because he lacked the manpower. On December 7 gunmen broke into the county jail again, releasing a man charged with murder. In this context a detachment led by Lieutenant Pritchett, attempting to arrest two young men charged with murdering a black couple in nearby Bosque County, rode to the house of Col. J. J. Gathings, the father of one of those charged. Gathings refused to let Pritchett search the house, declaring that he would not let it be searched by "your damned negro police." The lieutenant searched the house anyway. Later, a large group of men from the county, including Gathings and his relatives, seized Pritchett and his men and took them to Hillsboro, where word of their detainment had produced a mob. In front of the rabble, a local justice arraigned the policemen for entering Gathings's house without a warrant and then released Pritchett on bond.

At this point Pritchett informed the Adjutant General Davidson that he believed he had been detained to allow the parties charged with the murder of the black couple to escape. Once again local citizens had interfered with the efforts of authorities. This time Governor Davis declared martial law and sent Davidson to the county backed with fifty men from the State Guard. There he found the local sheriff powerless to act against Gathings and his supporters. State police officers and members of the State Guard quickly arrested Gathings and others responsible for seizing Pritchett. The prisoners pled guilty before a quickly constituted court-martial, which imposed a fine of three thousand dollars. In a move that proved controversial, Davidson used the money to pay for the expenses of the State Guard. Nevertheless, two days after arriving, Davidson had restored order and declared martial law lifted.

The Hill County affair was followed by another intervention, this one in Walker County in February, 1871. Once again the conflicting goals of politicians produced different interpretations of what happened, though the basic events are clear. In this instance a preliminary hearing found probable cause for holding three young men arrested by the state police for the murder of a black man. When the judge ordered them held for trial, a shooting fray broke out. The young men had been armed by friends, and they made their escape with their assistance and the refusal of local citizens to try to stop them. That evening an effort was made to assassinate the judge. Davis responded by declaring martial law, and Davidson and elements of the State Guard went into the county. Twenty persons, including one of the men who had escaped from the court, were arrested and tried before a military commission. The commission fined those charged with aiding in the escape. The young man charged with murder was sentenced to prison, though the sentence later was reversed and a trial before a civil court ordered. This time Davidson imposed a levy on the people of Walker County to pay for the expenses of the troops.

Finally, in October of that year, the governor used the guard for the last time when he sent it into Freestone and Limestone Counties. At Groesbeck, in Limestone County, a fight on September 30 between officers of the special police who had been appointed to supervise the upcoming election and two white men whom they tried to arrest had led to the death of one of the whites. The county had a history of hostility to the police, and the death provided the catalyst for a mob to gather. Subjected to threats, the mayor ordered the arrest of the policemen, who initially refused to surrender, but then agreed to be taken into custody by a member of the state police and removed to the county seat at Springfield. Violence continued, however, leading to wholesale intimidation of black voters in the congressional election held on October 3. To assure the prosecution of members of the mob, on October 8 Governor Davis declared martial law and sent in a large contingent of the State Guard. The militia's presence quickly suppressed the mob.

Overall, the actions of the state police and the State Guard appear to have suppressed the level of violence in some parts of the state. Davis secured little benefit from the good accomplished, however, as both the police and militia became the focus of a concentrated attack by his political opponents. When the bills first appeared in the legislature, Democrats had charged that the governor wanted the police and militia for political reasons, alleging that they were intended to suppress the Democratic opposition and impose a tyrannical regime on the people of Texas. They now looked to the actual operations of both to find proof of their accusations. The actions of policemen like Jack Helm gave them some measure of support. They found the ultimate justification for their claims, however, in the activities of the police and militia in the counties where Davis declared martial law. In January, 1871, the editor of the Democratic *State Gazette* at Austin sounded the theme taken up by the party press across the state. Their stories on the Hill County troubles confirmed their opinions on the character of E. J. Davis. "We have never known in the history of America," the editor wrote, "such flagrant abuse of power—such an open and bold violation of the rights of liberty and property of citizens." [2]

Another major part of the governor's attempts to bring peace to the state was initiated in 1870, with his efforts at providing protection against Indians along the frontier. These proved less controversial than the law-and-order measures aimed at interior counties, but they helped contribute to future administration problems. The basis for Davis's action was the bill passed by the legislature on June 13, 1870, providing for the creation of twenty ranging companies on the frontier. If fully organization, the frontier force would have consisted of 1,240 rangers signed up for one year's service. The state was to support them through the issue of state bonds. These units also came under the command of Davidson, and he proved equally aggressive in their organization. By the end of the summer of 1870, he had created fourteen of these companies, approximately 868 men. His plan for frontier protection was similar to that employed by the U.S. Army prior to the Civil War, placing these units in twelve counties along the frontier, where they patrolled in an effort to intercept raiding parties.

At the end of 1870, Davis had failed to sell the frontier bonds. The opposition of Sen. Morgan Hamilton had undermined all of his efforts in the East. Unable to provide for the existing force, the administration discontinued the ranging companies. In 1871 the legislature created a new frontier organization composed of twenty-four companies of minutemen; each was to have twenty-one men. The new force differed considerably from the first. These men signed up for service in the county of their residence. To save money, the companies were to go on active service only when needed, and an individual minuteman could not be on active duty more than ten days per month. The first companies saw service on the northwestern frontier in early 1872. Other units continued to be formed until all twenty-four were organized that August. The legislature amended this law in 1873 to allow the governor to create additional companies in any county where they were needed.

These frontier organizations aggressively worked to limit Indian incursions into the interior, but solving this problem proved far beyond the resources of the state. Indian raids in Texas at this time presented a challenge as complicated as that of domestic violence lawlessness. The Indian threat came from two sources. Along the northwestern frontier, farms and ranches faced depredations primarily from bands of the Kiowa and Comanche tribes (consisting in 1872 of approximately thirty-five hundred persons), often in conjunction with Cheyenne, Apache, and Wichita bands located in the Indian Territory (present-day Oklahoma). Most of these raiders were parts of tribes that had signed treaties with the United States in 1867 and were actually settled on a reservation near Fort Sill, Indian Territory. Under these treaties, raiding was to cease, but tribal organization meant little for some of these groups, particularly the Comanches, with their numerous subdivisions of distinct bands. As a result, treaty obligations were difficult to enforce. Groups often left the reservation to hunt, but outside the reservation they did not hesitate to take cattle, horses, and mules that could be sold or traded, often for arms and ammunition.

The second major Indian frontier was along the Rio Grande, across which Kickapoos, sometimes supported by Mescalero Apaches, raided. Responding to incursions from that quarter was particularly difficult, for the Kickapoos had treaties with Mexico that protected them. They were able to move across the international boundary for their raids and then hurry back to safety within Mexico. In 1868 Congress appropriated money to be used to encourage the Kickapoos to move back into the United States and settle on lands in the Indian Territory. Later reports suggested, however, that Mexican merchants encouraged them to remain in Mexico since their raiding provided the basis for a lucrative cattle business.

The state force, while well intentioned, faced an impossible task. It could not attack the Indians where they lived. Pursuing them along the northwestern and northwestern frontier required crossing over into Indian Territory, beyond the jurisdiction of the state. In the case of the Kickapoos, the international border provided safe haven for the raiders and a barrier to pursuit. This problem left the frontier units with the extremely difficult task of intercepting marauders within the vast frontier of Texas. Nonetheless, the adjutant general reported that in 1870 rangers had killed twenty-one Indians intercepted on raids and recovered horses and mules. In the years that followed, the minute companies also stopped some incursions and pursued and punished the raiders. While the actual numbers of Indians encountered were small, reports from the frontier suggest that the presence of the Texas units had the effect of discouraging some Indians and that, through the Davis years, the actual number of raids on frontier communities declined.

The limits on possible direct action by the state government forced the Davis administration to devote much of its activity concerning the Indians to influencing the federal government. In this area they found the situation almost as frustrating as conditions on the frontier. Disagreements among officials and agencies and unclear jurisdictions produced an Indian policy that seemed incapable of dealing with the raids. Indian affairs at this time were under the supervision of the U.S. Department of the Interior. Most of the agents who dealt with the Comanches and Kiowas believed that the only way to stop marauding bands was punishment. Interior's agents did not have this power, and those in the field recommended that the War Department send troops for this purpose. Treaties, however, prevented the army from pursuing raiders back to reservation land. As a result, during the Davis years, raids persisted when they might have been more easily suppressed by the use of troops in the Indian Territory.

The most notorious case in which state authorities found themselves thwarted by federal policy came in 1871, when they tried to punish two Kiowa chiefs, Santanta and Big Tree, for their role in an attack upon a wagon train resulting in the deaths of seven men near Fort Richardson on May 18, 1871. In this particular case the Indian agents arrested the chiefs on the reservation near Fort Sill and returned them to Jack County for trial. A jury found the Indians guilty, and the court sentenced to death. At this point federal authorities intervened, believing that the execution of the two would produce trouble with the reservation Indians. First, federal officials pressured Governor Davis to commute the death penalty imposed by the district court and place the chiefs in the state penitentiary for life. By 1872, fearing a potential Indian uprising and hoping to use the two chiefs to force the Kiowas on to reservations, federal authorities then placed further pressure on Davis to release the two and, before securing the governor's consent, promised the Kiowas that the chiefs would be released. Davis and most other Texans opposed this, but after a conference in Indian Territory, the governor received assurances that, upon the return of the chiefs, the Kiowas would move to and remain on their reservation. The federal government promised to enforce the agreement. Davis gave in to the pressure and released the chiefs in October, 1873.

But the Kiowas continued to raid, and federal officials remained frustrated in their efforts at bring the forays to an end. Given the situation, the state government could do little other than continue its attempts to intercept raiding bands along the frontier. The end of Indian incursions did not come until the

Davis administration was gone. Then, rather than anything the state did, the raiding stopped as railroads and farms began to occupy the lands across which the Indians moved and Washington changed its policies. In the mid-1870s the army began an aggressive campaign against the Indians along the western frontier that destroyed major raiding bands and forced the rest back to the Indian Territory's reservations.

At the same time that the Davis administration engaged in the creation of its police force, the militia, and the frontier force, it also moved ahead with the creation of a school system. The schools were a particularly critical part of the Republican effort. Party leaders saw the institutions as crucial to bringing about economic growth and social change within the state. Like those institutions designed to promote law and order, the schools also were successful in achieving their goals of expanding education within the state, though productive of considerable criticism. Despite the fact that the school system brought education to a larger proportion of the state's children than at any previous time in Texas history, it became the focus of considerable hostility almost from the day classes began.

The first Republican-sponsored school act failed to produce an effective organization. The law passed in 1870 placed the initiative for forming schools in local hands, but few communities responded. New legislation in 1871 gave the power to create a school system through a state board of education that included the governor and a superintendent of public instruction. The law empowered the board to create an administrative apparatus, establish basic rules and procedures for the operation of schools, and even test the qualifications of the system's teachers. Funding would come from state revenues distributed on the basis of students rather than from revenues generated solely within each county.

Davis immediately named Jacob C. DeGress as superintendent of public instruction. Originally from Germany, DeGress had lived in Missouri before the Civil War and had commanded Union cavalry during that conflict. He came to Texas in 1865 on the staff of Gen. Joseph A. Mower, served for a time as a staff member of the Freedmen's Bureau, then commanded black troops at Fort Duncan. He resigned the latter command because of recurring health problems caused by a wartime wound. DeGress had what amounted to a high school education in Germany, but the skills Davis's appointee brought to the job were those of an organizer and administrator. He summed up his basic goals for the schools in his first report, writing: "In the Southern States especially is there both room and necessity for advancement, and to the schools and institutes must we look for those influences that shall impress themselves upon the rising generation and prepare them to enter upon the arena of the battle of life with confidence, ability, energy, and knowledge."[3]

James DeGress, Republican superintendent of public education, 1870–74.
PICB-00960 Austin History Center, Austin Public Library

DeGress started his job on May 5, 1870, and began work immediately. He quickly found that no information existed on the prior educational work of the state and that no plan for creating a system other than the basic outline provided in the constitution and the school law. DeGress looked for guidelines from school systems across the nation, and by the end of August, he had put together an organizational program. He appointed, with the governor's approval, school supervisors for the thirty-five judicial districts and also named local district supervisors. The superintendent carried out a scholastic census and announced a set of rules and regulations for the operation of schools. He also created traveling boards of examiners to certify teachers who wanted positions in the new system.

DeGress's regulations created a standardized academic year. Schools were to open on the first Monday in September and continue until the thirtieth of June, establishing a ten-month term. Schools were supposed to hold sessions twenty-one days in short months and twenty-two in the longer ones. Operating rules even prescribed the length of the school day, which was to be divided into two sessions: The first began at 9:00 A.M. and continued to noon. The second session began at 1:00 P.M. and closed at 4:00 P.M. The term was particularly novel since few schools in the state previously had such lengthy sessions.

The rules of the new system also provided for graded schools consisting of four classes. The entering class, called the fourth class, studied spelling, writing, and reading. The work of the third class continued with these areas and added arithmetic, geography, and penmanship. The second class curriculum involved the same courses at a higher level, plus English grammar and American history. The first-class schools added composition, modern history, and instruction in the U.S. Constitution. These classes compared roughly to the curriculum in the modern elementary and junior high schools. It was supported by the use of standard texts across the state. These included series widely used in other state systems nationwide, such as Watson's readers and spellers, Clark's grammars, Quackenbos's arithmetic (plus his *Lessons in Composition and Rhetoric*), Perkins's *Algebra, Geometry, and Trigonometry,* and Barnes's *History of the United States.*

DeGress justified this standardization by arguing that, with a highly mobile population, the use of common texts and a common curriculum made it possible for children to move from district to district and advance their education without having to accommodate themselves to different books or a new course of studies. The use of systemwide texts also allowed the board to contract with publishers at lower costs. The books then were stored around the state at depositories, where individual districts could purchase them. The savings on the texts alone was considerable. DeGress reported that his system made it possible for the local districts to acquire books at 30 percent below published rates.

Another innovation in the school law was the requirement that teachers conform to certain guidelines. They had to show themselves qualified to teach each grade. They also had to demonstrate that they possessed good moral character as well as competency in their subject matter, temperate habits, and belief in a Supreme Being. They had to believe in God, but they were forbidden to exercise any sectarian influence in their schools. In his first report on the development of the schools in December, 1871, DeGress bemoaned the fact that many educators had not qualified under these provisions. Of 2,489 prospective teachers who had taken the test by August, 1871, 30 percent had failed. Nonetheless, he reflected the administration's view of that situation when he observed that "poor teachers speedily bring reproach upon any system of public instruction" and noted his intention of sticking with the guidelines.[4]

While representing a major innovation in local education, Texas schools were far from revolutionary in a social sense and did nothing to put white and black children together, despite repeated charges by administration opponents that the Republicans intended to create integrated schools. Two systems had been created under the 1871 legislation, one for whites and one for blacks; lawmakers actually toyed with the idea of creating separate schools for men and women as well. Relative to women, the perception of a woman's place in society that was central to the system may be seen in the fact that needlework was a recommended course for all females who were in school.

Many of the existing private schools, the few public schools, and the freedmen's schools organized by the Freedmen's Bureau quickly became part of the state system, which produced an almost immediate success, at least in providing education for the state's children. By the end of the first semester of the 1871–72 year, the superintendent reported that 1,324 schools had been opened. The 63,504 pupils listed as attending represented 28 percent of the school-aged population at that time. By the end of the spring term in 1872, completing the first full year of operations, the effort appeared even more successful. DeGress reported that by that time 2,067 schools had organized within the system, with 127,672 enrolled students taught by 2,625 teachers. This number represented 56 percent of those eligible to attend classes. Even while criticizing DeGress and various provisions for the new schools, hostile newspapers often recognized the accomplishments of the system.

Like every other Republican program, the public school system's successes did not deflect criticism by the opposition. Critics complained about its centralization and the lack of local control. They often charged that the curriculum and texts did not reflect the interests of the local community, pointing especially to history and geography books that provided a northern rather than southern view of the nation. Some nonpolitical opposition to the schools also emerged. Roman Catholics and some ethnic groups protested that the academic program aimed at destroying their religious or ethnic identity. Some teachers complained about the provisions requiring them to pass tests. Ultimately, the greatest criticism came to focus on the costs of the schools, with opponents arguing that the expenses did not justify the education provided. This argument frequently masked an appeal to white racism, suggesting that the education of blacks was an unjustified part of the plan. This became a major issue in the Democratic-backed taxpayers' revolt that took place in 1871, leading to the withholding of funds and the rapid unraveling of the new system.

When schools organized in September, 1872, the effect of their politicization had become apparent. Only 1,165 organized, down nearly 1,000 from the end of the 1871–72 academic year. A similar decline in the number of teachers in the system was apparent, with only 1,359 signed up for the system. Only half the number of students enrolled. Numbers improved after the harvest ended in 1872, but the recovery never brought the system back up to the size of its first year. Year-end reports in the spring of 1873 showed an increase to 1,824 schools, with 2,182 teachers and 83,082 students by December, 1872. But the growing revolt against state taxes in general began to squeeze the schools. DeGress found it almost impossible to pay his teachers by the spring of 1872, and many of them concluded that the system would collapse and abandoned it. Nonetheless, for a short time the public schools appeared destined to advance the education that its creators had believed essential for the future prosperity and peace Texas.

As the Davis administration moved forward in creating institutions designed to promote law and order and to educate the state's children, the Republican railroad program spurred private enterprise to move forward with construction. Unfortunately for Davis, those companies managed to get even more from the state than the governor had wanted. They advocated and secured a policy that brushed aside the cautious approach urged by Davis. As a result, the governor found himself in a conflict with the railroads that made his political situation even more delicate.

The action that produced the most immediate effect was the legislation that had provided relief for the Houston and Texas Central. Following the war, that company had received the financial backing of prominent Republican investors in the North and had almost immediately initiated the repair of track and equipment and the expansion of its system. By 1870 it had extended its mainline from Houston to Millican in Brazos County and on to Calvert, about fifty miles farther inland. In addition, they were able to pursue the Washington County Railroad, giving them a branch line at Hempstead to Brenham. By the end of 1870, the Central had established itself as the principal means of hauling cotton from the heart of the old cotton-growing region along the Brazos River.

The railroad's power and especially its support from Republicans outside the state had secured the passage, over the governor's veto, of the bill that allowed the road to refinance its debt to the school fund, validate its payment of state warrants to the fund during the war, and confirm its right to land granted in the original company charter. The road's directors had promised this measure would allow its rapid expansion northward. The relief made that and even more possible. By the end of 1871, the Houston and Texas Central had completed a spur from its mainline at Hempstead to Austin. At the end of 1873, its mainline from Houston had been extended another two hundred miles from Calvert, passing through Dallas and Sherman to a new terminus at Denison along Red River.

The state bonds the legislature had provided for the International Railroad also generated increased activity. Promised ten thousand dollars in bonds for every mile constructed, the company immediately took advantage of the opportunity. The projected route of the International was from the Red River to the Mexican border. It began construction of the first part of the project in 1871 at Hearne, along the route of the Houston and Texas Central, and immediately found itself in conflict with Davis, who wanted the road begun at Red River and initially refused to issue the promised bonds. Eventually, the two sides compromised, but the governor won no friends with the road and ironically contributed to opposition charges of corruption by his compromise. After Davis agreed to provide the bonds, the state comptroller then refused to issue them. Nonetheless, the International moved forward on the promise of state support, and by 1872 it had completed approximately 150 miles of track to Longview, where it intersected the Memphis and El Paso. By 1873 the International also had expanded its mileage by consolidating with the Houston and Great Northern, assuming control over the latter's rails from Palestine to Houston, thus providing direct access to Houston, and purchasing the Houston Tap and Brazoria, connecting the mainline at Houston with Columbia and providing a link into the cotton belt.

Governor Davis had supported the construction of a great trunk-railroad line across Texas, but he had always believed the state could not afford to back more than one such road. But pressure had grown to the point that, by the legislature's 1871 session, a combination of Republicans and Democrats in the assembly provided additional railroad aid. The most important subsidy went to the Southern Pacific and the Memphis, El Paso, and Pacific Railroads, operating now under the congressionally chartered Texas and Pacific. The roads' planners proposed operating along two parallel routes to Fort Worth, the Southern Pacific coming from Texarkana and the Memphis line coming from Marshall. From Fort Worth the projected route was to El Paso and west. For construction of this road, lawmakers authorized what could have been up to sixteen million dollars in bonds. Again, the governor vetoed the bill, but this time the legislature overrode it and then passed other bills too. As in the case of the International, the bond subsidy became involved in litigation that kept state funds out of the railroads' hands, but the promise of support encouraged construction, and by the end of 1873, the Texas and Pacific had more than 250 miles of track in service, with the mainline of the old Memphis and El Paso completed from Marshall to Dallas.

No single action of the government had been looked to as a greater instrument of change than its encouragement of railroad construction. Support of such enterprises was among the only policies emerging from these years that drew almost universal approval; indeed, many Democratic legislators proved more supportive of extravagant grants to railroad projects than did Republicans. Despite the constitutional problems, the effort had produced considerable development by the end of Reconstruction. The activity of the Texas Central, the International, the Texas and Pacific, and other lesser roads had produced a construction boom. In 1865 only about 341 miles of railroad remained in operation in the state. By 1870 the number of miles had increased to 711. That was only the beginning, however, and following the passage of bills that provided state aid and relief, the companies expanded even more aggressively. From 1870 to 1873, the companies doubled the amount of track in operation, the total nearly stretching 1,600 miles.

The legislature's encouragement of railroads had more of an influence than just the laying of more rails, however. It provided the ground work for a major social revolution in Texas that would not be realized fully during Reconstruction; its full effect ultimately would not be felt until the beginning of the next century. These roads overcame barriers of space and time that had produced a culture of rural isolation. They ultimately overcame this isolation and integrated all Texans into a broader state and national community. The schedules of the various roads tell the story. Prior to the railroad, the 150-mile trip from Houston to Austin by stage or on horseback took nearly two days, averaging a speed of 4 miles per hour. The arrival of the Houston and Texas Central at Austin in March, 1872, reduced the time by three-fourths. A traveler could board a train at Houston and, having moved across the prairies at the remarkable speed of 16 miles per hour, reach Austin nine and a half hours later. Future development linked the people of the state together even more.

A final aspect of the implementation of the Republican program begun in 1870 was the creation of a tax plan. In 1870 the governor had told Texans that, if they were to achieve progress, they would have to pay. The negative aspect of the Republican effort to expand the state government to achieve major social and economic goals was the need to raise taxes. That they unquestionably did. The Twelfth Legislature passed a revenue act in the summer of 1870 intended to take care of the broad needs of government. For state purposes, the tax law provided for the levying of an ad valorem tax on real and personal property of approximately .5 percent on each hundred dollars of assessed value. It also imposed a one-dollar poll tax to be used for supporting education. In addition, the law levied a 1 percent tax on the gross receipts of railroad and telegraph companies. It also established special occupation and licensing taxes.

The legislators also gave the counties power to raise property taxes potentially to an even higher level than the state. The law providing for local taxation authorized the county courts to levy taxes up to 1 percent ad valorem for general expenses. They also had the discretion to impose a 1 percent ad valorem tax for the improvement of public roads and another 1 percent for the construction of schools. Additional legislation allowed counties and incorporated towns power to subsidize railroad construction with bonds, which could be repaid with special ad valorem taxes of up to 2 percent.

The result was an immediate increase in taxes. The state property tax went up over 300 percent, rising from an average of about fifteen cents ad valorem at the beginning of Reconstruction to fifty cents. Ultimately, the real problem was not the state tax but the even more rapid increase in local taxes in some counties, where the local courts took advantage of the law to build roads and schools and to subsidize railroads. Typically, county taxes had been lower than state taxes before the war. This had meant a combined state and local tax burden of .3–.5 percent. By 1871, combined with the state levy of .5 percent, taxes in a county like Harrison, where the court undertook road improvements, construction of a school, the building of a new jail, and a subsidy for the Texas and Pacific Railroad, had reached 1.5 percent plus the one-dollar poll tax by 1871.[5]

The tax burden was increased further in some counties as courts reassessed the value of property upward after 1870. Across the state, property assessments had fallen drastically after the Civil War, and values continued to drop through the years of Congressional Reconstruction. A recovering economy probably did not justify the assessments in place in 1870, but the need by both state and local officials to raise additional revenues further encouraged the process. A look at assessments in two of historian Randolph B. Campbell's sample counties, where local county courts were in Republican hands and attempted to carry out the various improvements allowed by the tax law, shows what happened. In Colorado County lands had been valued at $2,107,005 in 1861 and remained at $2,100,568 in 1865. During the brief Throckmorton years, local officials reassessed, and in 1870 land values were at $913,350. Local courts reassessed land values heavily upward after 1870 so they reached $2,144,640. In Harrison County land had been at $2,153,458 before the war. There, reassessment had reduced overall value to $1,189,648 in 1865 and $1,030,821 by 1870. Republican reassessment brought land values back up to $2,414,958. Obviously, local taxpayers were concerned not just with tax rates but also with who controlled the assessments of property.

As the Republican agenda went into effect, the immediate political problem faced by the Davis administration and the party was whether or not the programs would produce results that justified to the public the increasing taxes. The expansion of government had raised taxes to a level never previously experienced. The governor had argued that this was necessary if Texans were to sleep under more than Mexican blankets. Republicanism's fate depended heavily on whether or not the party's efforts brought about economic prosperity and social change of the sort that would create a larger constituency supporting its basic philosophy.

Chapter 10

REPUBLICAN TEXAS

The ambitious program undertaken by Edmund Davis and pushed through the legislature in 1870 had significant implications for the lives of Texans almost from the beginning. Much of the Republican program aimed at creating conditions that would promote economic growth in the state. Railroads, education, and the restoration of law and order were the linchpins of the agenda. Assessing the individual effect of each of these efforts on the people of Texas is impossible, for they worked together and in conjunction with broader social and economic trends present at the time. Still, early 1870s Texans witnessed steady economic growth in their state, the emergence of new social trends, and a growing sense of stability and public order. The Davis administration could not take full credit for these developments, but neither could its accomplishments be ignored. It had worked to put measures in place to encourage these developments.

The clearest changes within the state came as a result of the rapid spread of railroads produced by the favorable policies implemented by the Twelfth Legislature. To a considerable degree, the railroads fueled the economic activity of the Davis years. They produced swift changes in agriculture and promoted its recovery. In turn, this recovery encouraged the development of prosperity in other economic sectors, especially commerce. The railroads affected much more than the state's economic life, however. Ultimately, the growth that they fostered encouraged major social changes as well, changes that pushed the state toward modernity.

The most obvious economic consequence of railroad expansion was the movement of cotton cultivation into the state's interior and toward the frontier. Through the antebellum period and into the postwar years, transportation had been a major factor limiting where cotton could be grown in the state. Much of Texas was capable of sustaining cotton culture, but hauling costs had restricted cotton growing to those areas along the coast or along the Red River in the northeast that were readily accessible to markets. Railroads brought with them relatively inexpensive shipping costs and easier access to market. Texans had continued to believe that money could be made with cotton, and whenever tracks tied new areas to markets, the state's farmers began growing more of it.

The shift to cotton production often was striking, and its expansion in the upper Brazos River valley produced some of the more remarkable results. Robertson, Limestone, Navarro, and Ellis were typical of the counties in that area experiencing a revolution. In all four, antebellum agriculture had been dominated by livestock raising and the cultivation of grain. Between 1870 and 1872, each was crossed by the Houston and Texas Central's mainline as it moved beyond Brazos County toward Dallas. In every one of these counties, the amount of cotton produced increased between 1869 and 1879. While across the state cotton production grew at a pace of 130 percent during these years, these counties demonstrated a much greater rate of expansion. Robertson County, crossed not only by the Central but also the International, grew 274 percent more cotton in 1879 than in 1869. In Limestone the cotton crop increased 165 percent; in Navarro, 218 percent; and in Ellis, 540 percent.[1]

As cotton spread into new territory, the line of counties that set the limits within which it was grown quickly moved farther west. The 1870 census had marked this frontier as it had existed since the antebellum period. Through these years, farmers grew cotton primarily in that part of Texas lying east of a line that ran southward from Montague County along the Red River to Atascosa, then eastward to Matagorda. Some 108,000 square miles were a part of this region. By the 1880 census, enumerators found that the line had moved west to Wichita County, southwest to Jones, then south to Uvalde, before turning east along the Nueces. The expanded cotton region now consisted of some 126,000 square miles.

The railroads not only encouraged cotton culture in a vastly expanded area but also promoted more intensive cultivation of the crop everywhere. This represented a major change in the character of agriculture for many. Most of the state's farms before the Civil War were not plantations, relying on both staple and cash crops instead. Limited markets for many of the products of these mixed farms put a premium on becoming as self-sufficient an operation as possible. This meant that much of their product directly went to support the farm family and its activities. Wheat and corn were grown to feed work animals, supply bread for the family, and to sell for cash in local markets. Winter wheat or rye was grown to provide pasturage for milk cows. A garden provided peas, squash, pumpkins, varieties of potatoes, and other vegetables to supplement the family table. On this type of farm, cotton was grown only after self-sufficiency had been achieved.

But the railroads shifted many farmers away from this. Cheaper transportation meant that merchants flooded markets with a wide variety of inexpensive goods. In Austin a local newspaper published prices for a variety of supplies in October, 1871, prior to the entry of the Texas Central the following December. At that time a sack of coarse Liverpool salt cost $4.50; northern butter in ten-pound cans cost forty-five cents per pound; northern "fancy" flour cost $15.00 per barrel. By March, 1872, three months after the arrival of the railroad, prices for all these products had fallen. Salt now sold at $3.40 per sack, butter at thirty-three cents per pound, and "fancy" flour at $13.00 per barrel.[2] In some cases merchants could sell goods at cheaper prices than it would take farmers to produce the same items themselves.

The greater availability of such food and supplies allowed small farmers to turn more of their efforts to producing a cash crop for market and to buy many of their other necessities from merchants. The chosen crop invariably was cotton. The change in emphasis could be seen in the mix of agricultural goods grown on the farms, especially the relative importance of the critical subsistence crop corn compared to cotton. A self-sufficient farm would necessarily devote more land to corn than to cotton, producing a high ratio of one to the other. As self-sufficiency became less important, the ratio of corn to cotton would lessen, showing more land had been devoted to the latter. Looking again at the four counties that had seen the entry of the Texas Central in the early 1870s, this trend is clear. In Robertson County along the Brazos, the one that had been most integrated into the antebellum commercial economy, the ratio of corn to cotton in 1869 had been 29:1. By 1879 it had dropped to 25:1. That of Limestone went from 56:1 to 37:1; Navarro from 75:1 to 40:1; and Ellis from 334:1 to 30:1. The figures show that farmers had intensified their efforts at growing the South's great cash crop at the sacrifice of traditional self-sufficiency.

The territorial expansion of cotton cultivation showed almost immediate results. Despite the problems that farmers had experienced in the first four years after the war, they continued their efforts to make money growing cotton. Even though many of the prewar plantation counties reduced their cultivation, the number of acres planted in cotton had steadily increased. One reporter estimated that in 1869 enough land had been planted in cotton to equal the crop of 1859. With an exception in only one year, Texas farmers continued to expand the amount of land devoted to the crop thereafter. In 1869 the commissioner of agriculture estimated that 720,000 acres had been planted. In 1870 almost 30 percent more land was in cotton, some 922,000 acres. The 1871 acreage was smaller at 867,000, but thereafter expansion continued. Cotton acreage reached 1,004,000 acres in 1872; 1,308,000 acres in 1873, a 30 percent increase; and then 1,384,000 acres in 1874.[3]

With more land being dedicated to cotton, the state's production of its one great cash crop began to recover to prewar levels. This comeback was particularly difficult because, from the end of the war to the end of the decade of the 1860s, farmers had been cursed by unfavorable conditions. Bad weather and the prevalence of the cotton worm had caused massive losses in 1866, 1867, and in 1868. The 1869 crop, for which as much land was under cultivation as in 1859, turned into another bad year, with a late spring delaying planting several months, heavy rains keeping workers out of the fields in June and July, and then the reappearance of the cotton worm to devastate many fields. Statewide the 351,000 bales harvested in 1869 represented approximately 80 percent of the harvest of 1859. In many counties, however, the crop surpassed or equaled that of 1859. Especially in the interior counties but also in some of the older plantation communities, the increased production was significant. Most of the older regions continued to lag behind in their recovery, however. Landowners insisted this reflected continued labor problems, but the bad weather may have been more of a factor.

During the next four years, the outlook for cotton continued to be optimistic, though farmers endured more bouts of bad weather, worms, and falling prices. In 1870 Texas farmers surpassed the harvest of 1859, sending over 532,000 bales to market. Unfortunately, this bounty produced a glut that then produced a price collapse. Cotton that had brought twenty-two cents sold for fifteen cents, and the value of the two crops was virtually the same, though a decade apart. The next year the natural risks of farming were once again apparent. A drought accompanied by high heat and then the early appearance of cotton worms in the summer seriously damaged cotton crops, especially along the Red River and in counties west of the Brazos. Estimates from some counties were that the weather was responsible for ruining as much as a third of the cotton that was in the fields, and overall production fell back to 370,000 bales. Prices did not recover, however, and as they remained low, Texas farmers harvested 468,000 bales of cotton in 1872, 592,000 in 1873, and 516,000 in 1874. Even though production recovered, farmers across Texas suffered from the vagaries of weather and a poor market. The combination was an unfortunate circumstance for the Davis administration, given the fact that the full effect of Republican taxes would be felt at the same time as the failure of cotton.[4]

There were nagging problems, however. Chief among them was the failure of some counties to recover at the same pace as the state as a whole. In particular, in many of the antebellum plantation counties along the lower Colorado and Brazos Rivers and in northeastern Texas, production lagged far behind that of the 1850s. There is no simple explanation for the failure of local farms to reach antebellum levels of cotton production. One possible cause was the continued friction between landowners and labor, though the reasons for that situation are not clear. Statistics for farm size in 1870 suggests that at least one element was a struggle between black laborers and landowners over the character of work. A comparison of economic conditions in Fort Bend and Washington Counties is suggestive. In Fort Bend, farm size had not decreased at all between 1859 and 1869, and reports indicate that planters there and elsewhere in the vicinity still wanted to work their plantations with gang labor. The 1869 crop there was two-thirds less than it had been in 1859. In Washington County, farm figures indicate that planters increasingly had abandoned large-scale operations in favor of sharecropping. The 1869 crop there was nearly equal to that in 1859.

In addition to labor problems, the failure of cotton to come back in some counties may also be related to the decision of many farmers to abandon the cultivation of the staple in favor of a greater emphasis on livestock. Colorado County was one of those where the 1869 crop came nowhere close to that of 1859. One of the top ten counties before the war, with a production of 14,438 bales, local farmers harvested only 2,796 in 1869. That year had seen floods on the lower Colorado River destroy an estimated one-half of the crop, but even if this had not taken place, an amount equal to only about 40 percent of the earlier harvest would have been taken in. Some farmers consciously looked for other opportunities. Isaac Towell, for example, grew one of the first rice crops in the county. More farmers probably took the course of Robert E. Stafford, who returned from the army and shifted to the cattle business. By 1869 the number of cattle in the county was almost back to prewar levels, and local livestock raisers were driving large herds to market.[5]

Another drag on the cotton economy was the problem of declining prices throughout this period. Unfortunately for Texans, the ultimate return of prosperity to the state's farmers depended on conditions beyond their control. While most quickly returned to prewar levels of productivity, many failed to achieve prewar levels of prosperity. Central to their failure was the change that had taken place in the textile market during the war years. Concerned even before the war with their reliance on American cotton, British investors had encouraged the development of plantations in India and Egypt. This cotton began arriving in international markets during and immediately after the war, helping force down prices. In 1869 the situation worsened when the completion of the Suez Canal allowed Indian cotton to arrive at European markets at the same time as that from America. The result for Texas farmers was steadily declining prices at the same time that they were increasing productivity.

Farmers understood the problem and had solutions, but this knowledge seldom helped. Monthly reports of the U.S. commissioner of agriculture provided warnings and suggestions that the local press passed on into the countryside. The message was for farmers to achieve self-sufficiency, growing enough food and forage to provide for themselves and their livestock, and to diversify production. Unfortunately, circumstances usually kept them from taking the necessary steps. While diversified agriculture represented an ideal situation, most farmers lacked a viable alternative to cotton as a cash crop. Corn, wheat, and other such grains were the only possibilities, and none of these had a market as good as cotton, even at the fiber's depressed prices. Self-sufficiency might also be desirable, but the indebtedness of most farmers, in some cases originating in the prewar years, forced them to sacrifice that goal in order to plant crops that would produce cash income. The idealized operations portrayed annually in the *Texas Almanac* never bothered to integrate the cost of debt into their projections of wealth.

Even taking into account all of these troubles, farmers could and did make profits, even if not as grand as they envisioned. Planters like John R. Hill of Waverly, San Jacinto County, successfully made the transition to fee labor, though he attempted to bring white labor in from the rest of the South and did attract several families of Polish immigrants. Using free labor and expanding his activities to include a part interest in a retail store, he kept his operations profitable until his death in 1878. Thomas Blackshear of Grimes County showed equal initiative, dividing one of his plantations into forty- to sixty-acre plots that he leased to whites and renting another of his plantations to three men who worked them with black laborers. Blackshear appears to have made profits but died in the yellow fever epidemic of 1867 before his plans could be fully realized.[6]

As the productivity of the farming sector of the agricultural economy recovered, another major development took place that added to the overall picture of growth. Livestock had been a major component of the agricultural economy before the war, but in the postwar years its importance became even greater. As early as 1866, speculators and packing houses began to take advantage of high prices for beef in northern markets to stage the first large cattle drives. In the immediate postwar period, cattle could be bought in Texas for between three and four dollars per head and would sell in the North at the same time for between thirty and forty dollars per head. Speculators, or drovers, purchased the cattle in Texas; drove them to Kansas, where they were wintered; and then sold to packing houses after having been fed out. In 1866 drovers sent an estimated 260,000 head of cattle overland from northern Texas to markets in Missouri and Kansans. Many on the first drive went to pens at Sedalia, Missouri. Later drives went mainly to Kansas, with Abilene becoming the major destination after 1869, then other towns opening as markets as the railroads pushed farther south. These drives continued to increase in size until 1871, when 700,000 Texas cattle went over the western trails to Kansas.

The economic significance of the cattle industry's revival was readily apparent. The market price in Texas for the 300,000 cattle put on the trail in 1869 was between one and one and a half million dollars. The 700,000 sent north in 1871 were worth from two to three million dollars. For those ranchers who drove their own herds to market, the potential for profits were infinitely greater. Profits spurred others to enter the business and, as in the case of farming, encouraged other aspects of the state's economic life.

Reconstruction policies contributed little directly to the emergence of the cattle industry, though the suppression of violence on the frontier and increasingly active policies aimed at displacing the Indians helped pave the way for the expansion of ranching. Many of the cattle taken to market in the early drives actually came from the coastal areas. Improving conditions brought larger herds into the counties along the farming frontier, then cattlemen moved even farther west. As early as 1872 the Skard Brothers pushed into Kiowa and Comanche territory in Wichita County, and shortly afterward pioneer cattleman Daniel Waggoner moved into the same area. By 1876 others, such as Charles Goodnight, had started running herds in the Panhandle, an area that Indians would have made untenable in earlier times.

The recovery of the state's farms and ranches and the evolving character of markets produced growth and important changes in other aspects of the state's economy. Commerce and business had suffered greatly during the war, but activity increased rapidly as the agrarian economy recovered. The movement of cotton through the port of Galveston illustrated this trend. In 1869 some 84,485 bales of cotton, valued at nearly ten million dollars, left the port. The next years saw a significant increase in the flow, and by 1873 the port shipped 333,502 bales worth in excess of thirty-two million dollars. For the city's businessmen involved in buying and selling cotton, ginning, compressing, warehousing, and shipping, the fees charged brought a proportional increase in their own profits.

The circulation of money into the countryside also added to business prosperity as it increased the demand for supplies and other goods. Retail merchants, wholesalers, and the railroads all benefited from the increasing traffic. Galveston wholesalers sent a wide variety of items to country merchants, including groceries, dry goods (including boots and shoes), drugs, hardware, crockery, farm equipment, and machinery. The volume of that city's commerce grew rapidly through the early 1870s. One of the best indicators of this was the value of goods brought into the port by local merchants. From a little over half a million dollars worth of goods between September 1, 1869, to September 1, 1870, imports increased to nearly two million dollars during the same period in 1871–72. Reports for this later period indicate that Galveston merchants sold over fourteen million dollars worth of goods locally and into the countryside.[7]

The Reconstruction era saw not only this simple increased volume but also witnessed a major restructuring of commerce as a result of the spread of railroads and, alongside the tracks, the telegraph. Prior to the Civil War, much of the cotton trade in the state's interior had been carried out by factors in Houston, Galveston, or New Orleans, the dominant market city for Texas goods throughout the antebellum era. Farmers and planters consigned their crop to these merchants, who then sold them. Usually, the same merchants advanced these planters and farmers supplies and credit for the next year's operation. With improved transportation and communication, the buying of cotton moved into the interior towns, where agents of the old cotton-buying houses, local buyers, or even general merchants purchased bales directly. Every depot along the railroads into the cotton country became a marketplace, with its buyers, compresses, and warehouses. Along with the merchants involved in this trade went retailers and agents of the wholesale houses of the larger towns to sell goods. The small railroad town became not only the place where cotton was bought but also a distribution point for merchandise. Towns across the state experienced an influx of merchants, bringing in peoples from places beyond the South and creating more-cosmopolitan populations.

In addition to the changes in the nature of commerce, the state experienced a major alteration in finance. The Constitution of 1845 had forbidden banking, but the practical aspects of banking had been carried out by factors who, in effect, loaned goods rather than money to farmers. The 1866 constitution did not have such a prohibitive clause, and many of the antebellum factors shifted to banking in the early 1870s. Consumers could now borrow money and buy supplies wherever they wished rather than being tied to a specific merchant. At Galveston the firm of Ball, Hutchings, and Company became the Hutchings-Sealy National Bank. The dry-goods merchant Henry Rosenberg helped organize Galveston's First National Bank and then the Galveston Bank and Trust Company. Other banks opened in many of the country-trading towns as well.

The recovery of agriculture and commerce represented the most significant economic trends during these years, but Texans also made some movement toward the creation of a more diversified economy. The ideal was for the state to develop manufacturing, bringing with it the increased income from producing finished products rather than raw goods and also the associated higher wages. Texans generally believed that the textile industry was the one that had the best prospects within their state. Entrepreneurs argued that factories located near the cotton fields could produce better and cheaper cloth, for the fiber used in the local mills would not suffer the damage and losses caused by baling and shipping. The mill also could make money by processing cotton-seeds into oil and cattle feed. Such enterprises provided an additional advantage to the farmers, who would not incur the heavy costs of process, shipping, and insuring their cotton.

Whether or not a government policy of tax breaks and other incentives helped generate this activity is unclear, but Texas manufacturing did show growth at the beginning of the decade and then through the 1870s. In 1869 the investment in manufacturing was $5.2 million; by 1879 the amount had increased to $9.2 million. During the same period, the value of goods manufactured in the state increased from over $11 million to over $20 million, some

80 percent. Most local manufacturing concerns were small, the average firm employing only four workers. Most were not highly mechanized and still used labor-intensive methods to produce flour, sawed lumber, clothing, shoes, leather goods, and numerous other similar products.

The state's efforts at acquiring the much desired cotton mills produced only mixed results. In 1870 the U.S. commissioner of agriculture reported that four mills had opened in Texas, suggesting a good start. These operated 8,328 spindles and produced over a million yards of material. The mills were at Houston, Waco, and in the state penitentiary at Huntsville. Among the larger of the private concerns was the Waco Manufacturing Company, organized by Nathan Patten, who had been a member of the Constitutional Convention of 1869. The Eureka Mills and the Houston City Cotton Mills in that city also were representative of the larger mills Texans sought. Unfortunately, few survived the 1870s, and the 1880 census counted only two mills still in operation.

The economic changes underway in the late 1860s and early 1870s had significant implications for the people of Texas. Relative to the rest of the South, the economic picture remained relatively good, and the promise of new opportunities attracted a constant flow of immigrants into the state. Beginning in the second year after the war's end, a steady influx of white families and individuals from the older states of the defeated Confederacy took place. These immigrants came for many reasons. Some feared for their futures in states with largely black populations. Others simply had returned to their homes after the war to find few opportunities and had set out to find a place where they could start again. The chance to begin again, for many to begin again free of their former slaves, lay primarily in western Texas, and many of the new immigrants settled in that and the northwestern regions of the state, along the edges of the farming frontier.

Almost alone among the former Confederate states, Texas experienced a rapid increase in population following the war. During the decade of the 1860s, the overall growth rate had been 34 percent, representing an increase of about 3.4 percent annually. By 1870 the census reported a total population of 818,579 compared to the 604,215 in 1860. The 1870s saw a more rapid pace, with the population reaching 1,591,749 in 1880, an annual increase of roughly 9.5 percent. The early years of the decade saw the highest rate, though. Between 1869 and 1872, the population expanded at a rate of 21.7 percent; the rate of growth between 1872 and 1875 was 22.5 percent.[8]

A heavy flow of immigrants into counties west of a line running southward from Grayson along the Red River to Williamson just north of Austin drove this population explosion. As the railroads prepared to advance to the north and northwest out of Houston and Galveston and westward through Dallas, thousands of new residents moved with them. The arrival of the railroads spurred the continued development of these counties through the 1870s, all of which outpaced the state's overall growth rate. Montague and Wise took the lead, their populations increasing over 1,000 percent during the decade. This particular movement had significant political implications. White immigrants constituted the majority of the new settlers, and many brought with them bitter feelings generated by the war and the destruction in their native states; some also carried a bitterness created by postwar politics. Whatever their reason, they often added to a growing population that had little interest in the Republican party's policies.

A second major trend was the steady growth of the state's towns and cities. In 1870 there had been only four cities with a population greater than 4,000 people—Austin, Galveston, Houston, and San Antonio. By 1880 there were eleven. The older cities nearly doubled in size during the 1870s, but railroad towns in the northwest showed the greatest development. Dallas had been only a village in 1870, but by 1880 it was the fifth-largest city in the state, with 10,358 inhabitants. Fort Worth, another village, was seventh with 6,663. Sherman, a major railroad center along the Red River, grew from 1,439 to 6,093.

These larger population centers were only the more successful of similar communities spawned along the routes of railroads throughout the state. Towns like Denison, the terminus of the Missouri, Kansas, and Texas, running south from St. Louis, and the Houston and Texas Central, entering the city from the south, sprung up almost overnight after the lines decided to locate there in 1873. Its development was typical as it quickly acquired a cotton compress, warehouses, and its share of cotton merchants. Within a year the town's population reached four thousand. It soon became a major interior market for cotton in north Texas. A visitor to Denison in 1874 found that, with the completion of the railroad, "Pullman cars were running through the untamed prairies. The gamblers and ruffians had fled. Denison had acquired a city charter, had a government, and the rabble had departed before law could reach them." [9] Railroads created but could also hurt a town. Denison's fate remained hinged to the trains, and the development of Sherman ultimately brought about a slowdown in its growth.

In addition to the population increase, Texas experienced important social changes as a result of conditions that were created during the Reconstruction years. Society was transformed for both whites and blacks. For whites, the uneven character of the agrarian economic recovery, the prosperity of the urban economy, and Republican programs created a highly unstable situation that challenged the antebellum social order. For blacks, the new circumstances made possible the emergence of a free society.

Among whites, the state's rural elites experienced some of the most momentous and threatening challenges to the antebellum status quo. Planters had dominated prewar society, but the Reconstruction years brought new conditions that challenged their wealth and power. What took place varied from community to community as planters had to adjust not only to free labor and declining prices but also to the environmental problems that affected each community differently. How planters responded to the challenges also varied individually, with everything from prewar debts to personality probably playing a role in their reactions. Even where they adjusted to the new circumstances successfully, rural elites remained pressed hard by economic conditions, and their very survival continued to be in doubt.

This uncertainty may be seen in the results of a study of six Texas counties, which has shown that between one-half and one-third of the richest 5 percent of residents remained within and part of the local elite between 1865 and 1880. Those areas with the highest persistence rates were comparable to rates found elsewhere in the country during the same period. Generally, the higher rates could be found in counties experiencing economic growth. A thriving economy may help explain the fact that in Dallas County more than half of the top 5 percent of taxpayers in 1865 remained in the county in 1880 and were still in that upper class. McClennan and Nueces Counties evidenced virtually the same results. Where the economy stagnated, however, the elites had a harder time. In Jefferson County only 42 percent of the 1865 elite remained in that group in 1880. The worst rates were in Colorado and Harrison Counties, where only one-third maintained their position.[10]

Little is known about what happened to white farmers who were not part of the highest class. In all probability they experienced the same pressures exerted on their wealthier neighbors, and the same various factors helped determine their fate. In Brazos County, for example, economic conditions favored elite survival. The survival rates of others in the community were not as good, as would be expected. Nonetheless, they persisted through the Civil War era at about the same level they had during the 1850s.[11]

The unsettled condition of white farmers, large and small, had significant political implications. No simple explanation exists for the failure of those farm families who did not survive. As has been seen, labor problems existed, nature dashed the hopes of many, and the value of cotton declined steeply as a result of the changing marketplace. The actual reasons were not important for the state's politics, however. All combined to threaten the very survival of this part of the population and pushed them into a desperate search for the means to keep going. They could do little about what they paid for marketing their crops, the fees for merchants, insurance companies, and shippers. They did have a say on the issue of taxation, however, and circumstances inevitably produced a climate of hostility toward the cost of Republican programs. Republicans might point to overall gains for the state that resulted from their actions, but this could mean little to farmers struggling for survival. It contributed to the creation of a particularly powerful enemy in the form of the rural elites.

Yet at the same time that farmers faced an increasingly unstable situation, the townspeople's prosperity grew. The result was not only the survival of much of the antebellum elite but also a steady increase in their economic and political power. The full story of the persistence of the state's wealthy merchants remains untold, but anecdotal evidence shows clearly their progress. Houston's Thomas W. House, one of the city's wealthiest individuals before the war, became even wealthier afterward with his activities as a wholesale merchant, private banker, sugar and cotton planter, rancher, and owner of the city's first public utility. Galveston's George Sealy demonstrated equal tenacity, shifting his focus from dry goods to banking and investments in railroads, manufacturing, insurance, and numerous other endeavors after the war.

While benefiting from postwar conditions and particularly from the support the Twelfth Legislature had provided for their railroads ventures, these successful urban leaders faced a difficult situation politically. Their economic interests lay in between the great rival political factions. The economic policies of the Davis administration and the national Republican party were to their advantage, but they still depended on the people of the countryside to produce the cotton they bought and sold and to buy the goods that they distributed. Ultimately, the latter determined their political course, and almost all of the urban elites linked themselves to the Democratic party and played a major role in that party through the rest of the century, even though some also provided strength to the Republican party after its later abandonment of its black constituents.

African Americans confronted their own uncertainty during the years of the Davis administration, but on the whole they made considerable progress toward establishing themselves as free in reality as well as in name. The policies of the government provided a framework favorable to this process, and their achievements were remarkable. While their efforts fell far short of achieving equality in any sense of the word, what was accomplished was all the more singular given the lack of resources with which they began, the unfavorable economic climate, and the efforts of many whites to prevent any change at all. Their successes reflected not only the encouragement given by the Republican regime but also their own tenacity and ingenuity in trying to establish themselves as truly independent.

From the beginning, most freedmen had believed that full liberty could be accomplished only when they were able to exercise control over their own lives, and for most that meant acquiring a farm. This belief had spelled the doom of white efforts at maintaining the old gang system of labor and fostered the various forms of tenant farming. The ultimate goal remained, however, not just farming on their own but actually owning the land that they cultivated. This was difficult to achieve. Many elements combined to thwart it. In some areas whites refused to sell land to freedmen. Sometimes their own immobility stood in the way. One observer noted that blacks in Colorado County could find land elsewhere, but a lack of transportation, the possession of at least some livestock that could not be moved, and a fear of leaving "the neighborhood where they have always lived" pinned them down in areas where they had no opportunity to acquire property.[12]

Still, at least some African Americans became landowners during this period. They acquired property in a variety of ways. In at least some cases former masters helped, a few actually giving them land. In 1869, for example, Swante Palm of Austin gave eighteen of his former slaves forty-acre tracts for farming and a half acre upon which to build a house on a large holding he owned in southwestern Colorado County. Palm apparently hoped they would create a viable farming community. This gift was not typical, however. Others may have helped favored slaves purchase farms too.[13]

The majority of former slaves received no such treatment and probably bought property on their own. Little is known about how they managed to do this, though the example of land acquisition by blacks at Kendleton in Fort Bend County may have been typical. In 1870 William Kendall, a planter in that area, decided to sell his plantation. He divided the land up into one-hundred-acre plots and sold them to freedmen with the assistance of Republican politician Ben Williams, charging between $.50 and $1.50 per acre, a relatively low price but still a considerable sum for those with limited resources. Kendall facilitated the purchases, however, by extending credit to the buyers.[14]

Landownership did not become prevalent, but given the fact that blacks had owned nothing in 1865, the extent achieved was remarkable. No statistics exist for black landownership at the end of Reconstruction, but those in the 1880 census show what had been accomplished. Scholarship that investigated six Texas counties has shown that in the three counties where the most people were engaged in agriculture, between 24 and 15 percent of those blacks who listed their occupation as related to farming owned land. Colorado County showed the highest ownership rate, with the holdings of black farmers averaging 65 acres. Harrison County had the lower rate, with black landowners there having farms that ranged in size from 15 to 240 acres. Landownership remained elusive, but hundreds had managed to achieve this goal.[15]

While property remained the object of many freedmen, the postwar economy offered new opportunities as well. Across the state, increasing numbers of blacks did not work in agriculture. Recent scholarship has shown that even in heavily agricultural counties such as Colorado, Harrison, and McClellan, large percentages of black workers were not engaged in farming. In Colorado about 33 percent had nonagricultural occupations; in Harrison, 38 percent; and in McClennan, 44 percent. In Dallas County, with its growing urban center, 65 percent of blacks worked in jobs other than farming. In Jefferson, the center of an emerging timber industry, 72 percent were nonfarm workers.[16]

Blacks engaged in all sorts of pursuits. Railroads offered men employment as construction hands and laborers. The timber industry hired men to work in sawmills and as shingle makers. The thriving livestock industry offered a source of employment for some blacks as well. Many African American women also entered this alternative labor force, especially in the towns, where they found employment as cooks and laundresses. Although the opportunities were more limited, at least a few secured jobs that would provide the core for the emergence of a black middle class. By 1870 in many towns African Americans could be found working as skilled craftsmen. There also were black ministers and teachers.

With economic independence envisioned as the key to full freedom, the desire expressed by many freedmen for their own and their children's education was unsurprising. The Freedmen's Bureau teachers had noted that blacks wanted education, but the bureau had never been able to create a system that could satisfy the demand. The new state public school system had that potential, however, and offered all African Americans the opportunity to get an education. Blacks rushed to respond, despite the barriers that poverty and racial violence presented. By December, 1871, the state superintendent reported nearly fifty thousand black children in the schools. In addition, often aided by northern religious groups, blacks in Texas began to develop their own teachers at institutions such as the Barnes Institute, created at Galveston in 1871; Paul Quinn College, created in Austin in 1872; and Wiley College, founded at Marshall in 1873.

The results of the effort at securing education, like that of finding economic independence, fell short of a revolution in the modern sense. But again, given where most blacks had been in 1865, the results were noteworthy. They acquired increased levels of literacy through the 1870s, and by 1880 24.6 percent of African Americans above the age of ten had learned to write. This figure was better among children, with 28.2 percent of those from age ten to fourteen being able to write.

African Americans remained relatively poor, but their successes made possible the development of their own social institutions. From the war's end, they had attempted to establish control over their own families, a process facilitated during the Davis administration. While the Freedmen's Bureau encouraged the regularization of prewar unions and established the first marriage regulations that applied to blacks, the state had refused to recognize these marriages, and until the ratification of the Constitution of 1868–69, many justices of the peace would not grant licenses to blacks or register their marriages. The new constitution legalized such unions, provided protection for parental rights, and provided the framework for the continued development of black family life.

As early as 1870, census statistics indicate the emergence of a black family culture that was virtually the same as that of whites. Scholarship has shown that by this time the traditional household, headed by a father, was the norm. The rate of households headed by a male, about 83 percent, was the same as among whites, where the father-dominated household was typical in 84 percent of the cases. In 1870 many households were composed of multiple families, but by 1880 the continuing development of black family life had produced the same type of nuclear family as prevailed among whites. Scholarship has shown that in almost every county examined, between 73 and 75 percent of black households consisted of a husband, wife, and children, with no other members. The one major difference, indicative of the financial position of many black families, was that more black than white women had to find employment outside of the home.[17]

Further illustrative of the development black culture and life during Reconstruction was the spread of African American churches. Once again, this took place despite the hostility of many whites, who saw these institutions as the spawning ground for political and social discontent. In some ways this assessment was correct, for black churches did become the center of community life and often produced some of the more important black community leaders, including state senator Matthew Gaines and the murdered George Brooks of Millican. In the face of violence aimed at these leaders and the destruction of their churches, blacks separated from white churches almost immediately after the war's end. With greater protection, their churches thrived.

By the mid-1870s thousands of blacks had joined Baptist churches. Some had been Baptists before the war, but the denomination's congregational organization, which provided greater autonomy, appealed to many freedmen following the war. Based upon later census figures, the number of black Baptists probably exceeded the combined total black membership of all other denominations. Other church organizations were significant, however. Particularly important were the various Methodist groups, including the African Methodist Episcopal Church, the African Methodist Episcopal Church Zion, and the Colored Methodist Episcopal Church. The formation of black institutions of higher education backed by these religious groups at the end of Reconstruction indicated the growing stability of the Davis years. The creation by Methodists of Paul Quinn College at Austin in 1872 and Wiley College at Marshall in 1873 signaled the increasing assertion of freedom by the African American Texans.[18]

The Texas that began to emerge in the early part of the 1870s differed considerably from that existing prior to the Civil War. The steady progress of African Americans toward consolidating their hold on freedom continued to be the most obvious social trend. Economic recovery also remained evident, though the returning prosperity of these years was not felt equally across the state, either geographically or socially. The social upheaval generated in those areas where the economy suffered may ultimately have been more significant than racism in creating a climate increasingly unfavorable to the Republican government that had, at least in part, helped pave the way for this new Texas. Added to the influx of hostile white immigrants, such problems made the task of maintaining Reconstruction even more difficult. Following the successful passage of Edmund J. Davis's agenda through the Twelfth Legislature and the subsequent expansion of institutions that legislation made possible, Republicans faced growing challenges that threatened all that had been accomplished and the future that had begun to unfold.

Chapter 11

The Collapse of Republican Government

The Davis administration and the Republican party moved forward with their agenda despite a mounting political assault on the legitimacy of the government, begun the moment Gen. Joseph Reynolds had announced the results of the 1869 election. That attack intensified through the legislative session of 1870 and into the election season of 1871. A. J. Hamilton had set the course for the opposition when he charged that Reynolds had counted Davis into the governorship and overridden the will of Texans. During the sessions of the Twelfth Legislature, the campaign continued as Hamilton Republicans and Democrats condemned the police measures, school system, railroad policy, and enhanced taxes of the administration, citing them as proof that Davis was unrepresentative of the interests of the people. Hamilton again served as principal opposition spokesman in accusing Davis and his party of suppressing the civil liberties of Texans, corruption, and the burdening of citizens with taxes that were both too high and unnecessary. The hostility of both Hamilton Republicans and Democrats had made it possible for the two to create an improbable fusion of interests and a powerful and dangerous opponent for the state government.

In 1871 the character of political struggles in Texas began to change. All four of the state's seats in the U.S. House of Representatives were up for election, making the year a critical one. Democratic leaders across the South and in the North as well had already begun to develop a policy known as the "New Departure" in their hopes of securing election victories from the state level to the presidency in 1872. The New Departure abandoned fusion and focused instead on a return to straight-out party organization, running Democratic candidates on Democratic platforms. Many thought that a reemphasis on the party's traditional states' rights ideas would mobilize its voters once again. At the same time, they dropped their opposition to black suffrage and the Reconstruction amendments, concluding that these now were irreversible and that continued agitation of the issue failed to turn out voters and potentially alienated Democratic moderates. In Texas the New Departure arrived with the congressional elections. While local Democrats followed the national party into support of the Republican Horace Greeley for president in 1872, the congressional elections of 1871 marked the return of the Democratic party in Texas and the first steps toward its recapturing political power the following year.

Since the war's end, Democrats had sought the means to regain control of government without provoking interference in state affairs by federal authorities. The principal strategy had been linking themselves to individuals or parties whose loyalty would appear unquestioned in Washington. They had even abandoned the use of the term "Democrat" to identify their party, calling themselves "Conservatives" instead. In 1867 they had formed a coalition with Unionist James Throckmorton. Then, in 1869, they had come to the support of A. J. Hamilton. The next year moderate Democrats, such as the longtime executive committee chairman William M. Walton, counseled continued cooperation with the Hamilton Republicans, who had now begun to associate themselves with the national Liberal Republican movement. The need for fusion, however, had passed. By 1871 the state had been back in the Union for a year and further intervention by the national government in its affairs was unlikely. The New Departure soon arrived in Texas.

Party leaders shifted Democratic strategy in early 1871. In January they held a state convention at Austin that stated the party's intention of returning to traditional Democratic issues. Their platform emphasized the doctrine of states' rights and condemned the centralizing tendencies of the Republican party. At the same time, it attacked the corruption and extravagance of the Davis administration. Noticeably absent was any mention of black suffrage or the Reconstruction amendments. It laid out future strategy when it declared the party's intention of supporting only Democratic candidates in the upcoming campaigns. District conventions followed that lead, choosing straight-out Democrats in three of the congressional districts. In the Second District the party renominated the incumbent Democratic carpetbagger from Indiana, John Conner. In the First the choice was William S. Herndon, a Confederate veteran who had been a railroad lawyer and developer at Tyler. The Third District candidate was Dewitt C. Giddings of Brenham, another former Confederate associated with the state's railroad interests. Only in the Fourth District, a Republican stronghold, did the Democrats compromise by selecting John Hancock, a Unionist turned Democrat, to run.

As a part of this effort, party leaders made arrangements at Austin for publishing a state newspaper, the *Democratic Statesman,* that would provide Democrats with a single statewide voice. In the *Statesman's* first issue, the editor made it clear that the aim of the paper was to bring unity to the party. In the years that followed, the *Statesman* became the chief vehicle through which the state party leadership communicated with the faithful elsewhere in Texas and maintained party orthodoxy. Its editorial pages set the tone of campaigns, stating the position of the leadership and providing information that other party newspapers then passed on. In 1871 the *Statesman* endorsed the New Departure, its editor writing, "We have nothing now to do with the Fourteenth and Fifteenth Amendments to the Federal Constitution." [1]

The editorial pages of the *Democratic Statesman* began setting the agenda for the campaign with its first edition on July 26. The New Departure prevailed as the editor emphasized traditional Democratic issues, throwing particular criticism at the national Republican party's shift of power toward the central government and its abuses of that power. The latter issue had taken on even more meaning at this time because of the increasing criticism by the northern press of the Grant administration and Congress's involvement with scandals and corruption associated with railroads. The Democratic press in Texas reprinted such charges, agreeing that this was to be expected from a drift away from states' rights. They welcomed the splintering away from the national Republican party of the Liberal Republicans. Events at the national level were taken to prove the validity of charges made against the Davis administration. Like Republicans everywhere, at least according to the Democratic press, Texas Republicans had raised taxes to enormous levels, succumbed to railroad corruption, and used the taxpayers' money dishonestly. The issue before the voters was no longer Reconstruction—it was returning government to the purity of the past by electing Democrats to Congress.

The tax problem in Texas was a perfect issue for the New Departure strategy. Most voters would be concerned with taxation, and charges that the tax burden was too high and made that way because of the corruption of the Davis administration would resonate. Through the summer, the Democratic press focused particularly on the issue of corruption. There were few specific examples to support these charges, though, for most of the rhetoric amounted to nothing more than insinuation. The editor of the *Statesman* proved a master at the indirect accusation. In his first editorial on the subject, he noted that under the Republicans, the cost of government had increased. "[C]an the administration be honest, which requires so much money to carry it on?" he asked rhetorically. His conclusion: "The answer is as ready as the inquiry. The administration is not honest." But the answer did not follow from the original premise. Such an approach, however, allowed Democrats to claim that they sympathized with many of the Republican-initiated programs; they only opposed the dishonest way in which the Republicans operated them. [2]

The public schools became the focal point of these Democratic accusations. The reason for this may simply have been that the schools were the more expensive of the programs. In one year the administration had created an administrative apparatus, hired teachers, purchased books and equipment, and authorized local school boards to raise additional local taxes for educational support and the construction of new buildings. The cost of the new system in its first year amounted to more than $1,200,000. At no time previously had more than about $100,000 been spent.

Democrats saw little that they liked in the new system, even criticizing the mandatory attendance policy as an infringement on personal liberty. Their most grievous charge, however, was that the money spent was being used to make school administrators wealthy and to create a party machine to subjugate Texans. Actual school operations provided little factual basis for these allegations, however. The purchase of slate boards furnished the principal source for these accusations of corruption, with Democrats claiming that the school administration spent exorbitant amounts of money for the boards. The charges actually proved false, for their basis was the warrants issued by the comptroller to pay for the purchase of the slate boards, but the amounts issued, totaling ten times their actual price, was an error, and the money never paid.

On the complaint that the administration used the system for political purposes, Democrats stood on somewhat firmer ground. Some of the thirty school-supervisor positions may have been given to party activists, and these men may have carried out party work, but no evidence exists that this was done in all cases or that any political test was applied to teachers within the system. The political rather than legal basis of Democratic assertions would become clear when a subsequent legislative committee found no basis for prosecuting anyone connected to the schools. Nonetheless, the Democratic-controlled committee refused to back away from the party's charges and insinuated that the failure to prosecute was simply because of a lack of hard evidence.

In addition to their focus on alleged Republican corruption in the school system, the Democratic leadership continued to criticize the Davis administration for abusing power to the point of imposing a tyrannical regime upon the state. To prove this point, they centered their attention on the police measures implemented in 1870. By the spring of 1871, the state police, the special police, and the militia had all seen service, and their actions offered a litany of grievances for Democratic editors. Declarations of martial law in Walker and Hill Counties provided the basis for charges that the governor had overridden the state constitution by suspending the writ of habeas corpus and by trying citizens before military tribunals. As in the case of the schools, no evidence existed of an actual abuse of power, but Democratic editors conjured pictures of a crisis of great proportion in which the governor used armed force to maintain his government in power. Three days after the *Democratic Statesman*'s editor had assailed the taxing policies of the Davis administration, he published a frightful prediction. "We are fully impressed with the conviction that constitutional government in this State is in danger of utter extinction," he wrote, "and that the cause of human rights and civil liberty were never in greater peril."[3]

The culmination of the Democratic campaign came with the meeting of the Taxpayers' Convention at Austin on September 22, 1871, just two weeks before voters went to the polls to elect their congressmen. On August 5 a committee in Austin called for meetings in every county in the state to express their opinion on the "exorbitant expenditures and enormous taxes" to which Texans were being subjected. This group also encouraged the selection of delegates to meet at Austin. Several prominent Liberal Republicans backed the move, former governors Andrew Hamilton and Elisha Pease and U.S. Sen. Morgan Hamilton being the most noteworthy; A. J. Hamilton and Pease would play active roles when the convention met. The great majority responsible for and involved in the convention, however, were Democrats. In taxpayers' meetings across the state that took place after the initial call, the political character of the movement became even clearer. Most of the men chosen to attend the convention at Austin were active Democratic politicians. An example of that party's role could be seen in Llano County, where all delegates chosen to go to Austin were members of the local Democratic executive committee.

The Taxpayers' Convention met for three days, during which leaders sought to meet with the governor, and publicized his refusals to accommodate them. But the results of the convention indicated that much more was on the minds of the delegates than taxation. A committee issued a report that condemned the Davis administration for an enormous increase in the cost in government, charged that these costs were greater than the needs of the state, and concluded that the higher taxes were unnecessary. The conclusion was a political one, for in itemizing taxes, the committee used the maximum rates allowed rather than those actually levied and included county taxes in the state total as well. A second committee moved beyond taxation, however, and catalogued what it called the governor's abuses of power. Its list included everything from the school law to the various police measures of the administration.

The convention produced enormous problems for Republicans. Its tax report questioned the constitutionality of the 1 percent county school tax and advised local citizens to take the matter to local courts, suggesting that they seek injunctions to block its collection until its legality could be tested. This lawsuit compounded the administration's political problems, for it raised the cost of the school system even further and forced the schools to borrow money to pay their costs. In addition, despite the bipartisan appearance of the convention, its report identified the Democratic party as the party of good government and fiscal conservatism while tarring the Republicans with charges of corruption just before the congressional elections. If voters believed the campaign rhetoric, the future was bleak for Republicans. The appeal being made was summed up in one of the major campaign documents to come out of the contest. In his *Review of the Laws of the Twelfth Legislature of Texas,*

Waco attorney and politician Charles B. Pearre insisted that under Republican taxation, "The cow which furnishes his babe with milk will be driven away and sold under the sheriff's hammer, for a song, while the tears of the distressed mother and her helpless children will have no effect on the rapacious tax gather."[4]

As the congressional campaign advanced, the moderation of the Democracy's New Departure began to fade. The issues of taxation and tyranny dominated newspaper coverage and official party propaganda. At the local level, however, party organs continued to play upon the racial fears of whites and insisted that the Republicans had created a crisis that threatened white supremacy. As in the case of taxes, the new public school system received particular attention as being at the heart of the danger. If newspaper editors remained relatively quiet on the subject, published letters to the editor contained frequent complaints that the schools were being used by Radicals to foment unrest among African Americans. The *Colorado Citizen* of Colorado County attacked the schools in May, 1871, as being used primarily to teach "negroes to be impudent to the white race." A correspondent of the *Dallas Herald* complained that the schools not only encouraged racial amalgamation but also encouraged African Americans to idleness and self-importance. Such a course made them "intolerable to all decent people around them."[5] While the *Democratic Statesman* remained quiet on the issue, papers like the *Neches Valley News* in Jefferson County had a solution. Its editor declared his paper the "White Man's Organ for the First Judicial District" and called for its voters to sustain "White Supremacy."[6]

The New Departure also did not limit the by-now traditional efforts by Democrats to control black voting. Violence aimed at the African American community and particularly at those blacks active in politics increased during the election season. One of the most violent places this time was Bastrop County. There, on May 28, disguised men burned an African American church used as a school and then destroyed a schoolhouse in the southern part of the county. In their attack they whipped one of the teachers. On June 13 and 17, other disguised bands whipped two black men and drove their livestock away from their farms. Finally, on July 1 a band of fifteen men rode into the small German community of Serbin, where they harassed local citizens. Republicans believed that the brutality in Bastrop was another part of a Democratic campaign strategy and charged that the Ku Klux Klan had reorganized in the state. Republican papers reported that witnesses described disguised men who told them they were hunting for "negro school teachers, mean negroes and Radicals."[7] A local grand jury failed to indict men arrested in the incident by the state police, offering Republican leaders further proof that what had taken place was politically motivated. Nothing could be done, however.

Attacks on black churches and schools took place elsewhere in 1871, but by this time overt violence was not the usual method local Democrats used to intimidate black or white Republicans. Testimony before a congressional committee examining contested elections in the First and Third Districts produced evidence that showed Democrats using the wide variety of more subtle means to control votes that they had developed in previous elections. White Republicans usually faced threats of economic boycott and social ostracism if they remained active in their party. One prominent party member reported that he was unable to secure credit for his business or any other backing as a result of his politics. Black Republicans found the usual economic coercion. Landowners informed their tenants that if they registered to vote or actually voted, they would have to look for new employment. The state police might restrain outright violence, but the not-so-subtle pressure exerted on voters by this time was much more difficult to control. Few affected probably ever complained—they simply did not vote.

The New Departure created serious problems for the Republican party. The renewed Democratic activity and the shift in strategy forced Republican leaders to respond with a transformation of their own efforts. Central to this alteration was the party's claim to be the people's bulwark against the depredations of the railroads, corporate monopolies, and land speculators that had taken over the Democratic organization. Political rhetoric argued that the railroads had driven up the cost of government, pushed corrupt deals through the legislature, and then, along with other rich men, did not want to pay the increased taxes; they were willing to sacrifice public safety and the future of the state's children to secure their end. The Republican press pointed to the governor's vetoes of railroad legislation and his efforts to prevent the delivery of state bonds into the hands of the International as evidence of the administration's actual policy.

The emphasis on economic issues made as much sense for the Republicans as it did for the Democrats. Amid the growing economic crisis in the countryside, the great mass of the state's farmers were not doing well. Anticorporate, antirailroad sentiment had already emerged in some areas and had led to the formation of agrarian political organizations. Republicans had as much right as, if not more than, the Democrats to claim that their policies worked to the long-term benefit of Texas. Governor Davis had tried to keep the railroads from bankrupting the state, and Democrats had helped railroad interests in the legislature overturn his efforts. If Republicans were going to secure votes with strategy, however, they would have to make gains among the thousands of white immigrants moving into Texas, most of whom were from the southern states to the east. If any hope existed for gaining that support, the racist fears of most of these people had to be addressed, which led to a subtle change in the position of the party's white leadership toward its black voting base.

Behind-the-scenes maneuvering indicated that Republican leaders realized the difficulty their party's biracial character presented to gaining support from poorer whites in the state. Some Republicans, such as Executive Secretary James Tracy and Secretary of State James Newcomb, who at the time also was the president of the state Union League organization, believed that the use of the secret league as one of the principal instruments for mobilizing voters kept many whites from joining the party. They thought whites would not work within this group because it was dominated by blacks. In the spring of 1871, leaders tried to solve their problem by deemphasizing the league and creating alternative organizations, such as the Grand Army of the Republic, which might attract Union Army veterans, or Republican clubs for other whites.

The shift of emphasis undertaken by Tracy and Newcomb posed serious problems since it took for granted black support at a time when Democrats continued their efforts at reducing black participation. Leading African American politicians, such as state senator Matthew Gaines, and whites tied closely to the Union League, such as Congressman George Whitmore, criticized the administration's effort at dismantling that organization. Tracy and Newcomb's efforts ultimately produced a challenge to party leadership, with local league chapters putting their own candidates up for the Republican nomination in two congressional districts. The biggest threat to the party leadership came in the Third District, where incumbent representative William T. Clark had been courting white business interests in Galveston and Houston, taking positions favorable to them in Washington. His course clearly reflected the new direction intended by Republican leaders. The revolt by Union Leaguers, however, confronted him with opposition from Louis W. Stevenson, a former Freedmen's Bureau official and an organizer for the league. Clark's problems forced the administration to use all of the tools at its disposal to ensure his nomination. Superintendent DeGress encouraged district school supervisors who were Republicans to back Clark. Adjutant General Davidson apparently appointed special police for the upcoming election to reward the congressman's supporters. At the district convention Davidson may also have used special police to keep anti-Clark delegates from their seats, though the accuracy of such charges is suspect since they came from the anti-Clark faction and the Democratic press that willing publicized anything giving credence to their allegations that the schools and police were politicized.

The direction of the public campaign became clear on the Fourth of July, when James G. Tracy gave the principal address at a celebration at Bryan. The executive-committee chairman called for unity among the discordant groups, especially the rival Clark and Stevenson elements, on the grounds that no matter what their differences, the situation would be worse if the Democrats won. He then moved on with the new emphasis on the Republican party as the party that looked after the interests of the common man. The speech

James G. Tracy, Republican senator from Houston, president of the Republican State Executive Committee, editor of the Houston Union. *Courtesy Texas State Library and Archives*

James P. Newcomb, secretary of state, 1869–74, Union League leader.
Courtesy Enderle Papers, Daughters of the Republic of Texas Library, CN-03.005

called on voters to consider how Republicans had established order for the first time since the war and how they had opened public schools. These were things designed to help all Texans, not just the special interests. The party promised opportunity for all. Tracy insisted: "It is the pride and boast of the Republican party that no differences are recognized in politics or before the law on account of race or color. We propose to give every man an equal chance in the race of life, and let those excel who can." As to taxes, he acknowledged that they were higher but argued that they fell primarily on those who had the resources to pay them. In a statement that clearly put forward the Republicans' new emphasis on being the party of the masses, he observed that if high taxes forced some landowners to place their holdings on the market, it would "equalize the possession of the soil which God intended not for a few but for all mankind."[8]

In an unusual move during a congressional election, Governor Davis personally entered the fray and campaigned across the state. His appearance was necessary, however, since his administration had become the focal point of Democratic attacks. He traveled extensively, beginning with a speech at the Travis County Republican Convention on July 27, then going to Galveston and speaking at key spots along the Houston and Texas Central line. Ultimately, his canvass took him on to Bonham, Dallas, and Tyler. That Tracy's Brenham speech represented the focus of the party was clear, for Davis sounded many of the same themes. He particularly defended the Republican government's increased taxes, arguing that his administration had worked for the good of all the people and that for the first time they were getting what their tax monies had gone to provide—protection, education, and economic development. At Galveston on August 16, he summed up his arguments: "If you live in a hut and sleep under a Mexican blanket, it will cost you less than if you fabricate an elegant building. If you have no government it will cost you nothing. If you have public schools and law and order, you must pay for it."[9]

This distancing from the league helps explain the extraordinary measures taken by Davis to protect the polls from violence as the election approached. On August 9 the governor placed all police forces throughout the state under his command. Local peace officers, the state police, and the State Guard were ordered to maintain order at voting places. Adjutant General Davidson issued extensive instructions on policing the election. The police were to inform persons who had voted to return to their homes and stay away from the polls thereafter. Guards were instructed to arrest persons who might "shout, jeer at, or in any way insult or annoy voters, or candidates for office." In addition, they were charged with dispersing any gatherings or assemblies that might take place for the purpose of intimidating voters. Public officials would replace the Union League in protecting black voters. Of course, Democrats responded by charging that Davis's actions simply proved their point—he was using the police for political purposes. The editor of the *Statesman* summed up this view when he described the police and militia as nothing more than a Radical club composed "of all the worthless scum of society who are willing to sell themselves as tools of an ambitious and heartless *TYRANT.*" [10]

The congressional elections took place between October 3 and 6. Accounts of what occurred at the polls varied. Democratic newspapers generally reported a peaceful election, though they complained that the state police harassed and intimidated white voters as well as those blacks who wanted to vote Democratic. Republicans reported considerably more trouble, especially in the race between Clark and Giddings in the Third District. In Grimes County large crowds of whites intimidated black voters. Democrats also provided a separate "white man's box" for Giddings supporters and threatened bodily harm and loss of employment to those not placing their ballots there. The registrar in Grimes County closed the polls as a result. Washington County officials also noted the use of a "white man's box." Republicans described similar intimidation throughout the district, with hundreds of whites camping around the polls. [11]

The most violent activity during the Third District election took place in Limestone and Freestone Counties, though the outbreak began before the polls opened and may not have been aimed specifically at disrupting voting. A riot took place at Groesbeck on September 30. The immediate cause was an effort by special state police, hired to protect the election registrars, to arrest a white who had been publicly threatening Republican politicians. In the ensuing melee another white was shot. A mob formed and attacked the police, who sought cover in the mayor's office and held out against the rioters until the arrival of additional policemen allowed them to withdraw safely from the town. Afterward, local Democratic officials secured warrants for the arrest of the officers involved in the affair, though they were unable to serve them. Large crowds of whites continued to gather at Groesbeck, and rumors spread that blacks intended to attack the town. Tension continued to increase, with local authorities and supporters of the state police trading countercharges. Mobs did not disperse, however, and on October 9 Governor Davis declared martial law in both Limestone and adjacent Freestone Counties. The election was held amid the unrest, with the mob seizing the ballot boxes and producing predictable results. In Limestone County William T. Clark had received 286 votes against Jacob Elliot's 337 in 1869; now Clark received only 28 votes, compared to Giddings's 1,153.

Initial results from the election showed that in every congressional district, the Democratic candidate won. These victories were decisive in three of the four races. In the First District, William S. Herndon beat Congressman George Whitmore by a vote of 16,238 to 11,572. Congressman John Conner won reelection in the Second District over A. M. Bryant with 18,285 votes to

5,948. In the Fourth, John Hancock received 17,010 votes to Congressman Edward Degener's 12,636. Only in the Third District were the results even close, with Giddings polling 21,172 votes to Clark's 20,342. There, Clark received the certificate of election from Governor Davis after the state election commission rejected returns in five counties. When Giddings contested the election in Congress, however, Clark did not respond. The House seated Giddings, completing the Democratic sweep of the 1871 election.

Violence and intimidation had happened across the state, but the figures suggest that the Democratic victories, except perhaps in the Third District, did not take place because large numbers of blacks were kept from voting. Instead, they took place because the Democrats turned out even larger numbers of white voters for their candidates. In the Third, for example, Clark actually received 23 percent more votes than he had in 1869; Giddings, however, received 138 percent more. The pattern was true in every district, with Republican candidates increasing their numbers but being outdone by the Democrats. Statewide, Republicans increased the number of votes they received by about 30 percent, but Democrats beat their earlier numbers by nearly 130 percent. Receiving roughly seven thousand more votes than the Democrats in 1869, Republicans fell behind by twenty-two thousand votes in 1871.

The reason for the heavy Democratic turnout can never been known with certainty, but the organizational efforts of the resurgent Democratic party were an important part of what happened. Democrats told voters that they were in the midst of a crisis. They insisted that taxation threatened the livelihood of all Texans. Behind the scenes, they warned about a threat to white supremacy. Democrats had long used race as an issue, but the addition of taxes may have been the missing ingredient that finally mobilized the great mass of white voters. When they chose to support the Democratic party, the majority white population of the state, grown even larger by recent immigration, simply overwhelmed the Republicans. Whatever the ultimate reason, the Democratic party had reasserted itself in a massive way, which changed the basic dynamic of Texas Reconstruction politics. A Democrat in Jefferson County would remember of this election: "Success in the . . . congressional campaign marked the beginning of the end of the carpetbag government in Texas. The spirit of lethargy which had come with the loss of power to shape their own destiny was shaken off, and progress, with increasing impetus, animated the good people of Texas." [12]

Politicians in both parties recognized what had taken place. Results continued on the course now set as they prepared for more important contests in the autumn of 1872. A presidential election would take place that year, and Texans statewide would vote to fill two seats in Congress gained as a result of the new census figures gathered in 1870. Most, however, saw much more at stake in the local elections, which included every seat in the state house of representatives, a third of the seats in the state senate, and most county officials. Democratic leaders gave every indication that they believed the tax issue had been the key to victory in 1871, and they further emphasized it in preparations for a campaign they hoped would bring a decisive victory the following autumn. Democrats continued to criticize Republican taxation and also took an active role in what became a taxpayers' revolt. They encouraged Texans not to pay questionable levies, especially the special school tax. Democratic lawyers took the lead in filing injunctions in counties across the state, but party leaders took the forefront in urging citizens to prevent the taxes from being collected while the question was still before the courts. Their efforts not only kept the tax issue before the public but also allowed Democrats to claim the role of protecting Texans from the corruption of the Davis administration.

Republicans had tried to counter the Democrats' use of the tax issue in 1871 but had failed to gain significant public support with their appeals. Now, many in the party panicked. The Twelfth Legislature had convened for its final session in September, before the congressional elections, but had awaited the election results before beginning business. The majority Republicans reacted with legislation that reflected their belief that the tax issue had been a critical element in the election disaster. They began to dismantle their own programs, even though Governor Davis tried to keep them from repudiating everything. Legislators replaced the permanent frontier force with minute companies to be paid only when called up. They reduced the size of the school system, cutting the number of districts and supervisors and saving at least those salaries. Republicans also joined with Democrats to repeal the laws that had allowed counties to raise special taxes to pay for public roads and buildings.

While Republicans in the legislature looked for ways to cut the cost of government and reduce taxes, party leaders prepared for the critical upcoming elections. The first necessary step was to assure their control over the party. The election had created uneasiness within the ranks and a belief by some at the local level that the party had to repudiate the Davis administration if it were to achieve success. The organization of the Liberal Republican party in New York in April, 1872, contributed to this movement. The Liberal Republicans had broken with the national party over the leadership of President Grant and the corruption associated with his administration and pushed a reform program that included civil service and tariff reform. The participation of influential German senator Carl Schurz of Missouri attracted many Texas Germans to the splinter group. For others, the attraction was that identifying with the Liberals might also divorce Texas Republicanism from the charges leveled against them by the Democrats. On April 6 a number of Republicans, including supporters of the Hamiltons and Pease, met at Austin and endorsed the Liberal movement.

Local supporters of the administration did not agree with this strategy. They devoted much of their organizational work in the spring of 1872 to making sure that Texas supported Grant in the party's national convention and that the delegates not repudiate the Davis administration. The greatest threat to these goals came in the heavily German Fourth Congressional District, where Liberal Republicanism had its greatest support. Party leaders used all of the usual mechanisms to organize their supporters, but in the Fourth District, Superintendent DeGress also used school supervisors to coordinate administration efforts and to control local conventions. His actions produced further criticism of the schools, but by the time of the party's state convention at Houston on May 14, the administration safely controlled the delegates.

The state Republican convention reaffirmed the course taken by Governor Davis in the 1871 political campaigns. In the party's platform the delegates expressed continued support for the public schools, though they promised to cut the expenses of the system through more-efficient administration and rigid economy. The delegates also stated their continued support for internal improvements, though insisting that state aid should be reasonable and that land grants be substituted for the issuing of state bonds to further this work. Overall, Republicans stated their approval of the general course of the Davis government, insisting that it promised the best future for the great mass of Texans. After endorsing Governor Davis, the convention proceeded to elect delegates to the national convention committed to the renomination of President Grant.

Davis and his supporters had held on to the party, but the future was not promising. Party leaders attempted to develop Republican organizations at the local level once again, but a lack of funds limited their activities. Governor Davis, Secretary of State Newcomb, and party chief Tracy all called upon the national Republican organization and its supporters for financial aid, but they received nothing. When they asked for funds from various railroad interests, national leaders refused to endorse the requests, citing their belief that the situation in Texas was not promising. The failure of the national party to provide support not only kept the administration from fully organizing the state party but also demoralized that effort, for it indicated that the nation's Republican leaders had given up on retaining power in Texas.

Democrats confidently prepared for victory, while the Republicans tried to prevent the complete collapse of their party. The Democratic convention at Corsicana on June 17 celebrated their resurgence. Many antebellum and wartime Democratic leaders appeared for the first time since the surrender and actively participated in the sessions. Still, the ideas of the New Departure prevailed. Nowhere did the platform adopted by the delegates mention Reconstruction, except to condemn the Davis administration for all of the tyranny and corruption they alleged were connected to it. On other issues the party's platform differed little from that of the Republicans, stating the party's support for education, law and order, and state support for internal improvements.

National politics complicated the course of the Democrats somewhat. By the time the Texas convention met, Liberal Republicans had nominated Horace Greeley as their candidate for president, and the national Democratic party had given its support to his candidacy as the best way to defeat Grant. Texas Liberals encouraged the Democrats to work with them as they had in 1869, endorsing Greeley and running fusion tickets for other offices. Democratic delegates agreed to follow the course of the national party and support Greeley. They refused, however, to agree on anything but a straight-out Democratic ticket in state and local elections. Even the moderate *Galveston News* agreed, informing the state's Liberal Republicans that they could never receive the support of the party unless they ran as Democrats.

The campaign leading up to the election looked much like that in 1871. Governor Davis actively participated around the state, urging voters to remember that the Republican party had brought an end to violence, provided education, and prevented the railroads from bankrupting the government. Republicans were the rightful representatives of the interests of the common people. The Democrats, however, claimed the same right, pointing to their party's opposition to the tyranny of Davis and its role in stopping the collection of taxes. At the same time, they also encouraged the usual efforts to limit the Republican turnout at the polls. The results were much like those in 1871 as well.

The 1872 elections presented Republicans with a disaster even worse than the previous year. Greeley secured 66,455 votes to Grant's 47,426. In the two congressional races, Democratic candidates won by similar margins. Local elections proved catastrophic. Democrats gained control over the state house of representatives and secured a one-seat majority in the state senate. Republicans could be relieved that the Democrats still lacked enough strength in the senate to override a gubernatorial veto, but that was true only because enough Republicans remained as holdovers from previous elections. At the local level Democrats made gains almost everywhere. Only in a few counties with African American majorities or predominantly German populations did the Republicans hold on. The election showed an even more ominous trend, for the number of Republican voters actually declined.

Ironically, following the election, the only proven case of malfeasance by anyone in the Davis administration became known. Adjutant General Davidson had resigned his position in the autumn of 1872 to run in a special election to fill a seat in the state senate and had been replaced by Frank L. Britton. Davidson lost the election and accompanied Secretary of State Newcomb to New York, where the latter had gone to try to sell state bonds. While Davidson was out of the state, Britton discovered that he had drawn warrants from the treasury amounting to over thirty-seven thousand dollars for services but had not documented the work done. Governor Davis immediately ordered the treasurer not to pay on the warrants, and the attorney general quickly secured an order for Davidson's arrest. The general never returned to the state, however, and actually fled the country. His rapid flight suggests he had never intended on returning.

The 1871 elections had brought the advancement of Republican programs to an end as party leaders paused to consider how to respond to the overwhelming Democratic victories that year. The 1872 elections ended the Republicans' ability to act at all on their programs, leaving Democrats in control of the legislature and many of the local offices across the state. Governor Davis remained in power, but he would be up for reelection the next year, and his defeat was a foregone conclusion. He could do little in the interim but await the inevitable. The efforts of Republicans to redirect the development of Texas had come to an end under a landslide of white votes. Whether issues of race, charges of tyranny, or economic concerns over taxes provided the most important force producing this turnaround cannot be known for certain. All played some part, however, and returned to power the Democratic party. Over the next years that party would push Texas along a new direction, carrying out a counterrevolution that attempted to reverse much that the Republicans had tried to achieve.

Chapter 12

CONSERVATIVE TRIUMPH, 1873–1900

When the Thirteenth Legislature gathered at Austin on January 14, 1873, the overwhelming dimensions of the electoral triumph by the Democrats was apparent. In the state house, where the Republicans had held fifty-five seats, they now numbered only twelve. In the state senate the Republican's razor-thin majority became a minority, and the fact that only one-third of the seats had been up for election gave the Republicans the ability to keep the Democrats from overriding gubernatorial vetoes. Recapturing the legislature marked the end of Radical efforts at constructing a new Texas. Neither the Republican minority nor Governor Davis could further advance the party's program. Instead, Democrats began implementing their own agenda, one that altered the course set by Republicans. Over the next few years, they carried out what amounted to a virtual counterrevolution, even though they could never completely reverse the changes that had taken place during Reconstruction.

Governor Davis's address to the new legislature attempted to convince the victorious Democrats to abandon the issues they had used to regain power and look to the welfare of the state as a whole. Every institution created by Republicans had come under attack during the political campaigns since 1869. The governor urged legislators to consider carefully what had been accomplished by each before they changed them. He recognized the problems with the existing school system but countered that it had effectively provided an education for more children than at any previous time in the state's history and urged that it not be done away with completely. The militia and police organizations had given cause for complaint, but again he pointed out that violence had been suppressed and asked lawmakers to retain some sort of system of state police. Davis went through Republican programs one by one, pointing out successes and counseling restraint. Opposition legislators listened politely, then began taking apart most of these institutions.

Democrats had campaigned promising to lower taxes and to end what they had charged had been the arbitrary and tyrannical rule of the Davis administration. These promises had been the key to their election victory, attracting the great mass of white voters, and the new lawmakers acted immediately, with legislation regarding the state police, the militia, the public schools, and election regulations. Cutting government programs also promised the tax relief they had guaranteed. Given their longstanding complaints against the state police, Democrats began by abolishing that organization. From every perspective, the state police had to go: it represented everything hated about the Davis government; had never been an agency intended just to run down bandits and other such lawbreakers; had been an extension of central authority intended to protect the civil and political rights of African Americans where local authorities would not act; had stood in the way of local whites who sought to deny these rights; actually had intervened in local matters, sometimes arresting those who broke the law; and had used black policemen to carry out its mission. The legislature repealed the police law. Governor Davis vetoed the repeal. Then, Democrats, with the aid of some Republicans, overrode the veto, ending the existence of the state police. Despite general agreement on the problem of continued violence, they did not replace it with another law-enforcement force.

The legislature followed this with a new militia law that merged the State Guard and the Reserve Militia into a single group. The new legislation put an end to the creation of biracial companies that had existed under the Republican law and replaced them with segregated units. While the Davis administration remained in place, the adjutant general saw that black units as well as white ones received weapons from the state's limited arsenal. Under the new act, Democratic adjutant generals initially armed only white units, though later in the century some black companies received weapons. In addition to these revisions in organization, the legislature also restricted the governor's power to declare martial law and use the militia to quell domestic disturbances.

The legislature also radically altered the state's educational system. Its new school law abolished the state school board, though maintaining the office of superintendent. The superintendent still had responsibility for organizing a system but virtually no power to do so. Almost every aspect of school organization now came under the authority of local school boards composed of elected directors for each county. All that remained from the earlier system were basic requirements for schools to receive public funds. The new law got rid of the common curriculum and textbooks that had existed under DeGress's oversight and reduced the required term for public schools from ten months to four. Defenders noted that this limited term was all the state constitution required and condemned those teachers who complained that such a system would not attract professional educators. In a typical attack an editor for the *Democratic Statesman* concluded that teachers would be better if they taught for four months and then did common labor the rest of the year.

"Your professional, life long, nothing else teacher is apt to become a mere Dominie Sampson, or something worse, with his mind running in a narrow channel, and. . . . unfited [*sic*] really to be a teacher in a common school."[1] A reduction in funding accompanied these changes. The legislature repealed county authority to raise additional taxes for school buildings, ceased funding schools from the general revenue, and restricted state support to revenue derived from a school fund created by the sale of one-half of the state's public lands. The funding measure offered a short-term fix for education, providing some support without having to impose taxes.

In addition to terminating the state police and radically altering the militia and state school system, the Thirteenth Legislature also took actions that had the potential effect of reducing the influence of blacks in state politics. Legislators changed election laws so that state officials could not exercise as much control over elections as they had. County clerks replaced the appointed voting registrars, and local justices of the peace rather than specially appointed officials formed election boards. Instead of voting only at the county seat, the new law provided for polls in each precinct. The latter provision made it almost impossible to provide adequate police protection for voters. As a whole, these procedural changes increased the ability of local whites to control black voting. In an additional action that clearly reduced the power of black voters, the legislature redistricted the state in such a way that African Americans found it more difficult to gain political office. The most significant result of this effort was ending the career of Matthew Gaines by changing his senate district from one that encompassed only Washington County, where blacks outnumbered whites, into one that included Burleson County, thus creating a new district in which whites outnumbered blacks.

The Thirteenth Legislature disposed of Republican measures and replaced them with their own, but its members also took actions that reflected the peculiar economic interests that provided the core of Democratic support. Chief among these were the planters. A jury law that excluded men who could not read and write from jury service increased the influence of planters in civil suits involving tenant contracts. Legislators' unsuccessful effort to pass a measure that allowed landowners to fence their holdings and sue the owners of stock that might get on to the land and damage crops provided further evidence of this relationship, for the bill appeared to be aimed specifically at African American farmers in the plantation counties. In addition to the fencing and suing provisions, the proposed legislation also required that all sheep, goats, or hogs be kept either in enclosures or in herds. For poorer farmers who were used to having livestock, particularly hogs, run loose on the land for forage, this bill would have been a severe blow, making them responsible for any damages their animals might commit and requiring them to build costly fences, which few of them could afford. Such costs had the potential of driving these small landowning farmers off of their property. Governor Davis vetoed the bill, however. It proved to be one of the few vetoes sustained by the legislature when some Democrats joined Republicans to support his action.

Legislation also showed the power the railroads had acquired within the Democratic party. Democrats chartered sixteen additional companies during the Thirteenth's session. Anticipating that the legality of the constitutional amendment passed in 1872 allowing railroads to be subsidized with public lands would be upheld by the courts, lawmakers awarded each of the new roads sixteen sections of land for each mile of track they completed. Texans could have their railroads without paying for them with taxes. Legislators also voted to substitute lands for the bonds awarded to the Texas and Pacific, allowing twenty sections of land for each mile built, and tried to force Comptroller Albert Bledsoe to deliver the bonds awarded to the International Railroad after that road refused to accept a bill similar to that for the Texas and Pacific. Davis vetoed most of these measures, only to have his veto overridden each time. By the end of the session, the governor estimated that if all of the new companies claimed the land granted to them, then most of the public lands of Texas had been given away.

The railroads succeeded, for the most part, in their endeavors to get favorable legislation passed, but lawmakers debated railroad affairs, a fissure became apparent within the Democratic coalition. Many of the farmers Democrats had mobilized to their side over the issues of taxation and corruption were not willing to give the railroads all that they wanted just because Democrats sponsored the legislation. They coalesced under the leadership of John Ireland of Seguin after Governor Davis asked the legislature to validate the constitutional amendment allowing the state to substitute land subsidies for bonds to encourage railroad construction. These agrarian Democrats tried unsuccessfully to stop validation, then tried to prevent the promise of land for the new roads chartered by the Thirteenth Legislature or the substitution of land for the bonds promised to the Texas and Pacific and to the International. Ireland even espoused repudiation of the International debt altogether. In every case the agrarians failed. The division was not one that could be easily reconciled, and it offered Republicans some hope that the successful coalition of 1871 and 1872 could be broken apart.[2]

A test of the permanence of the Democratic alliance would take place quickly. In his address to the legislature, the governor had indicated that his term and those of the state's other elected officers would expire in April, 1874, and called for a general election to fill these positions. Among their last acts, lawmakers set this election for December, 1873. In addition to the various executive offices, the act provided for the election of a new legislature and for a vote on four constitutional amendments. The proposed amendments carried forward the Democratic counterrevolution into areas that legislation alone could not. One removed the governor's ability to declare martial law and placed it in the hands of the general assembly. Another required that assessors and collectors of taxes be elected, thus ensuring that local interests would have greater control over the assessment process. A third increased the size of the state supreme court from three to five justices, not only allowing the court to better handle an expanded caseload but also allowing the new governor to appoint an entirely new bench. A final amendment restricted the legislature to consideration of general laws alone, specifically prohibiting it from considering local or special matters. Following passage of the election law, the Thirteenth Legislature adjourned.

The split among Democrats in the legislature gave Republicans cause for some hope, but most believed that Davis's chances for reelection were small. The party's problems even encouraged some opposition to the governor's renomination. The state executive secretary, James Tracy, even suggested that Republicans nominate no one in the hopes that the Democrats would start fighting among themselves. Supporters of Tracy's idea generally believed that this then would allow the Republican party to break away from its black constituency and form a coalition with the business and railroad elements of the Democratic party. Davis refused to abandon the blacks who had supported him opposed the idea of not running party candidates, pushed the executive committee to call a convention, and began preparing to run again for the governorship.

Throughout the summer, Davis's friends marshaled Republicans to his support. On July 3, blacks gathered at the "Colored Men's Convention" at Brenham. Senator Ruby had organized the affair, which turned out not only to be a rally for Davis but also an event that saw the reconciliation of many blacks who had felt the governor had abandoned them with his support for William T. Clark in the congressional elections the previous autumn. Senator Gaines, often a critic of the moderation of the administration on race issues, introduced a resolution calling the governor a friend of the black people of the state. A convention of Germans held at Austin on August 7 followed the Brenham gathering. The purpose of the meeting was avowedly nonpartisan, but the delegates passed resolutions that pledged themselves to supporting the traditional goals of the Republican party and condemned the Thirteenth Legislature for its assault upon public education and civil liberties.

Republicans held their convention at Dallas on August 19, and Davis clearly was in control. He addressed the delegates and received an overwhelming ovation when he told them it was their duty to nominate candidates. They did, and they chose Davis as their nominee for governor. Davis even found old enemies back in the party fold, including the Flanagans and A. J. Hamilton. The Republican platform was primarily an attack upon the record of the Thirteenth Legislature, condemning it for increasing taxes, giving away the state's lands, destroying the school system, and exposing Texas to a return of violence. In turn, the party promised that if returned to power, Governor Davis and a Republican legislature would restore the schools, protect the people of the state, and lower taxes. The platform was similar to those of previous years, though the promise to lower taxes was a clear appeal to that class of Texans who had been won over to the Democrats by the tax issue in the past.

Democrats held their convention at Austin on September 5, showing signs of serious discontent among the faithful. The revolt against the prorailroad activities of the leadership in the legislature had intensified through the summer. Some Democratic journals criticized the party's leaders as dictatorial and in the service of the railroads. The editor of the *Victoria Advocate* typified those critics who portrayed the divisions within the party as a class issue, a fight between capital and labor. Its editor charged, in terms reflecting the radicalism of the agrarians, that most of the party's newspapers were "allied with the bond holding human oppressors of the land." The *Advocate,* however, represented "the honest farmer" who had no real choice between the existing political parties.[3] The appearance in Texas of the farm organization known as the Grange in the summer of 1873, even though declaring itself nonpartisan, seemed to indicate even more-widespread unrest.

The party's leadership worked through the summer to prevent the agrarians from gaining control over the upcoming convention. They most feared their threats of repudiating the bonds that had been issued to the International since it would not only scare away other railroad developers but also undermine the state's credit. The editors of the *Austin Democratic Statesman,* reflecting the thoughts of Democratic leaders, devoted much time to explaining to its readers why repudiating the International bonds would be disastrous for Texas. The potential for political problems was immense. If leaders could not keep the agrarians under control, Republican hopes of attracting some of the Democrats' support might come true. Railroad advocates in San Antonio, concerned that if the International bonds were repudiated the road would not be built to their city, let it be known that if the agrarians gained control of the convention, they would withdraw from the party.[4]

Democratic leaders not only appealed to reason but also played on the fears of members to maintain unity. Since 1869 they had insisted that the Republican party and the Davis administration represented a threat to the well being of white Texans. Now they used the same strategy to demand unity from those that might threaten the party on the eve of full victory. The editor of the *Democratic Statesman* provided the lead in addressing the split between railroad and antirailroad interests. He personally favored honoring the debts of the state rather than repudiating them, but he accepted the fact that some might disagree. The differences had to be put aside, however, because much more was at stake. "The democracy must free Texas and the whole country from the blighting curse of radicalism," he wrote, "before they commence quarrelling [*sic*] and squabbling about railroad bonds." The real threat lay in the Republican party. After all, he continued, the very problems the state now faced had been created by the Republicans in the Twelfth Legislature, a body made up of "reckless Northern carpet-baggers, dirty Southern scalawags, and poor ignorant negroes, who were made the mere tools of others, and all together commenced a system of extravagance, appropriation and pillage, previously unknown."[5]

Whether or not the party's leadership had the situation under control was still unclear when the convention assembled. Numerous railroad lobbyists were present to make sure that they did not, however. John Ireland openly sought support for the gubernatorial nomination based on his desire to repudiate the railroad debt, but he faced opposition from men like James Throckmorton and John Reagan who had longstanding ties to railroad interests. Railroad men would not accept Ireland. The agrarians made it clear they would not vote for either Throckmorton or Reagan in the general election. To make the peace between the rival factions, the convention turned to Richard Coke. A lawyer from Waco, a Confederate veteran, and a justice on the state supreme court under Throckmorton, Coke's chief appeal was that he had not taken a stand on the railroad issue that made him unacceptable to either faction. Behind the scenes, he may have promised the International lobbyists that he would support their claims to the state bonds in return for their support.

The Democratic platform reflected the triumph of the railroad interests, regardless of how Coke secured the nomination. It congratulated the Thirteenth Legislature for its success in dismantling Republican programs, then stated strong support for a liberal policy of state aid to foster the construction of railroads. In addition, the platform declared that the party had no intention of repudiating the railroad debt; agrarians had succumbed. The leadership that had come to be known by this time as the Bourbons or Redeemers had consolidated their control over the party. At the end of the meeting, the Redeemers tried to secure the patched-up coalition when they pushed through a resolution requiring all delegates to pledge their support to use all honorable means possible to secure the election of all of the convention's nominees.

Campaigning for the December election had been ongoing even before the actual nominating conventions, but it intensified afterward. Davis opened his drive for reelection at Austin on September 6 and delivered a speech that set out the themes he used over and over as he traveled about the state. Democrats had attempted their New Departure, but the governor accused the party as being nothing more than the secessionist Democracy of 1861. It had added to its support of slavery and treason an unrelenting hostility to the freedmen and those who attempted to protect them in their rights. But it was not just

Richard Coke, Democratic governor of Texas, 1874. Courtesy Texas State Library and Archives

blacks who would be their victims, however. Davis charged that the Democratic party was out to oppress the poor, regardless of color, in order to protect the special interests that supported it. If reelected governor, he promised to do all he could to protect the civil rights of all Texans and stand up against the railroad interests that threatened the state.

Republican leaders apparently believed that the railroad issue was one that might secure their resurgence. Davis returned to it in his canvass across the state. Then, on the day before the election, the party placed in local Republican newspapers a full-page defense of the governor's stand on the railroads and an attack upon that of the Democrats. It reviewed every vote that had taken place in the legislature in 1870 and 1871 and showed that Democrats had provided the critical votes in every case where Davis's veto of a railroad matter had been overridden. Democrats had made it possible for those companies to plunder the state of its assets and had made them totally unaccountable to the public despite the aid provided. Davis had tried to protect the funds of the state and now was all that stood between the railroads and their complete triumph. Republicans offered Davis as the only defense against the future depredations of the railroads.

Coke responded with the tried-and-true rhetoric of previous Democratic campaigns. Tyranny and corruption were the recurring themes. Davis was a traitor who had abandoned his state in 1861 and then come back to punish it with an oppressive regime. To keep himself in power, Davis had based his support on a combination of ignorant blacks and corrupt whites. He and the Republicans had imposed the state police and the integrated-militia system on the people of the state. They had created a school system to reward Davis's political allies and were responsible for the lavish support given to railroads. They had raised taxes to support their machine to a level that threatened the livelihood of most Texans, a claim made even more relevant by the national panic of 1873. The Democratic party had broken the chains of tyranny, but the reelection of Davis threatened to place the state's people back under his power. Coke and the Democratic newspapers simply ignored Davis's arguments that claimed that good had been accomplished by the state police, militia, and public schools and that Democrats had been responsible for the plundering by the railroads.

All voters did not believe the Democratic rhetoric, however. As the campaign progressed, Redeemer leaders found that the agrarian element within their party remained dissatisfied. Democrats claimed in their campaign that they represented the taxpayers of the state, but their state convention had promised to honor the warrants provided to railroads; it had committed the party to continuing liberal support for the railroads. This did not work to the advantage of Republicans, but it did threaten to draw away possible Democratic voters and might allow some Republicans to be elected in local races. The center of discontent was in the farmlands to the east and south of Austin, and this discontent grew to the level of a revolt. In Fayette County dissatisfied farmers met and denounced the Democratic party, though at the same time criticized Republicans—the Republicans were simply selfish officeholders and the Democrats were the agents of organized capital. The group encouraged the formation of a "people's Movement." In the senate district encompassing Bastrop and Fayette Counties, disgruntled farmers actually organized what Democrats referred to as a "Radical Farmer's" party that put forward candidates for state office.

Farmer discontent may help account for an even greater appeal to racial fear by Democrats than had been used in the New Departure campaigns of 1871 and 1872. The party's newspapers portrayed Davis's reelection as presenting so great a threat that racial issues had to take precedence over economic ones, white unity had to be maintained. Editors charged that the governor was the black man's candidate and as such represented a threat to whites everywhere. They linked his support of equality before the law to integration and claimed that had he gotten his way, Davis would have created a community in which blacks and whites would have mixed in perfect equality. The result would have been demeaning to whites and ultimately resulted in a mongrel society of mixed races. The racist editor of the *Clarksville Standard,* Charles DeMorse, was perhaps the most vitriolic of all the Democratic newspapermen. He summed up all of the charges leveled against Davis when he wrote that the governor's greatest sin was that "he endeavored to place us beneath the feet of the brutish negroes, who have been our slaves."[6]

For the first time since the war years, Texans went to the polls in December, 1873, without the presence of federal troops or the state police. The polls were relatively quiet, though as usual much of the intimidation of voters had taken place before the election actually began. In Liberty County, for example, officials had arrested a Republican organizer for "exciting Negroes" and ordered him out of the county. When he continued his efforts at organizing blacks, the man simply disappeared. For black voters, the message was clear. President Grant received 274 votes there in 1872; Davis received none in 1873. In Smith County local officials failed to stop the lynching of a black man just before the election; Davis received 150 fewer votes in 1873 than the Republican candidate for Congress in 1871. Across the state, poll watchers reported a consistent trend—black turnout had declined.

At the same time that black voters began to stay away from the polls, white turnout continued to increase. Democratic strength grew, especially in the counties along the farming frontier. Agrarian discontent did not notably cut into Richard Coke's totals. Republicans had been unable to convince white voters that they best represented their interests and had failed to benefit from the dissension within the Democratic party. The result was a Republican catastrophe. Coke received 85,549 votes to Davis's 42,663. Democratic candidates swept into all of the state offices and secured total control of the state legislature. All four constitutional amendments passed. The election had eliminated the last remaining element of Republican government.

Only one barrier remained. As soon as the polls closed, the state supreme court began hearing a challenge to the legality of the election. The case of *ex parte Rodriguez,* usually called the "Semicolon Court," could potentially block the inauguration of Coke and the seating of the new legislature. The lawyers for Joseph Rodriguez of Houston, who had been arrested for voting twice, challenged his arrest on the grounds that the election was not legal. Their claim centered on the constitutionality of the election law passed by the Thirteenth Legislature. The state constitution had said that elections would be held at the county seats of the counties "until otherwise provided by law; and the polls shall be opened for four days." Not only had the legislature allowed precinct voting, as authorized in the constitution, but it had also reduced the days the polls should be opened to one. According to Rodriguez's lawyers, the constitution did not allow the legislature to change the days of the election since the semicolon turned the phrase into two independent clauses. The legislature could change the place of the elections; it could not change the number of days.

When the supreme court ruled in favor of Rodriguez, it effectively nullified the election. Democrats determined to organize the Fourteenth Legislature anyway and confronted Governor Davis with either enforcing the decision of the court or giving in. Davis decided to enforce the court's ruling, setting up a confrontation with the new legislature when it assembled in January, 1874. The situation was awkward since Davis's term actually extended to April, four years from the date he officially took office as governor under the new constitution. At first members of the newly elected legislature believed that a deal might be reached with Davis to allow them to organize without opposition. Fearing trouble, however, Democratic leaders determined to organize the legislature regardless and immediately inaugurate Coke. They argued that since General Reynolds had appointed Davis provisional governor in the month of January, his actual term expired then. The decision led to the brief and over-dramatized Coke-Davis Imbroglio.

Davis tried to stop the organization of the Fourteenth Legislature when its members appeared at Austin in January and even called up units of the state militia to help enforce order in the capital. Democrats refused to delay, however, and confronted the governor with the option of giving in or using force. Davis did not have the military resources to stop them, and he appealed to President Grant for aid. The Grant administration had little heart for intervention, however, as public interest in maintaining Republican government in the South had waned amid the economic problems and disillusionment with the administration in the North. Local Democrats knew that Grant would not become involved and pressured Davis to recognize the legislature. Davis's supporters and the forces of the legislature and Coke exchanged words and threats, but when the president offered no aid, Davis had little choice. The Fourteenth Legislature met on January 13, organized, and then inaugurated Richard Coke as governor. Davis left the governor's mansion, protesting the illegal organization of the legislature and the inauguration of Coke before his own term had expired.

With the demise of the Davis administration, the Texas Democratic party took over the reins of government and controlled them virtually unchallenged until the middle of the twentieth century. At least through the nineteenth century, the Redeemer Democrats who represented the plantation, merchant, and railroad interests that had come to dominate the party by the end of Reconstruction remained in control and shaped not only party policy but also that of the state government. Their basic positions on public affairs began to be formed almost immediately during the sessions of the Fourteenth Legislature as party leaders attempted to secure three major goals. The first was to lower taxes as much as possible, a purpose that cemented small farmers to the party and fulfilled the desires of the large landed interests of the state, including planters and by this time the railroads. The second objective was the continued encouragement of economic development through aid to railroads and other such endeavors, though without raising taxes. And the third was securing the state's landed interests' control over labor. A new constitution in 1876 provided the institutional framework that assured that the Redeemers achieved these ends. Democratic politics throughout the rest of the century revolved around the use of whatever means were needed to maintain power to meet the party's aims.

The Fourteenth Legislature began the process necessary for Democrats to gain their political goals, but from the beginning, party leaders realized that achieving them required changes in the basic institutions of government. As a result, during the first session, they initiated efforts at writing a new constitution. Governor Coke and other Democratic leaders originally wanted lawmakers to carry out this task, avoiding the costs of a convention and also limiting the possibilities that an open fight would take place between the party's regular leadership and the agrarians. A committee drafted a document that differed from the Constitution of 1869, before its amendment, primarily in its provisions for supporting internal improvements and carrying out elections. The proposal confirmed the use of land grants as a means of encouraging the development of a transportation system, maintained a system of voter registration, and added the requirement that all voters had to pay a poll tax, a feature clearly intended to restrict black participation. What would have been the Constitution of 1874 failed to pass both houses of the legislature, however. This led to a constitutional convention in 1875.

The convention met at Austin on September 6, 1875, and remained in session for almost three months. Democrats dominated the proceedings, and even though disputes developed between the delegates who represented the controlling interests of the party and agrarians—possibly forty of the ninety delegates were members of the Grange—they produced a draft constitution

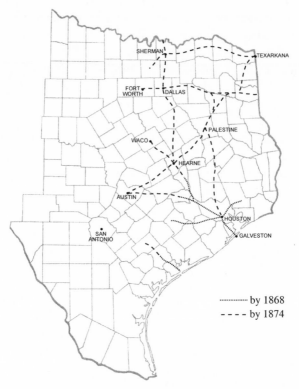

Railroads in Operation by the End of the Republican Era

that proved agreeable to both. The substance of change incorporated into the proposal was to limit the power of the state government, particularly its taxing power, and to move many functions located in the state authority by the Constitution of 1869 to local governments. In February, 1876, voters approved the new constitution by an overwhelming majority of 136,606 to 56,653.

The provisions constraining the powers of the state in the newly adopted constitution were numerous. The governor's term was reduced from four to two years, making it difficult for any single individual to develop and pursue a personal agenda. The ability of the governor to lead the state was restricted further by removing other executive offices from his control, making the critical offices of attorney general, treasurer, comptroller, and commissioner of the land office elected positions. A reduction in the governor's salary from five thousand dollars to four thousand dollars ensured that only those with ample personal resources would even run. The new constitution also restricted the powers of the legislature. In addition to limiting terms of office and reducing pay, it placed a debt ceiling of two hundred thousand dollars on the state, restricting the legislature's ability to finance state operations through bonds, and capped state taxes, though the legislature could still use public lands to encourage railroad construction. It even affected the power of the judiciary, removing its ability to act either independently or in a nonpartisan manner by making judicial positions elected and with a term of office. The most limiting feature of the new constitution ultimately proved to be its inclusion of what typically would have been legislative provisions, requiring many future changes to be done by constitutional amendment, a process that seriously hindered responses to changing conditions.

While restricting the power of state government, the constitution shifted to the resources of county government many of the activities previously assumed by the state. It virtually abolished a state educational system, even though providing for a state school superintendent. The actual operations of the schools were put into the hands of county authorities who determined everything from the division of school funds to who would teach. Local officials could not raise money for their schools, however. The state provided for school funding with a poll tax of up to one dollar, the appropriation of up to one-fourth of the general revenue, and income from a special school fund created by the lease of lands dedicated to support education in 1866 and the sale of additional lands from the public domain. The constitution also placed greater power in the hands of local justice courts, giving them the authority to hear a wide variety of minor criminal cases.

Agrarian interests coincided with those of the Redeemer leadership for the most part, but the former did put their unique imprint on the constitution. When black-belt delegates tried to impose a poll tax as a requirement for registration, a requirement that might well have removed many blacks and poor whites from the rolls, the Grange element in the convention combined with Republicans to defeat it. They also managed to include provisions that allowed the legislature to pass laws regulating railroads, including setting passenger and freight rates.

The new constitution provided the framework within which Democratic leaders pursued their chief goals over the next decades. Taxes on property remained low, at the cost of most public services. Paying for the state debt forced legislatures to keep ad valorem tax rates at roughly the same level between 1874 and 1881. In 1881, however, the legislature reduced the tax from .5 percent to .4 percent while increasing poll and occupation taxes. The next year they reduced property taxes even further, to .3 percent. Taxes remained at these low levels throughout the rest of the century. The cost to Texans of these low taxes was significant, for the state failed to support education and law enforcement. Frontier protection consisted of little more than that offered by the Republicans.

Reduced state revenues effected public education possibly more than any other state institution, for schools cost more than any other of the state's endeavors. State support had remained at one-fourth of the general revenues up until 1879, when Gov. Oran M. Roberts proposed that the amount be reduced to one-fifth. The legislature responded by reducing it to one-sixth. This meant state support, other than the revenues of the school fund, declined drastically since this reduction came at the same time that tax rates were cut. In 1878–79 the state had provided $600,000 for education. In the 1879–80 school year, state funding fell to $410,000, then in 1880–81 to $275,000. The lease of school lands and the sale of some public lands helped but did not solve the problem of adequate funding for education.

For Texans, the state's reluctance to spend money meant that education suffered everywhere, but poor rural districts suffered the most. As late as 1900, counties with large urban populations funded their schools at $8.35 per student, while rural counties spent only $5.01. This meant that urban schools were staffed increasingly by full-time, professionally trained teachers, while teachers in rural schools often worked only part time and often possessed little more education than their students. The urban pupil attended school on the average of eight months per year; his rural counterpart, less than five. Schools for African Americans fared worse relative to those for whites. The legacy of neglect for both rural and black children left a population ill prepared for the nonagricultural world emerging at the end of the century and created a barrier to economic development. Roughly 45 percent of blacks still remained illiterate around 1900. Of course, the landed interests responsible had little interest in disrupting its labor force by creating new opportunities nor had they any real concern with economic development beyond that benefiting them.

Democratic legislatures kept taxes low, serving propertied interests throughout the state. At the same time, they provided a favorable climate for railroad development. Under the new constitution, which allowed the donation of public lands to railroads for construction of new track, they were particularly generous. By 1882, land grants had potentially obligated the state to give railroads eight million more acres than remained in the public domain, a liability that did not include grants to other companies that secured support for building canals and roads. In addition to this carefree use of public lands to encourage the expansion of the rail system, the legislatures generally favored railroad interests. Time and time again legislators extended deadlines set in railroad charters that companies had to meet to qualify for their land grants. The Texas and Pacific was particularly successful in obtaining such concessions, allowing it to collect over five million acres from the state. Farm interests forced legislatures to impose some regulations, but throughout the nineteenth century, the state never possessed the power to police what the railroads did.

This sort of generosity finally paved the way for the settlement of one of the state's potential financial problems, the debt that might be incurred if the International Railroad received its bonds. The International had repeatedly resisted the substitution of land grants for loans and had used considerable pressure to force the legislature to require the comptroller to deliver the promised notes. As the International extended its lines, however, the potential state liability increased, and those concerned with taxes refused to give in and blocked the company's efforts. The potential cost for the state was enormous. Texas ultimately would be repaid its loan to the road, but in the meantime it had to pay interest on the bonds, which by 1874 would have been equal to all other expenses of the state government. In 1875 the International and the state finally agreed to a deal in which the government gave the road a grant of twenty sections per mile instead of the bonds. The sections were to be located in blocks, so that the land could be sold more easily. The legislature also relieved the International from any state taxes for twenty-five years. This tax break in the long run cost the state more in lost revenue than it would have had to pay on the bonds, but the legislature had ensured that no immediate tax increases had taken place.

The final area in which the Redeemers worked to create conditions favorable to their supporting interests was their efforts at ensuring the presence of an inexpensive and quiescent workforce for the state's planters. The failure to provide adequate education for the poor or police protection did much to accomplish this goal, but legislation aimed directly at limiting the legal rights of agricultural workers also helped secure the same ends. Since African Americans provided the main source of farm labor, the restricting of black political power and the relegation of blacks to second-class citizenship also helped achieve this purpose.

The most important action directly giving landlords greater power over their workers was taken by the Fourteenth Legislature when it passed the Landlord and Tenant Act, which had been considered in the previous legislature. That measure gave landlords the first claim on the crop produced by a tenant for repayment of rents owed on the land or advances in supplies. To assure that end, the law required tenants to have the permission of the landlord in order to sell a crop. It also gave the landlord the right to have the local sheriff or other law-enforcement officers seize the property of the tenant to secure payment. The tenant, in turn, had virtually no power to seek redress in grievances with the landlord.

As for blacks, Democratic legislatures made repeated efforts through the rest of the century to reduce their power in the community. Only the fear of some whites that the measures could be used to limit their own power blocked repeated efforts in the 1870s and 1880s to make payment of the poll tax a requirement for voting. This also prevented legislators from imposing property requirements on voters. Yet even though they could not deny blacks political rights of citizenship, legislators successfully reduced African Americans to second-class citizens as they moved toward a segregated society. Legislative mandates requiring segregated schools and lawmakers' refusal to police local authorities assured that black schools received an unequal share of school funds. By the 1880s legislators had begun efforts to force blacks into separate facilities almost everywhere in public, with laws that first allowed and then forced railroads to provide separate facilities for black travelers.

Remarkably, in the face of Democratic efforts at restricting the power of black workers and voters, the course set by Reconstruction could never be reversed completely. African Americans retained the right to vote, even in local elections, and though restricted from participating in the politics of the Democratic party by provisions passed during the agrarian upheaval at the end of the century, they never lost that right. Blacks continued to make economic progress based upon the gains made through the end of Reconstruction, with an increase in the number of landowning blacks and the emergence of a black middle class in the state's towns and cities. Despite white hostility, blacks successfully created their own community and an awareness of that community's interests by the end of the century.

For the Redeemer leadership of the Democratic party, politics through the end of the nineteenth century involved hanging on to power so that the interests of their chief supporters could be maintained. This became increasingly difficult as agrarian radicalism intensified and movements emerged among small farmers that challenged Redeemer control. From the late 1870s, Democratic leaders confronted the efforts by "agrarians" to seize control of the party from them or to challenge their control of government. The Greenback movement was the first, beginning in 1878, nearly seizing control of the governorship when Republicans agreed to support its candidate in 1882. During the mid-1880s, Democrats faced challenges to their control over county governments with the appearance of numerous independent movements. The rising power of the Farmers Alliance after 1886 again challenged Redeemer control of the party, and the Populists received 44 percent of the vote in 1896. In the end, however, none of these succeeded in supplanting the Redeemers.

Redeemers held on to power in part through careful concessions to their agrarian challengers. Primarily, however, they were able to maintain control over both party and state through the same techniques they had used to defeat the Republicans in the early 1870s. The use of violence against blacks, as well as whites who would work with them politically, remained a critical tool. They frequently resorted to appeals for racial solidarity, for whites to remain united under their leadership to prevent a return to the evils of black power during Reconstruction. The latter appeal helped permanently fix the Democratic version of Reconstruction as the "true history" of that era. In election after election Democratic speakers cast back to the Davis years to warn white voters of what might happen if any but the Democratic party controlled the state. They hung on to power and left Texas with its tradition of limited government that provided few public services and worked primarily to the benefit of the economically powerful interests that dominated the state.

The Redeemer legacy ultimately ran even beyond the institutional structure that it left. The story of Reconstruction used to defeat the Republicans in 1871, 1872, and 1873 and then to put down the host of agrarian challenges through the rest of the century became the generally accepted history of that era. In 1898 Dudley G. Wooten published the first attempt at writing a comprehensive history of Texas up to that time. The man chosen to write on the state's political history was Oran M. Roberts, chairman of the state's secession convention, Conservative delegate to the Constitutional Convention of 1866, Democratic party activist in the early 1870s, justice of the state supreme court following the downfall of the Davis administration, and Redeemer governor for two terms after 1878. By the end of the century, however, he was considered an elder statesman and a respected faculty member of the University of Texas Law School, and his account of Reconstruction strongly influenced the scholarly history that followed. On the one hand, it is hardly surprising that this first history of the period would condemn the whole of Reconstruction and conclude that the end of the Davis years "redeemed" the state "from the ignominy and ruin with which it was threatened by the continuance of such Republican rule."[7] On the other hand, the story scarcely reflects the complex reality of those years. A century later Roberts's peculiar interpretation still holds sway over many, especially the popular image of the state's history. Recognition of the more tangled reality of Texas after the Civil War is long overdue.

NOTES

INTRODUCTION

1. Charles W. Ramsdell, *Reconstruction in Texas* (New York: Columbia University Press, 1909), 315.

2. For an overview of this literature, see Edgar P. Sneed, "A Historiography of Reconstruction in Texas: Some Myths and Problems," *Southwestern Historical Quarterly* 72 (April 1969), 435–48; Barry A. Crouch, "'Unmanacling' Texas Reconstruction: A Twenty-Year Perspective," *Southwestern Historical Quarterly* 93 (January 1990), 257–302.

CHAPTER I

1. The question of how many soldiers fought for the Confederacy is one of some controversy. A good discussion of the literature may be found in Ralph A. Wooster, ed., *Lone Star Blue and Gray: Essays on Texas in the Civil War* (Austin: Texas State Historical Association, 1995), p. viii n. 1. For a revised estimate, see Randolph B. Campbell, "Fighting for the Confederacy: The White Male Population of Harrison County in the Civil War," *Southwestern Historical Quarterly* [hereafter cited as *SWHQ*] 104 (Apr., 2000): 23–40.

2. A historical problem of equal difficulty is determining the number of casualties suffered by Texas troops. These figures are based on casualty rates discovered by Campbell in the only systematic study of the social history of Texas troops. "Fighting for the Confederacy," p. 37.

3. There is little written on the state's antebellum economy. The discussion of this economy and the statistics presented draw primarily on the publications of the U.S. Bureau of the Census, particularly the census of agriculture. See, in particular, U.S. Bureau of the Census, *Agriculture of the United States in 1860; Compiled from the Original Returns of the Eighth Census* (Washington: Government Printing Office, 1864), pp. 140–51, 216–17, 222, 240–42, 247. Useful statistics and discussions of the economy may be found in the various contemporary editions of the *Texas Almanac*.

4. *Texas Almanac for 1867* (Galveston: Richardson, 1866), p. 197.

5. See Randolph B. Campbell and Richard Lowe, *Wealth and Power in Antebellum Texas* (College Station: Texas A&M University Press, 1977), p. 80. For this particular definition of a plantation, the traditional number of twenty slaves was multiplied by Campbell's estimate for Harrison County of 0.89 bales of cotton on the average per slave, indicating that on the average, twenty slaves would produce 17.8 bales of cotton (rounded for convenience to 20). Given cotton production averaging about 0.6 bales per acre, this would have required about thirty-six acres of land devoted to cotton alone.

6. *Texas Almanac for 1869* (Galveston: Richardson, 1868), pp. 100–101.

7. For a discussion of slavery during the war, see Randolph B. Campbell, *An Empire for Slavery: The Peculiar Institution in Texas* (Baton Rouge: Louisiana State University Press, 1989), pp. 231–51.

8. Randolph B. Campbell, *A Southern Community in Crisis: Harrison County, Texas, 1850–1880* (Austin: Texas State Historical Association, 1983), pp. 385–94; idem, "Fighting for the Confederacy," pp. 38–39. For other studies showing similar results, see Jonathan Wiener, *Social Origins of the New South: Alabama, 1860–1885* (Baton Rouge: Louisiana State University Press, 1978); idem, "Planter Persistence and Social Change, 1850–1870," *Journal of Interdisciplinary History* 8 (1976): 235- 60; Dwight B. Billings Jr., *Planters and the Making of a 'New South': Class, Politics, and Development in North Carolina, 1865–1900* (Chapel Hill: University of North Carolina Press, 1979); Lee W. Formwalt, "Antebellum Planter Persistence: Southwest Georgia—A Case Study," *Plantation Society* 1 (1981): 410–29; Kenneth S. Greenberg, "The Civil War and the Redistribution of Land: Adams County, Mississippi, 1860–1870," *Agricultural History* 51 (1978): 292–307; Carl H. Moneyhon, *The Impact of the Civil War and Reconstruction on Arkansas* (Baton Rouge: Louisiana State University Press, 1994).

9. *Galveston Weekly News,* Mar. 3, 1857, quoted in Campbell, *Empire for Slavery,* p. 256.

CHAPTER 2

1. Andrews's observations on the immediate situation in Texas may be found in a speech he made at Brenham on July 20, 1865, and in his General Orders No. 3, issued at Houston on July 26. *Galveston Daily News,* July 23, 27, 1865. Other examples of the military's efforts at creating policy toward the freedmen may be found in General Orders No. 3, Post of Houston, July 22, 1865, and Circular, Office of the Provost Marshal, Galveston, July 28, 1865, in *Galveston Daily News,* June 23, July 1, 1865.

2. For examples of local orders, see Circular, Office of the Provost Marshal, Galveston, June 28, 1865; and General Orders No. 3, July 22, 1865, Post of Houston. For observations on persistent opinions on slavery's survival, see Elisha M. Pease to J. H. Starr, Aug. 19, 1865, James Harper Starr Papers, Center for American History, University of Texas at Austin; and B. F. Barkley to A. J. Hamilton, Oct. 30, 1865, Governors' Papers, Texas State Archives, Austin.

3. For the details of Hamilton's ideas, see "To the People of Texas, July 25, 1865," in *Flake's (Galveston) Daily Bulletin,* July 26, 1865; "Proclamation of the Governor, August 19, 1865," in *Galveston Daily News,* Aug. 25, 1865; various speeches, in ibid., July 23, Sept. 20, 1865; *Galveston Daily News Supplement,* Aug. 6, 1865; Hamilton to Johnson, July 24, Aug. 30, Sept. 23, Oct. 21, Nov. 27, 1865, Andrew Johnson Papers, Library of Congress, Washington, D.C.

Little has been written about the early concerns expressed by many northerners about the president's Reconstruction policies, though that concern appears to have emerged soon after his first provisional governors went south. There is no question that this concern had coalesced into opposition as early as September, but Hamilton would have been aware of the discussion as it emerged. For a discussion of the early reaction to southern events, see Michael Perman, *Reunion without Compromise* (Cambridge: Cambridge University Press, 1973), pp. 13–25; J. Michael Quill, *Prelude to the Radicals: The North and Reconstruction during 1865* (Washington, D.C.: University Press of America, 1980), pp. 127–30; and Eric Foner, *Reconstruction: America's Unfinished Revolution, 1863–1877* (New York: Harper and Row, 1988), pp. 222–27.

4. Hamilton to Johnson, Nov. 27, 1865.

5. See *Galveston Daily News,* Sept. 28, 1865.

6. *Flake's (Galveston) Daily Bulletin,* Sept. 19, 1865.

7. Randolph B. Campbell's work reconstructing the character of district and local officeholding is critical to understanding Hamilton's goals. See particularly his "Grass-Roots Reconstruction: The Personnel of County Government in Texas, 1865–1876," *Journal of Southern His-*

tory 58 (Feb., 1992): 99–116; "The District Judges of Texas in 1866–1867: An Episode in the Failure of Presidential Reconstruction," *SWHQ* 93 (Jan., 1990): 357–77; and *Grass-Roots Reconstruction in Texas, 1865–1880* (Baton Rouge: Louisiana State University Press, 1997).

8. For the text of the proclamation, see *Galveston Daily News,* Aug. 25, 1865.

9. A. J. Hamilton to A. Johnson, Aug. 30, Oct. 21, 1865, Johnson Papers; S. S. Cox to William E. Chandler, Oct. 14, 1865, William E. Chandler Papers, Library of Congress.

10. The character of postwar violence has been a major concern of historians. Charles Ramsdell concludes that Radical officials overestimated the amount of violence and what did occur was random or connected either to the breakup at the war's end or to frontier conditions. *Reconstruction in Texas* (New York: Columbia University Press, 1910), pp. 66–67. Nora Estelle Owens tends to agree with Ramsdell by concluding that the loss of respect for the law produced by the war played a central role in what took place. "Presidential Reconstruction in Texas: A Case Study" (Ph.D. diss., Auburn University, 1983), p. 252. In a similar vein William L. Richter emphasizes the reaction of Texans to military occupation as a major force in producing violence, though seeing expressed concerns as a mask for racial hatred. *The Army in Texas during Reconstruction, 1865–1870* (College Station: Texas A&M University Press, 1987), pp. 187–96.

More-recent scholars have emphasized the central role of racism in producing much of the violence that occurred. See Alwyn Barr, *Black Texans: A History of Negroes in Texas* (Austin: Jenkins, 1973), p. 43; and James M. Smallwood, *Time of Hope, Time of Despair* (Port Washington, N.Y.: Kennikat, 1981), pp. 32–33.

The argument presented here is based on the close parallel between major outbreaks of violence and critical periods in the cotton cultivation season, especially when landowners and laborers signed contracts, and then again at harvest.

11. U.S. House of Representatives, *Reconstruction,* 39th Cong., 1st sess., H. Rpt. 30, vol. 2, p. 46.

12. Estimates of the size of the army varies. Smallwood places the number at about five thousand. *Time of Hope, Time of Despair,* p. 39.

CHAPTER 3

1. Editorials discussing the course of Reconstruction appeared frequently in the *Galveston Daily News* and should be examined for insight into the view of moderate Democrats. *Galveston Daily News,* Sept. 26 (first quote), Sept. 9 (second quote), 1865.

2. Ibid., Nov. 2, 1865.

3. U.S. House of Representatives, *Letter from General Grant,* 40th Cong., 2d sess., H. Exec. Doc. 57, p. 109.

4. Modern historians have been perplexed as well. Ramsdell attributes the turnout to bad weather. Historian John Carrier may have been more insightful in his observation that it "indicated the general demoralization of the people." James W. Throckmorton believed that the people had no interest in the election because they would not be allowed to express their true sentiments. "They think we go there [to the Austin convention] simply to register the edicts of our masters." John Carrier, "A Political History of Texas during the Reconstruction" (Ph.D. diss., Vanderbilt University, 1971), p. 35; Ramsdell, *Reconstruction in Texas,* p. 89; James W. Throckmorton to B. H. Epperson, Jan. 21, 1866, B. H. Epperson Papers, Center for American History, University of Texas at Austin.

5. At least one historian believes that the convention of 1866 proceeded with the Civil War as the principal frame of reference for deciding what course to take in Reconstruction. See Carrier, "Political History of Texas during the Reconstruction," pp. 41–42.

6. See Owens, "Presidential Reconstruction in Texas," p. 124.

7. Carrier, "Political History of Texas during the Reconstruction," pp. 54–55. Ramsdell

also suggests at least that opponents of *ab initio* were driven by the desire not to admit the illegality of their actions. *Reconstruction in Texas,* pp. 97–98.

8. *Galveston Daily News,* June 17, 1866.

CHAPTER 4

1. U.S. House of Representatives, *Report from Benjamin C. Truman,* 39th Cong., 1st sess., H. Exec. Doc. 43, p. 13.

2. U.S. House of Representatives, *Freedmen's Affairs,* 39th Cong., 2d sess., H. Exec. Doc. 6, p. 146; Smallwood, *Time of Hope, Time of Despair,* p. 44.

3. Quoted in Smallwood, *Time of Hope, Time of Despair,* p. 56.

4. See *Flake's (Galveston) Daily Bulletin,* particularly its Saturday business sheet, for this period.

5. William L. Richter, *Overreached on All Sides: The Freedmen's Bureau Administrators in Texas, 1865–1868* (College Station: Texas A&M University Press, 1991), p. 111.

CHAPTER 5

1. The actual number of cases in which Griffin intervened is not known, although ultimately the army held over one hundred of these trials. Richter, *Overreached on All Sides,* p. 252, provides evidence of many of these, including the Robertson County case.

2. Historians have generally concluded that these removals represented a political triumph for the Republicans. John Carrier observes that "the last vestige of state constitutional government disappeared." "Political History of Texas during the Reconstruction," p. 162. Randolph B. Campbell notes that military authority had "substantially altered the personnel of state and local government," even though recognizing that the military tended to keep in place officers who showed any sign of cooperation. *Grass-Roots Reconstruction in Texas,* p. 15. Richter observes that, following removals by Griffin and his successor, Joseph J. Reynolds, "The miracle had happened—the Republicans were entrenched in state government as never before." *Army in Texas during Reconstruction,* p. 124.

An examination of the actual numbers removed, however, brings into question the extent of change. Carrier points out that one Republican claimed that only 306 removals among 2,500 state and local officers had taken place as late as May, 1868. "A Political History of Reconstruction," p. 203. Richter indicates that military authorities removed only about 600 officials but does not discuss how many were ever replaced by military appointees. *Army in Texas during Reconstruction,* pp. 115, 124. Scholars have long recognized the trouble Republicans had in securing officials. Both Charles Ramsdell and Campbell have noted the lack of available candidates. Ramsdell, *Reconstruction in Texas,* pp. 174–75; Campbell, *Grass-Roots Reconstruction,* pp. 116, 152. A report by a committee in the Constitutional Convention of 1868–69 showed that the military had appointed 796 men to the 2,377 elective offices in the state but that only 402 loyal appointees ever took office, leaving most in the hands of incumbents. See Carl Moneyhon, *Republicanism in Reconstruction Texas* (Austin: University of Texas Press, 1980), pp. 69–70.

3. Concerning the growing violence in 1866 and 1867, Charles Ramsdell provided the standard interpretation when he attributed lawlessness in part to the demoralization of the courts caused by the Jury Order, the interference of the military in civil matters, and the growth of party rancor. Finally, he saw state authority crippled when the military began to appoint unpopular men perceived as minions of military power into local offices. Ramsdell concludes, "it was next to impossible for the officials to maintain order, not because the people were 'disloyal' to the United States government, as the Radicals asserted, but because the very foundations of order had been taken away." *Reconstruction in Texas,* pp. 160, 176 (quote).

4. See J. W. Throckmorton to Ashbel Smith, Apr. 5, 1867, in *Houston Daily Telegraph,* Apr. 12, 1867.

5. The issue of white registration was not only important in contemporary politics but also became central to the interpretation of Reconstruction by subsequent historians. At the time, Conservatives argued that large numbers of whites were disfranchised as the result of the oath required by Congress and by the character of the registration boards. This claim became a central component in their charges against the legitimacy of subsequent Republican governments.

Scholars, however, have long recognized that limited registration among whites often was a result of their own choice. Charles Ramsdell, for example, found whites refusing to register to make political or racial statements. *Reconstruction in Texas,* p. 162. See also Richter, *Army in Texas during Reconstruction,* p. 129. For an example of the registration in one county, see Campbell, *Southern Community in Crisis,* pp. 276–77.

Dale Baum's important scholarly assessment of the question, using modern statistical analysis, has shown that white underregistration was not general but focused primarily in counties along the lower Brazos and Colorado Rivers and in the group of counties surrounding McLennan County in north-central Texas. Why this is so is not clear, though Baum speculates that it resulted from a the despair whites had of carrying elections in these black-majority counties. See *The Shattering of Texas Unionism* (Baton Rouge: Louisiana State University Press, 1998), p. 171.

6. The percentages are based upon the numbers of white males over the age of twenty-one listed in the census in 1870. The 51,062 African Americans probably are fewer than the number actually living in the state at that time; 136,270 whites may be closer to the actual population. The numbers in both groups probably had grown between 1868 and 1870, but the percentages give at least a rough estimate of the effectiveness of the political parties in getting their people to register.

Explanations for the low white turnout have varied. Contemporary whites contended that many refused to register because they did not wish to humiliate themselves by appearing before a black voting registrar. The best discussion of voter registration is Baum, *Shattering of Texas Unionism,* p. 172.

7. The character of evidence for most of the violence during this period makes a definitive assessment of causation difficult. Regarding the Marshall Riot, for example, Charles Ramsdell accepts Conservative newspaper assertions that the meeting was broken up by a drunken man who fired a pistol. *Reconstruction in Texas,* p. 189. More-recent examinations have accepted the accounts of Judge Colbert Caldwell, the commander of the military post, and an investigation by a representative of General Hancock that the Marshall chief of police had fired the shot and tried to break up the meeting. Campbell, *Southern Community in Crisis,* pp. 283–85; and *Grass-Roots Reconstruction,* p. 116. For a discussion of the positive relationship between violence and political events, see Gregg Cantrell, "Racist Violence and Reconstruction Politics," *SWHQ* 93 (Jan., 1990): 349.

8. Almost nothing is known about local league organization in Texas. For some of the few insights, see Campbell, *Southern Community in Crisis,* p. 284; Barry Crouch, *The Freedmen's Bureau and Black Texans* (Austin: University of Texas Press, 1992), p. 111; and Campbell, *Grass-Roots Reconstruction,* p. 118.

9. Jerry Moore quoted in Campbell, *Southern Community in Crisis,* p. 291.

CHAPTER 6

1. Ramsdell recognizes the political element in the violence but blames it on the "manner" in which blacks asserted their new rights. *Reconstruction in Texas,* p. 230.

2. For an example of this type of activity, see H. C. Pedigo to E. M. Pease, Sept. 11, 1868, Governors' Papers, Texas State Archives, Austin.

3. Contemporary papers are filled with information on the Democratic efforts to either organize or intimidate black voters. For the examples above, see *Galveston Daily News,* July 2, 16 (quote), 1868.

4. *Flake's (Galveston) Daily Bulletin,* Jan. 23, 1868.

5. *Galveston Daily News,* Sept. 3, 1868.

6. *Texas Republican,* quoted in Ramsdell, *Reconstruction in Texas,* p. 231.

7. Quotes from the constitution are taken from William F. Swindler, ed., *Sources and Documents of United States Constitutions,* vol. 9, *South Dakota, Tennessee, Texas, Utah, Vermont* (Dobbs Ferry, N.Y.: Oceana, 1979).

CHAPTER 7

1. Scholars have differing views on what pushed the Radicals to compromise. Charles Ramsdell and W. C. Nunn conclude that they had to take this measure in order to maintain support with the president and with Congress. Ramsdell, *Reconstruction in Texas,* p. 271; Nunn, *Texas under the Carpetbaggers* (Austin: University of Texas Press, 1962), p. 350. John P. Carrier suggests that the compromise was achieved because the Radicals desperately wanted office and also represented a recognition that virtually no whites within the party supported the positions the Radicals had taken previously. "Political History of Texas during the Reconstruction," pp. 350–51. Moneyhon views the movement as generated within the party out of a real concern with the effect of a division on the character of the government that would be elected in 1869. *Republicanism in Reconstruction Texas,* pp. 109–11.

2. Quoted in *Galveston Daily News,* June 8, 1869.

3. Ashbel Smith et al. to Oran M. Roberts, Feb. 12, 1869, O. M. Roberts Papers, Center for American History, University of Texas at Austin.

4. M. A. Harrison's testimony before a congressional investigating committee examining the election in the Second Congressional District in 1869 appears to be both believable and that of a witness hostile to Republican aims. See U.S. House of Representatives, *Papers in the Contested Election of Grafton vs. Conner,* 41st Cong., 2d sess., H. Misc. Doc. 14, pp. 15, 16. This document details more broadly the problems of the 1869 election.

5. Ibid., p. 12.

6. Considerable attention has been devoted to the reasons for Reynolds's shift from Hamilton to Davis. In *Reconstruction in Texas,* p. 274, Ramsdell concludes, based upon an interview with Jack Hamilton's daughter, that the change came as early as June, after Hamilton turned down Reynolds's proposal to serve in the U.S. Senate. According to Ramsdell, Reynolds subsequently played a major role in undermining Hamilton in Washington. Nunn expands on this, concluding that Hamilton's decision on the proposal for a senate seat "infuriated Reynolds, who deserted the Conservative faction of Hamilton and gave his support to the radicals." *Texas under the Carpetbaggers,* p. 15.

More-recent scholarship has seen Reynolds's motives as more complex than simple personal pique. John Carrier believes that Reynolds may have changed his mind when he saw the national administration shifting its support or that he was actually concerned with growing Conservative support of Hamilton. "Political History of Texas during the Reconstruction," p. 369. In *Republicanism in Reconstruction Texas,* pp. 114–15, Moneyhon concludes that Reynolds had never made a clear decision on which faction to back and was involved in efforts at reconciling them as early as June, suggesting that Reynolds's own indication that he denounced Hamilton because he had resisted reconciliation may have been a serious consideration in the choice.

7. *Dallas Weekly Herald,* Oct. 2, 1869.

8. The fairness of the registration has been a source of some historical debate. Ramsdell believes that there was considerable fraud in the registration process. *Reconstruction in Texas,* p. 281. Nunn agrees. *Texas under the Carpetbaggers,* p. 16. More-recent scholarship has dismissed the charges on the grounds that the Conservatives benefited more from the registration than the Radicals. See Ronald N. Gray, "Edmund J. Davis: Radical Republican and Reconstruction Governor" (Ph.D. diss., Texas Tech University, 1976), p. 176. Baum, however, suggests that there is no strong evidence that policy swayed the registration. *Shattering of Texas Unionism,* pp. 185–86.

Historians differ on the number of voters registered. Baum, based on the printed *Tabular Statement of Registration and Voting,* provides these figures. *Shattering of Texas Unionism,* p. 184. Using the same source, Carrier and Gray both show that the registration added 20,558 whites and 7,648 African Americans to the lists, bringing the total to 81,960 whites and 53,593 blacks. Carrier, "Political History of Texas during the Reconstruction," p. 390; Gray, "Edmund J. Davis," p. 176. Ramsdell reports 78,648 whites and 56,905 blacks. *Reconstruction in Texas,* p. 283.

9. Historical assessment of the character of the election has relied heavily on contemporary newspapers, and almost all of them supported Hamilton. These universally contended that the election was one of the most peaceful that had occurred at any time since the end of the war. Ramsdell agrees that the election was a quiet one. *Reconstruction in Texas,* pp. 283–84. Richter supports this conclusion. *Army in Texas during Reconstruction,* p. 184.

A closer examination of what took place at the local level suggests a much different picture of events. Although the charges are unsubstantiated, the testimony by supporters of the Republican congressional candidate B. F. Grafton offers a perspective of the 1869 election that appears to be an accurate one, for it shows actions very similar to those in previous elections. See House of Representatives, *Papers in the Contested Election of Grafton vs. Conner.*

10. The statistics here and cited subsequently are drawn from or based upon the materials provided in Baum, *Shattering of Texas Unionism,* pp. 180–228.

11. Ibid., pp. 203–4, 212.

12. William P. Ballinger to Fletcher Stockdale, Dec. 20, 1869, William P. Ballinger Papers, Center for American History, University of Texas at Austin.

CHAPTER 8

1. *Texas House Journal,* 12th Legislature, 1st sess., p. 14 (first quote), p. 15 (second quote).

2. Davis's speech was published in the *Austin Daily Republican,* May 2–5, 1870, the *(Austin) Daily State Journal,* and the journals of the legislature.

3. See these newspapers in particular for the period April 29–May 2: *Galveston Daily News,* Apr. 30, 1870; *Austin Republican,* May 2, 1870; *Flake's (Galveston) Daily Bulletin,* May 1, 1870.

4. Davis provided considerable insights into his views on the necessity of the police measures and his strategy for pushing the measure through the legislature in a speech that he gave in Austin on June 28. His quote is from that speech, published in the *(Austin) Daily State Journal,* June 30, 1870.

5. For an example of this speculation, see *Galveston Daily News,* Apr. 30, 1870. For observations on the racial character of the new militia, see *(Austin) State Gazette* quoted in *(Austin) Daily State Journal,* May 8, 1870.

6. Texas newspapers carried extended coverage of the debates from the bill's introduction in May through its passage in late June.

7. These included E. L. Alford, Thomas Baker, John G. Bell, Web Flanagan, John S. Mills, Mijamin Priest, and Boliver J. Pridgen.

8. J. W. Flanagan to E. J. Davis, July 29, 1870, in *(Austin) Daily State Journal,* Aug. 4, 1870; and in *Houston Weekly Telegraph,* Aug. 1, 1870.

9. *Speech of Governor A. J. Hamilton, Delivered in the Hall of the House of Representatives, on the Evening of 23d July, 1870* (Austin: Austin Republican Office, 1870).

CHAPTER 9

1. The state police force attracted more criticism than any other agency created by the Republican government. The basic facts about the police are well known, but interpretation of the meaning of these facts have varied among scholars. Early historians were particularly critical. The most serious charges against the state police came in Ramsdell, *Reconstruction in Texas*, p. 302; and Nunn, *Texas under the Carpetbaggers*, pp. 43, 74.

Recent published scholarship has called into question many of the conclusions reached by earlier historians. Ann Patton Baenziger, "The Texas State Police during Reconstruction: A Reexamination," *SWHQ* 72 (Apr., 1969): 470–91; and William T. Field Jr., "The Texas State Police, 1870–1873," *Texas Military History* 5 (fall, 1965): 139–41, raise serious questions about the traditional interpretation of the police. A more definitive defense of the police remains (at this point) in manuscript form, Barry Crouch and Donaly Brice's "The Governor's Hounds."

2. *(Austin) Tri-Weekly State Gazette*, quoted in Nunn, *Texas under the Carpetbaggers*, 79.

3. *First Annual Report of the Superintendent of Public Instruction of the State of Texas* (Austin: J. G. Tracy State Printer, 1872), p. 203.

4. Ibid., p. 5.

5. The full story of Reconstruction taxation remains untold. Randolph B. Campbell shows that taxes varied considerably from county to county because of the great differences in local taxes levied by the county courts. See his discussion of taxes for each of his six sample counties in *Grass-Roots Reconstruction*, passim.

CHAPTER 10

1. Campbell, *Grass-Roots Reconstruction*, pp. 94, 162.

2. *(Austin) Tri-Weekly Democratic Statesman*, Oct. 5, 1871, Mar. 12, 1872.

3. Annual figures for cotton production in Texas have been difficult to acquire. The annual reports of the commissioner of agriculture provide information on every crop but cotton. The statistics on acreage and production presented here come from U.S. Department of Agriculture, *Cotton Acreage, Yield, and Production, 1866–1938, by State; and Related Data* (Washington, D.C.: Government Printing Office, 1940). The figures here differ from those provided by S. S. McKay, "Economic Conditions in Texas in the 1870s," *West Texas Historical Association Year Book*, 15 (Oct., 1939): 87.

4. See *(Austin) Tri-Weekly Democratic Statesman*, Aug. 19, 29, 1871, for reports from the countryside concerning the drought and subsequent injury to crops in counties from Smith and Lamar in the northeast to Ellis in the northwest, Gonzales in the southwest, and Washington in the settled parts of the state.

5. There are few studies of local communities that provide insight into agriculture's problems. Among the best is Bill Stein, "Consider the Lily: The Ungilded History of Colorado County, Texas," *Nesbitt Memorial Library Journal: A Journal of Colorado County History*, 9 (Jan., 1999), pt. 7:3–39; 10 (Jan., 2000), pt. 8:3–62. For the stories of Towell and Stafford, see ibid., 9 (Jan., 1999), pt. 7:31–33.

6. The economic successes and failures of postwar Texas farmers has not been examined. There is anecdotal material on some of those who succeeded. See, in particular, Robert A. Calvert, ed., "The Freedmen and Agricultural Prosperity," *SWHQ* 76 (Apr., 1973): 461–72 n. 6; and William Warren Rogers, "From Planter to Farmer: A Georgia Man in Reconstruction Texas" 72 (Apr., 1969): 526–30.

7. *The Texas Almanac for 1873* (Galveston: Richardson, 1872), pp. 43, 39–40.

8. Homer L. Kerr, "Migration into Texas, 1860–1880," *SWHQ* 70 (Oct., 1966): 185–80, 209.

9. Edward King, *Texas: 1874* (Houston: Cordovan, 1974), p. 147.

10. The only study of elite survival can be found in the work of Randolph B. Campbell, particularly *Grass-Roots Reconstruction.* For his discussion of the problem of comparative statistics, see ibid., p. 228 n. 2.

11. No significant amount of research has been done on the effect of war and Reconstruction on Texans below the elites. These observations are based on a preliminary examination of Brazos County as reported in Carl Moneyhon, "Reconstruction in Texas" (unpublished lecture to Texas State Historical Association, Seminar in Texas History, summer, 1997).

12. S. T. Burney to E. J. Davis, June 22, 1870, Governors' Papers, quoted in Campbell, *Grass-Roots Reconstruction,* p. 59.

13. For the story of Palm's gift, see Stein, "Consider the Lily," 9 (Jan., 1999), pt. 7:24.

14. For the example of Kendleton, see Smallwood, *Time of Hope, Time of Despair,* p. 50.

15. Campbell, *Grass-Roots Reconstruction,* offers the only statistical examination of this development. Of his studied counties, Colorado, Harrison, and Jefferson were the most agriculturally focused.

16. Again, Campbell offers the only systematic effort at assessing black employment characteristics. These statistics and the following information are based on his analysis.

17. Campbell provides information on 1880 family life. The information on conditions in 1870 comes from James Smallwood, "Emancipation and the Black Family: A Case Study in Texas," *Social Science Quarterly* 57 (1977): 849–57. The findings of both scholars contradict popular ideas that a matriarchal family emerged among freedmen in the years following slavery.

18. Little research has been done on the development of African American churches in Texas. For an overview of what has been done, see William E. Montgomery, "African-American Churches," *The Handbook of Texas Online* <http://www.utexas.edu/handbook/online/articles .html>.

CHAPTER II

1. See *(Austin) Tri-Weekly Democratic Statesman,* Sept. 2, 1871. For a discussion of the New Departure at the national level, see Michael Perman, *The Road to Redemption: Southern Politics, 1869–1879* (Chapel Hill: University of North Carolina Press, 1984), chap. 1.

2. *(Austin) Democratic Statesman,* July 26, 1871.

3. Ibid., July 29, 1871.

4. Pearre quoted in Carrier, "Political History of Texas during the Reconstruction," p. 482. Pearre's pamphlet, printed in Baltimore, may actually have been for northern rather than local consumption. See *A Review of the Laws of the Twelfth Legislature of the State of Texas, Enacted in the Years 1870 and 1871, and the Oppressions of Governor E. J. Davis' Administration Exposed* (Baltimore: J. D. Lipscomb, 1871).

5. See *Weekly Dallas Herald,* Aug. 26, 1871; *Colorado Citizen,* May 11, 1871, quoted in Campbell, *Grass-Roots Reconstruction,* p. 49.

6. *Neches Valley News,* Jan., 1871, quoted in Robert J. Robertson, *Her Majesty's Texans: Two English Immigrants in Reconstruction Texas* (College Station: Texas A & M University Press, 1998), p. 53.

7. Reported on the *(Austin) Daily State Journal,* Aug. 6, 1871.

8. Ibid., July 19, 1871.

9. *Galveston News,* Aug. 17, 1871.

10. *(Austin) Democratic Statesman,* Aug. 5, 1871.

11. Modern scholarship has been uncertain as to what happened. Carrier believes that the election was relatively peaceful. "Political History of Texas during the Reconstruction," pp. 493–94. For both sides of the story provided by contemporaries, see U.S. House of Representatives, *Papers in the Case of Giddings vs. Clark,* 42d Cong., 2d sess., H. Misc. Doc. 163; and idem, *Whitmore vs. Herndon,* 42d Cong., 2d sess., H. Misc. Doc. 182.

12. Robertson, *Her Majesty's Texans,* p. 56 (quote).

CHAPTER 12

1. *(Austin) Democratic Statesman,* July 17, 1873.

2. For Ireland's position, see ibid., July 30, 1873.

3. Few smaller newspapers exist for this period, but their views often may be seen in those papers printed in the larger towns. For the *Victoria Advocate,* see *(Austin) Democratic Statesman,* July 22, 1873.

4. For an example of the conflict that emerged, see *(Austin) Democratic Statesman,* July 9, 1873.

5. Ibid., July 23, 1873.

6. *Clarksville (Tex.) Standard,* Nov. 15, 1873.

7. Oran M. Roberts, "The Political, Legislative, and Judicial History of Texas for Its Fifty Years of Statehood, 1845–1895," in *A Comprehensive History of Texas, 1685 to 1897,* ed. Dudley G. Wooten (Dallas: William G. Scarff, 1898), p. 198.

Annotated Bibliography

Introduction

The following bibliography provides information on the literature from which the basic information and narrative on each chapter are drawn. Where individual works offered an interpretation used in this book, they are cited in the notes. This bibliography is not intended to be comprehensive and does not cite unpublished manuscripts except in cases where they provide the only information about a topic. For more-complete bibliographies, see Edgar Sneed, "A Historiography of Reconstruction in Texas: Some Myths and Problems," *Southwestern Historical Quarterly* [hereafter cited as *SWHQ*] 72 (April, 1969): 435–48; and Barry A. Crouch, "'Unmanacling' Texas Reconstruction: A Twenty-Year Perspective," *SWHQ* 93 (January, 1990): 275–302.

The standard work providing an overview of the Reconstruction era up through the end of Congressional Reconstruction remains Charles Ramsdell, *Reconstruction in Texas* (New York: Columbia University Press, 1910). W. C. Nunn's *Texas under the Carpetbaggers* (Austin: University of Texas Press, 1962) picks up the story with the election of 1869 and carries it through the end of the Davis administration. Both of these studies are dated, written before the explosion of revisionist literature that emerged during the 1960s and afterward. For a thoughtful assessment of this literature and its persistence, see Randolph B. Campbell, "Carpetbaggers Rule in Reconstruction Texas: An Enduring Myth," *SWHQ* 98 (April, 1994): 587–96.

Chapter 1

The military history of the Civil War in Texas has received extensive scholarly attention, but there is less on other aspects of the state's wartime story. Politics has received the most coverage, especially secession and wartime dissension. Considerable background to the politics of wartime may be found in Walter L. Buenger, *Secession and the Union in Texas* (Austin: University of Texas Press, 1984). Stephen B. Oates, "Texas under the Secessionists," *SWHQ* 67 (October, 1963): 167–212, offers a good overview of the war years. See also Nancy H. Bowen, "A Political Labyrinth: Texas in the Civil War," *East Texas Historical Journal* 11 (fall, 1973): 3–11. Although primarily concerned with military affairs, Robert L. Kerby's *Kirby Smith's Confederacy: The Trans-Mississippi South, 1863–1865* (New York: Columbia University Press, 1972) also offers insights into wartime conditions within the state.

James Marten, *Texas Divided: Loyalty & Dissent in the Lone Star State, 1856–1874* (Lexington: University Press of Kentucky, 1984) provides extensive coverage of the nature of political dissent within the state, beginning with the antebellum years and running through Reconstruction. The character of Unionism in Texas, in particular, has been a major topic of interest. Claude Elliott, "Union Sentiment in Texas, 1861–1865," *SWHQ* 50 (April, 1947): 449–77, was among the first efforts at identifying the sources of Unionist sentiment.

Alan C. Ashcraft, "Role of the Confederate Provost Marshals in Texas," *Texana* 6 (1968): 390–92, offers some perspective on the controversy within the state produced by wartime dissent. Alwyn Barr's editing of the "Records of the Confederate Military Commission in San Antonio, July 2-October 10, 1862," *SWHQ* 70 (1966–67): 93–1009, 289–313, 623–44; 71 (1967–68): 247–78, documents the brutal persecution of those suspected of wartime Unionism.

Virtually nothing exists on the wartime economy and society, although Charles Ramsdell's speculations in *Texas Reconstruction* have provided a basis for much subsequent generalization.

CHAPTER 2

There is no published general study of Reconstruction politics in Texas, but John Pressley Carrier, "A Political History of Texas during the Reconstruction, 1865–1874" (Ph.D. diss., Vanderbilt University, 1971), provides a detailed picture of events and a considered analysis. Gov. Andrew J. Hamilton played a critical role in Texas Reconstruction, and his course helped produce subsequent developments. John L. Waller, *Colossal Hamilton of Texas: A Biography of Andrew Jackson Hamilton, Militant Unionist and Reconstruction Governor* (El Paso: Texas Western, 1968), provides a fair assessment of Hamilton's overall career, though room remains for an extended treatment of his Reconstruction activities. Further insights into his administration are offered by Alan C. Ashcraft, "Texas in Defeat: The Early Phase of A. J. Hamilton's Provisional Governorship,

June 17, 1865, to February 7, 1866," *Texas Military History* 8 (1970): 123–34; and Richard Moore, "Radical Reconstruction: The Texas Choice," *East Texas Historical Journal* 16 (spring, 1978): 15–21. A discussion of the sources of Hamilton's support may be found in Robert W. Shook, "Toward a List of Reconstruction Loyalists," *SWHQ* 76 (January, 1973): 315–20.

Most of the events of the Hamilton administration have been dealt with only tentatively. Randolph B. Campbell's various works dealing with local government are critical to understanding the governor's goals and activities. See particularly his "Grass Roots Reconstruction: The Personnel of County Government in Texas, 1865–1876," *Journal of Southern History* 58 (February, 1992): 99–116; and *Grass-Roots Reconstruction in Texas, 1865–1880* (Baton Rouge: Louisiana State University Press, 1997).

The history of the freedmen and their adjustment to the postwar world has attracted some of the most important scholarship of the last three decades. This revisionist work began with James Smallwood, *Time of Hope, Time of Despair: Black Texans during Reconstruction* (Port Washington, N.Y.: National University Publications, 1981). Smallwood covers every aspect of black history during this period. This study was one of the earliest revisionist works that saw blacks as responsible citizens of the state who possessed legitimate interests.

Closely associated with the study of black history has been the extensive work on the Freedmen's Bureau by William L. Richter and Barry Crouch. Richter's *Overreached on All Sides: The Freedmen's Bureau Administration in Texas, 1865–1868* (College Station: Texas A&M University Press, 1991) provides the best picture of the bureau organization and the views of its leaders on the freedmen and on political conditions at the time. Richter also has contributed significantly to our understanding of the bureau at the local level with an extensive literature that includes "'The Revolver Rules the Day!': Colonel DeWitt C. Brown and the Freedmen's Bureau in Paris, Texas, 1867–1868," *SWHQ* 93 (January, 1990): 303–32. Barry Crouch, *The Freedmen's Bureau and Black Texans* (Austin: University of Texas Press, 1992) is a significant effort at moving beyond institutional history to see what the bureau meant for the people it intended to serve. Like Smallwood, Crouch has written extensively on local bureau affairs, including his "The Freedmen's Bureau and the 30th Sub-District in Texas," *Chronicles of Smith County, Texas* 11 (spring, 1972): 15–30; and "View from Within: Letters of Gregory Barrett, Freedmen's Bureau Agent," ibid. 12 (winter, 1973): 13–28. Although supplanted by this revisionist work, Claude Elliott's "The Freedmen's Bureau in Texas," *SWHQ* 56 (July, 1952): 449–77, still provides a useful short overview of the organization's history.

There are numerous useful local studies of the Freedmen's Bureau, including Diane Neal and Thomas W. Kremm, "'What Shall We Do with the Negro?': The Freedmen's Bureau in Texas," *East Texas Historical Journal* 27 (1989): 23–33. James Smallwood has also contributed to this literature with "Charles E. Culver, a Reconstruction Agent in Texas: The Work of Local Freedmen's Bureau Agents and the Black Community," *Civil War History* 27 (December, 1981): 350–61; and "The Freedmen's Bureau Reconsidered: Local Agents and the Black Community," *Texana* 11 (1973): 309–20.

Alton Hornsby Jr., "The Freedmen's Bureau Schools in Texas 1865–1870," *SWHQ* 76 (April, 1973): 397–417, documents one of the most important aspects of the Freedmen's Bureau's efforts, its educational program. Also see James Smallwood, "Early 'Freedom Schools': Black Self-Help and Education in Reconstruction Texas: A Case Study," *Negro History Bulletin* 41 (January/February, 1978): 790–93; and "Black Education in Reconstruction Texas: The Contributions of the Freedmen's Bureau and Benevolent Societies," *East Texas Historical Journal* 19 (spring, 1981): 17–35.

The U.S. Army played a major role in Texas from the end of the Civil War through the end of Reconstruction. William L. Richter, *The Army in Texas during Reconstruction, 1865–1870* (College Station: Texas A&M University Press, 1987) follows that history through the inauguration of the Davis administration, synthesizing and stating the central theme that the army contributed to resistance against Reconstruction by its authoritarian style and peculiar view, which Richter has advanced in numerous previous articles on this topic. The latter include "'Devil Take Them All': Military Rule in Texas," *Southern Studies* 25 (April, 1986): 5–29; and "Spread-Eagle Eccentricities: Military-Civilian Relations in Reconstruction Texas," 8 (1970): 311–27. Other useful insights are provided by Robert W. Shook in "The Federal Military in Texas, 1865–1871," *Texas Military History* 6 (spring, 1967): 3–53; and "Military Activities in Victoria, 1865–1866," *Texana* 3 (winter, 1965): 347–52.

CHAPTER 3

Dale Baum, *The Shattering of Texas Unionism: Politics in the Lone Star State during the Civil War Era* (Baton Rouge: Louisiana State University Press) is an essential work for understanding Reconstruction politics, providing a systematic analysis of elections and thoughtful interpretation of what took place in elections during this period. The only work on the broader issue of Presidential Reconstruction that touches on the politics of Conservative resurgence is Nora Estelle Owens, "Presidential Reconstruction in Texas: A Case Study" (Ph.D. diss., Auburn University, 1983).

CHAPTER 4

The events of the Throckmorton administration have received only limited attention. James Throckmorton was a critical figure in the state's history during this era and deserves fresh attention, though sources may be inadequate for an expansion beyond Claude Elliott's *Leathercoat: The Life History of a Texas Patriot* (San Antonio: Standard Printing, 1938).

The activities of the Eleventh Legislature have attracted little scholarly attention. The "black codes" that it considered and passed have been examined in Barry Crouch, "All the Vile Passions: The Texas Black Code of 1866," *SWHQ* 97 (July, 1993): 13–34.

Randolph B. Campbell's "The District Judges of Texas in 1866–1867: An Episode in the Failure of Presidential Reconstruction," *SWHQ* 93 (January, 1990): 357–77 is the only study of this period that attempts to get beneath the story of the Eleventh Legislature and the governor, focusing on the judges selected in the 1866 elections.

William Richter's previously cited studies provide considerable information on the conflict between Governor Throckmorton and military authorities. For his in-depth examination of probably the single most-important basis for the governor's charges against military officials, see "The Brenham Fire of 1866: A Texas Reconstruction Atrocity," *Louisiana Studies* 14 (1975): 286–314.

Little has been written on social and economic trends during this critical period. Nancy Cohen-Lack, "A Struggle for Sovereignty: National Consolidation, Emancipation, and Free Labor in Texas, 1865," *Journal of Southern History* 58 (February, 1992): 57–98, assesses the efforts of blacks in the first year of the war to establish economic independence. James Smallwood, "Perpetuation of Caste: Black Agricultural Workers in Reconstruction Texas," *Mid-America* 61 (January, 1979): 5–23, looks at the darker side of the transition and the early development of tenant farming. Many of the ideas presented here by Smallwood appear in his later *Time of Hope, Time of Despair.*

On broader economic events, the best study of the changing conditions in the cotton industry is L. Tuffly Ellis, "The Revolutionizing of the Texas Cotton Trade, 1865–1885," *SWHQ* 73 (April, 1970): 478–508.

CHAPTER 5

The emergence of the Republican party may be followed in Carl H. Moneyhon, *Republicanism in Reconstruction Texas* (Austin: University of Texas Press, 1980). This study follows Republican politics through the end of the Davis administration and is important to understanding the politics of the convention of 1868–69, the state election of 1869, and the subsequent Davis administration. Further information on the beginnings of the Republican party may be found in James Alex Baggett, "Birth of the Texas Republican Party," *SWHQ* 79 (July, 1974): 1–20; and "Origins of Early Texas Republican Party Leadership," *Journal of Southern History* 40 (August, 1974): 441–50. William Richter, "'We Must Rubb out and Begin Anew': The Army and the Republican Party in Texas Reconstruction, 1867–1870," *Civil War History* 19 (December, 1973): 334–52, explores the military's role in Republican politics during this period.

Merline Pitre, *Through Many Dangers, Toils, and Snares: The Black Leadership of Texas, 1868–1900* (Austin: Eakin, 1985), provides insights into the black leaders who began to appear with the organization of the Republican party. This study is an important one that explores the continued role of African American leaders through the rest of the Reconstruction years and afterward. Pitre explores the way black politicians emerged in "The Evolution of Black Political Participation in Reconstruction Texas," *East Texas Historical Journal* 26 (1988): 36–45. A further look at the broader political viewpoint of these black leaders may be found in Barry Crouch, "Self-Determination and Local Black Leaders," *Phylon* 39 (December, 1978): 344–55.

George T. Ruby is the only one of these black leaders about whom much has been written. See, in particular, Carl H. Moneyhon, "George T. Ruby and the Politics of Expedience in Texas," in *Southern Black Leaders of the Reconstruction Era*, ed. Howard N. Rabinowitz (Urbana: University of Illinois Press, 1982), 364–78; James Smallwood, "G. T. Ruby: Galveston's Black Carpetbagger in Reconstruction," *Houston Review* 6 (winter, 1983): 24–33; and Randall B. Woods, "George T. Ruby: A Black Militant in the White Business Community," *Red River Valley Historical Review* 1 (autumn, 1974): 269–80. A brief look at the more radical Matt Gaines appears in Ann Patton Malone, "Matt Gaines: Reconstruction Politician," in *Black Leaders: Texans for Their Times*, ed. Alwyn Barr and Robert A. Calvert (Austin: Texas State Historical Association, 1981), pp. 49–81. A lesser-known figure is examined in Merline Pitre, "Richard Allen: The Chequered Career of Houston's First Black State Legislator," *Houston Review* 8 (1986): 79–88.

Even less has been written about significant Republican politicians. Dale A. Somers, "James P. Newcomb: The Making of a Radical," *SWHQ* 72 (April, 1969): 449–69, attempts to explain how this southerner became a part of the Republican party. Randolph B. Campbell, "George W. Whitmore: East Texas Unionist," *East Texas Historical Journal* 28 (1990): 17–28, deals with an important local politician elected to the U.S. Congress in 1869. Ronald N. Gray, "Edmund J. Davis: Radical Republican and Reconstruction Governor of Texas" (Ph.D. diss., Texas Tech University, 1976) is the only biographical study of this particularly important figure.

Chapter 6

The only work examining the broader history of the Constitutional Convention of 1868–69 is Betty J. Sandlin, "The Texas Reconstruction Constitutional Convention of 1868–1869" (Ph.D. diss., Texas Tech University, 1970).

Many aspects of the convention have not been explored, including the long-term debate over *ab initio.* The one issue that has received considerable attention is "division," and the definitive book on that topic is Earnest Wallace, *The Howling of the Coyotes: Reconstruction Efforts to Divide Texas* (College Station: Texas A&M University Press, 1979).

There have been numerous efforts at explaining the violence that beset the state during Reconstruction. Barry Crouch, "A Spirit of Lawlessness: White Violence, Texas Blacks, 1865–1868," *Journal of Social History* 18 (winter, 1984): 217–32, attributes it to the racism of contemporary whites and the breakdown of social order that took place at the war's end. His conclusions are supported by James M. Smallwood, "When the Klan Rode: White Terror in Reconstruction Texas," *Journal of the West* 25 (October, 1986): 4–13. Billy D. Ledbetter, "White Texans' Attitudes toward the Political Equality of Negroes, 1865–1870," *Phylon* 40 (September, 1979): 253–63, provides insights into the racist ideology that provided the framework for this type of violence. Gregg Cantrel, "Racial Violence and Politics in Reconstruction Texas, 1867–1868," *SWHQ* 93 (January, 1990): 333–55, has offered an alternative explanation in this study, which links violence primarily to contemporary politics. The previously cited Smallwood, *Time of Hope, Time of Despair,* and Richter, *Overreached on All Sides,* and *The Army in Texas during Reconstruction* provide extensive details of the violent outbreaks.

Chapter 7

The best overview of the politics of the election of 1869 and the historical debates surrounding it may be found in Baum's *Shattering of Texas Unionism* and his "Chicanery and Intimidation in the 1869 Texas Gubernatorial Race," *SWHQ* 97 (1993): 37–54. William R. Russ Jr., "Radical Disfranchisement in Texas, 1867–1870," *SWHQ* 38 (July, 1934): 40–52, attempts an estimate of the number of whites who actually were disfranchised at the time of this election and that for the constitutional convention in 1868.

The conservative character of Republicans elected to Congress in the 1869 election and at the subsequent first session of the legislature may be seen in Philip A. Avillo Jr., "Phantom Radicals: Texas Republicans in Congress, 1870–1873," *SWHQ* 77 (April, 1974): 431–44.

The history of the significant court cases that ultimately brought an end to the *ab initio* controversy can be found in William W. Pierson's dated but still very useful "Texas *versus* White," *SWHQ* 18 (1914–15): 341–67; 19 (1915–16): 1–36, 142–58.

Chapter 8

The character of black Republicans in the state legislature after 1870 has been one of the few topics concerning the state government that has received attention. Alwyn Barr, "Black Legislators of Reconstruction Texas," *Civil War History* 32 (December, 1986): 340–52, is a useful supplement to Merline Pitre's previously cited *Through Many Dangers, Toils, and Snares.*

Little has been written about the activities of these Republican legislators, however. James A. Baggett, "Beginning of Radical Rule in Texas: The Special Legislative Session of 1870," *Southwestern Journal of Social Education* 2 (spring/summer, 1972): 28–38, documents the activities of the session called in the spring of 1870 to ratify the Fourteenth and Fifteenth Amendments and to elect U.S. senators.

Although this study disagrees with some of his conclusions concerning the relationship of the militia bill and the railroads, John Brockman offers the most insightful and detailed examination of railroads and Reconstruction politics in the Twelfth Legislature in "Railroads, Radicals, and the Militia Bill: A New Interpretation of the Quorum-Breaking Incident of 1870," *SWHQ* 25 (October, 1987): 105–22; and "Railroads, Radicals, and Democrats: A Study in Texas Politics, 1865–1900" (Ph.D. diss., University of Texas, 1975).

Chapter 9

The implementation and operations of various Republican programs has received some attention from revisionists. The state police have received significant reexamination. Ann Patton Baenziger's "The Texas State Police during Reconstruction: A Reexamination," *SWHQ* 72 (April, 1969): 470–91 was among the earliest revisionist works dealing with Texas. Baenziger's study, along with William T. Field Jr., "The Texas State Police, 1870–1873," *Texas Military History* 5 (fall, 1965): 131–41, have provided an interpretation of the police that suggests the organization was not as bad as contemporary Democrats suggested. Walter Prescott Webb,

The Texas Rangers: A Century of Frontier Defense (Austin: University of Texas Press, 1965), remains useful on the collapse of the police and the development in its place of the Texas Rangers.

Militia operations also have received some attention, particularly in Otis Singletary, "The Texas Militia during Reconstruction," *SWHQ* 60 (July, 1956): 23–35.

The creation of a pubic school system has received the least attention of all Republican programs. Frederick Eby's *The Development of Education in Texas* (New York: Macmillan, 1925) remains a useful study, providing the details of that effort, though it is an interpretation that fits within the pre-revisionist school of thought.

Little has been written on the judiciary during this period, despite the fact that Republican judges were the objects of extensive criticism. James R. Norvell, "The Reconstruction Courts of Texas, 1867–1873," *SWHQ* 62 (October, 1968): 141–63, offers an overview of the courts throughout the period. For a look at the types of men Governor Davis appointed, see Randolph B. Campbell, "Scalawag District Judges: The E. J. Davis Appointees," *Houston Review* 14 (1992): 75–88.

Railroad policy and its results may be followed in S. G. Reed, *A History of the Texas Railroads and of Transportation Conditions under Spain and Mexico and the Republic and the State* (Houston: St. Clair, 1941); and C. S. Potts, *Railroad Transportation in Texas* (Austin: University of Texas, 1909).

CHAPTER 10

The postwar economy remains largely unexplored. One of the few efforts at identifying trends and explaining them is Winston Lee Kinsey, "The Immigrant in Texas Agriculture during Reconstruction," *Agricultural History* 53 (January, 1979): 125–41.

Much remains to be done on the social history of African Americans in postwar Texas, however, there are major works dealing with this topic. Barry A. Crouch, "The 'Chords of Love': Legalizing Black Marital and Family Rights in Postwar Texas," *Journal of Negro History* 334–51, examines efforts at stabilizing family life in the postwar years. His article with Larry Madaras, "Reconstruction Black Families: Perspectives from the Texas Freedmen's Bureau Records," *Prologue* 18 (summer, 1986): 109–22, provides further insights into this process. In addition to his *Time of Hope, Time of Despair,* James Smallwood's important "Emancipation and the Black Family: A Case Study in Texas," *Social Science Quarterly* 57 (March, 1977): 849–57, offers a statistical assessment of the character of black families and the rapidity that characterized their stabilization through this era.

On the development of a broader community among African Americans, Michael R. Heintzen, *Private Black Colleges in Texas, 1865–1954* (College Station: Texas A&M University Press, 1985), offers insights into the origins of higher education within that community.

How the war and Reconstruction affected whites remains largely unexplored, though the general social history of Texas after the war has received increased attention. The one major exception in efforts to identify the social implications of the war and the years afterward is Randolph B. Campbell, *A Southern Community in Crisis: Marshall, Texas, 1850–1880* (Austin: Texas State Historical Association, 1983). Campbell offers one of the few revisionist studies of a county during the Reconstruction years, at a time when many other such works continued to provide an interpretation within the Ramsdell-Nunn framework. His "Population Persistence and Social Change in Nineteenth-Century Texas: Harrison County, 1850–1880," *Journal of Southern History* 48 (May, 1982): 185–204, offers a more limited look at the statistics of change. Another noteworthy exception to the traditional-interpretation county history is Bill Stein, "Consider the Lily: The Ungilded History of Colorado County, Texas," *Nesbitt Memorial Library Journal: A Journal of Colorado County History* 9 (January, 1999), pt. 7: 3–39; 10 (January, 2000), pt. 8: 3–62.

An early study of broader social history is Seth S. McKay, "Social Conditions in Texas in the Eighteen Seventies," *West Texas Historical Association Yearbook* 14 (October, 1938): 32–51. McKay's view has been expanded greatly by John Austin Edwards, "Social and Cultural Activities of Texans during the Civil War and Reconstruction, 1861–1873" (Ph.D. diss., Texas Tech University, 1985).

CHAPTER II

Little has been written about the politics of Democratic redemption, though there have been a number of biographies of Democratic politicians. John Anthony Moretta's *William Pitt Ballinger: Texas Lawyer, Southern Statesman, 1825–1888* (Austin: Texas State Historical Association, 2000) is the most recent. Elizabeth Silverthorne, *Ashbel Smith of Texas: Pioneer, Patriot, Statesman, 1805–1886* (College Station: Texas A&M University Press, 1982); Louis Horton, *Samuel Bell Maxey: A Biography* (Austin: University of Texas Press, 1974); and Ben H. Procter, *Not without Honor: The Life of John H. Reagan* (Austin: University of Texas Press, 1962) should also be consulted. Patrick George Williams, "Redeemer Democrats and the Roots of Modern Texas, 1872–1884" (Ph.D. diss., Columbia University, 1996), offers considerable insights into the era and its politicians and should fill the absence of published material in the not too distant future.

For an examination of Democratic tactics against Republicans, see Carl H. Moneyhon, "Public Education and Texas Reconstruction Politics, 1871– 1874," *SWHQ* 92 (January, 1989): 392–416.

On the emergence of the Ku Klux Klan, see a contemporary's view, W. D. Wood, "The Ku Klux Klan," *The Quarterly of the Texas State Historical Association* 9 (1905–1906): 262–68. Allan W. Trelease, *White Terror: The Ku Klux Klan Conspiracy and Southern Reconstruction* (New York: Harper and Row, 1971), provides an overview of the Klan in the state, but a closer examination remains to be done. Although primary sources, some of the best insights into the critical 1871 elections may be found in congressional documents that record testimony on what took place in the First and Third Districts. See "G. W. Whitmore vs. W. S. Herndon," 42d Cong., 2d sess., *House Misc. Doc.* 182; and "D. W. Giddings vs. W. T. Clark," 42d Cong., 2d sess., *House Misc. Doc.* 163.

CHAPTER 12

The end of Reconstruction and the removal of the Davis administration has received considerable attention. See, in particular, Carl H. Moneyhon, "Edmund J. Davis in the Coke-Davis Election Dispute of 1874: A Reassessment of Character," *SWHQ* 100 (October, 1996): 131–45; and George Shelley, "The Semicolon Court of Texas," *SWHQ* 48 (April, 1945): 449–68.

The period following the end of Reconstruction has received less attention from historians than any other era in the state's history. Alwyn Barr, *Reconstruction to Reform: Texas Politics, 1876–1906* (Austin: University of Texas Press, 1971), remains the only work to provide an overview of the politics of this critical era, though there are quite a few studies that look at the farm movements in the 1870s and 1880s.

Our knowledge about the writing and purposes of the Constitution of 1876 is dated. John E. Ericson, "The Delegates to the Convention of 1875," *SWHQ* 67 (July, 1963): 22–27, provides a relatively modern view of the membership, but Seth Shepard McKay's dated "Making the Constitution of 1876" (1924) remains the only examination of the work of that convention and assessment of its product. John Walker Mauer, "State Constitutions in a Time of Crisis: The Case of the Texas Constitution of 1876," *Texas Law Review* 68 (June, 1990), offers the most recent assessment of that document.

John Stricklin Spratt's *The Road to Spindletop: Economic Change in Texas, 1875–1901* (Dallas: Southern Methodist University Press, 1955) offers the most comprehensive assessment of major economic trends during the post-Reconstruction years.

Studies of the social history of this period remain relatively few in number. The most important of these is Lawrence D. Rice, *The Negro in Texas, 1874–1900* (Baton Rouge: Louisiana State University Press, 1971), which chronicles the struggle of African Americans in the context of the oppressive conditions that developed following Reconstruction's end. The steady emergence of segregation from 1865 can be followed in Barry A. Crouch and L. J. Schultz, "Crisis in Color: Racial Separation in Texas during Reconstruction," *Civil War History* 16 (March, 1970): 37–49.

INDEX

Page numbers in *italic* type refer to illustrations.

Caldwell, Colbert, 84
Campbell, Don, 128
Campbell, Randolph, 16, 33, 153
Canby, E. R. S., 100
carpetbaggers: in constitutional convention, 88; in legislature, 127–28; significance, 88
cattle industry: conditions in 1860, 90; expansion into black belt, 159; postwar cattle drives, 160; prices, 160; problems during war, 9–10
Cheyene Indians, 144
Chiles, John, 32
civil rights, 93
Civil Rights Bill of 1866, 52
Clark, William T.: contests 1871 election, 183; defeated for reelection, 182; elected to Congress, 116; Radical Republican congressional nominee, 111; supports white Republican party, 178
class and status: in antebellum Texas, 14, 16; postwar developments, 164–66; wartime issues, 15
Clayton, Powell, 130
Coke, Richard, *195;* Democratic gubernatorial candidate, 194; election campaign in 1873, 196; inauguration in 1874, 198
Coke-Davis Imbroglio, 198–99
Colorado County: black landownership, 167; social conditions, 165; taxation in, 153
Colored Men's Convention, 192
Colored Methodist Church, 169
Comanche Indians, 144, 145
commerce and trade: exports through Port of Galveston, 161; postwar volume, 161; railroad impact upon, 156–57; restructuring of, 161–62; wartime conditions, 12–13
Confederate troops, 8
Conner, John C.: Democratic congressional nominee, 113; elected to Congress, 117; reelected to Congress, 182; renominated to Congress, 172
Conservative party: convention of 1868, 83; delegates in constitutional convention of 1868, 89; election strategy in 1868, 82, 83; organization in 1868, 83
Conservative Reconstructionist party, 83
Conservative Republicans, 135

Conservative Union party: election of 1866, role in, 49; moderate Democrats in, 40; platform in 1866, 47–48; rhetoric of states' rights, 41; roots, 38
Constitutional Convention of 1866: *ab initio* in, 45–46; assembled, 43; called, 32; civil rights for freedmen, position on, 46–47; character of delegates, 44
Constitutional Convention of 1868: action against violence, 96; assembled, 87; business finished by E. R. S. Canby, 100; delegates, 87–89; election results, 85; first session adjourned, 96; second session adjourned, 100
Constitutional Convention of 1876: assembled, 199; delegates, 199–200
Constitution of 1866, 46–47
Constitution of 1868: Bill of Rights, 100; civil rights limits, 101–102; education, 101; executive branch provisions, 100–101; Republican contributions to, 100; suffrage provisions, 102
Constitution of 1876: agrarian influence on, 201; compared to that of 1869, 199–201
contract law, 60
cotton: crop conditions, 25, 55, 79, 158; expansion of growing area, 155, 156; harvest, 10, 64–65, 79, 158; land in cultivation, 157; prices, 23, 36, 65, 159–60; ratio of cotton to corn, 157
courts, state: appointments, A. J. Hamilton's to, 31; expansion of system, 140; failure to protect freedmen, 37
Craig, Samuel H., 64
Curtis, Stephen, 75

Dallas County: employment opportunities for blacks, 167; social conditions, 165
Davidson, James: adjutant general, 138; fraud committed, 186–87; management skills, 140; role in Republican politics in 1871, 178
Davis, Anne Briton, 135, *136*
Davis, Edmund J., *119;* address to Thirteenth Legislature, 188; appointed governor, 118; black constituents, loyalty to, 192; in campaign of 1869, 113–14; in campaign of 1872, 185; in campaign of 1873, 194–95; commander 1st Texas Cavalry, U.S., 18; in

Congressional campaign of 1871, 181; Conservative press early attitudes towards, 124; constitutional convention of 1866, delegate to, 46; constitutional convention of 1868, delegate to, 88; elected president of constitutional convention of 1868, 89; enclosure law vetoed, 191; and George T. Ruby, 97; inaugurated governor, 119; legislative program of, 119–23; opposes constitution of 1869, 103; protection of polls, 181; Radical Republican gubernatorial nominee, 107; on railroad debts, 113; recognized by Republican National Executive Committee, 109; release of Santanta and Big Tree, 145; renominated governor, 192; veto of railroad legislation, 134, 151, 191

Degener, Edward: elected to Congress, 117; defeated in 1871, 183

DeGress, Jacob C., *147;* educational ideas, 147–48; Freedmen's Bureau agent, 66; named superintendent of public instruction, 146; political role in election of 1872, 185

Democratic party: agrarian discontent within, 191, 196; and Andrew J. Hamilton's reconstruction policies, 28; antebellum position, 17; anti-agrarian strategy of, 204; attacks on state police and militia, 182; on black disfranchisement, 98; campaign strategy in 1871, 173–74; campaign strategy in 1872, 184; campaign strategy in 1873, 193–94; connection to Ku Klux Klan, 110; convention of 1868, 98; convention of 1871, 172; convention of 1872, 185; convention of 1873, 193–94; and *Democratic Statesman,* 172–73; efforts to secure black voters, 94; election strategy in 1868, 95, 98; election strategy in 1869, 109, 110, 113; increased votes for, in 1871, 183; and New Departure, 171–72; platform in 1871, 172; Redeemer control and goals, 199; reorganization for presidential election (1868), 94; support of Andrew J. Hamilton for governor in 1869, 113; support of railroads, 152, 193

Democratic Statesman: created by Democratic party, 172; public school system attacked by, 189–90

Denison, 164

disfranchisement, 90

division of state: Congressional bill to, 103, 104; issue in constitutional convention (1868), 92–93, 99; Radical Republican support for, 107; Ulysses S. Grant's failure to support, 104

Dohoney, E. L., 117

education: Constitutional Convention of 1876 provisions for, 201; corruption of system charged, 173–74; curriculum in, 148; political criticism of public schools, 149; political use of school system, 174; after Redemption, 201–202; revised school bill passed, 135; schools organized, 146; segregation of, 149; students attending, 149, 150; support by Edmund J. Davis, 122; taxpayer's revolt, impact on, 150, 184; teacher qualifications, 148–49; and Thirteenth Legislature, 189; and Twelfth Legislature, 132

Election for constitutional convention, 1866, 42–43, 50–51

Election for constitutional convention, 1868, 84

Election of 1866, general, 47–51

Election of 1869, general: called, 102; delayed by Ulysses S. Grant, 110; Democratic strategy in, 98; Radical Republican voting strength, 116; Republican canvass, 107–109; results, 116; voter turnout, 116

Election of 1871, Congressional: racial fears played upon, 176; results, 182–83; tax issue in, 174–75; violence and intimidation in, 176–77, 182–83

Election of 1872, general: Democratic gains in, 183; Democratic strategy, 184; local issues important, 186; results, 186

Election of 1873, general: Democratic strategy in, 193–94; racist appeals during, 197; results, 197

Election on secession, 1860, 17

Ellis County, 156

Emancipation Proclamation: cost to slaveholders, 8; proclaimed in Texas, 7

Epperson, Benjamin H.: candidate for U.S. Senate in 1866, 53; Congressman, unrecognized, 62

Eureka Mills, 163
Evans, A. J., 117
Evans, Lemuel D.: delegate to constitutional convention of 1868, 89; on state division, 92
ex parte Rodriguez, 198

Falls County: election fraud in, 115; reduced black voting, 107
Fanin County, 107
Farmers Alliance, 204
farming: antebellum and wartime character, 10–12; definitions of farm and plantation, 11; postwar shift to commercial farming
farm labor: contracts, 23; delays in contract signing in 1865–1866, 24; emergence of share cropping, 24–25, 58; shortage of, 24, 56; white complaints concerning, 25, 55, 80
farm wages: in 1865, 24; in 1866, 58
Fayette County, 196
Fifth Military District, 70
First National Bank of Galveston, 162
Flanagan, James W.: appointed lieutenant governor, 118; candidate for lieutenant governor, 107; elected to U.S. Senate, 118; opposes constitution of 1869, 103; in Radical Republican convention of 1869; reconciliation with Edmund J. Davis, 192; schism with Edmund J. Davis, 134
Flanagan, Webster: and militia bill, 131; reconciliation with Edmund J. Davis, 192; Republican state senator, 127
Fort Bend County: attack on Freedmen's Bureau schools, 96; black landownership, 167; violence against Republicans, 96; voter registration (1868), 70
Fountain, Albert J., 117
Freedmen's Bureau: complaints against, 55; educational efforts, 34–35, 58–59; judicial and police efforts, 66; labor policies, 33, 56; manpower, 56; organized, 33
Freestone County: election violence in 1871, 142–43, 182; martial law declared, 182
frontier protection: bond sales prevented, 143; frontier force legislation, 132; minute companies created, 143–44; ranging

companies created, 143; reliance on federal government to secure, 145

Gaines, Matthew, *126*; district gerrymandered, 190; minister, 169; Republican state senator, 124; resists Republican strategy in 1871, 178; supports reelection of Edmund J. Davis in 1873, 192
Galveston Bank & Trust Company, 162
Gathings, J. J., 141
Geological Survey, 132
German convention, 192
Germans: antebellum social order, place in, 14; wartime conditions of, 15
Giddings, DeWitt C.: constitutional convention of 1866, delegate to, 45; Democratic nominee for Congress, 172; elected to Congress, 183
Goodnight, Charles, 161
Grand Army of the Republic, 178
Granger, Gordon, 7
Grant, Ulysses S.: concerns with Texas political situation, 111; delay calling Texas election, 106; local Republicans endorse in 1872, 185; presidential candidacy, 96–97; withdraws support for Edmund J. Davis in 1874, 198
Greely, Horace, 172, 186
Greenback movement, 204
Gregory, Edgar M., 21, 33, *34*
Griffin, Charles C., *71*; civil courts, intervention in, 70–72; death of, 77; Elisha M. Pease, appointed governor, 76; freedmen, concerns for, 75; James W. Throckmorton, removal of, 76; military commander in Texas, 70; removal of state and local officials, 70, 77; voter registration, policies for, 72, 78
Grimes County, 182
Groesbeck Riot, 182

Hamilton, Andrew J., *26*; *ab initio,* position on, 91; appeals 1869 election, 117; appointments of local officials, 29–30; attack on Davis administration, 135; Conservative Union party, role in, 39; constitutional convention of 1866, message to, 45; delegate to constitutional convention of 1868, 88; on division of the

state, 93, 99, 104; fraud charged in 1869
election, 171; gubernatorial candidate,
106, 108; and Liberal Republicans, 184;
named military governor, 18; named
provisional governor, 7; opposition to
Throckmorton government, 73; plan
for reconstruction, 25–28; prosecution
of Confederate authorities, ideas concerning, 40; racial attitudes, 27; reconciliation with Edmund J. Davis, 192;
as refugee, 18; and Taxpayers' Convention, 175; on white enfranchisement,
99, 112

Hamilton, Morgan: on *ab initio,* 90; break
with Edmund J. Davis, 134; calls Radical
Republican convention, 107; civil rights
position, 93; elected U.S. Senator, 118;
and frontier bonds, 143; and George T.
Ruby, 97; and Liberal Republicans, 184;
refused to pay state officials, 90; and Taxpayers' Convention, 175

Hancock, John: ally of Andrew Johnson, 83;
candidate for U. S. Senate, 53; Democratic nominee for Congress, 1872;
elected to Congress, 183

Hancock, Winfield Scott: blamed for increased violence, 94; constitutional convention of 1868, ordered by, 82

Harrison County: African-American schools
attacked, 96; African-American voting in
1868, 85; political violence, 84; removal of
officials, 77; social conditions, 165; taxation in, 153

Helm, Jack, 139, 143

Herbert, Claiborne C., 62

Herndon, William S.: Democratic Congressional nominee, 172; elected to Congress,
182

Hill County: election fraud in, 115; militia
sent to, 141–42

Hill, John R., 160

Homestead Law, 61

Honey, George W., 118

Hopkins County, 115

House, Thomas W., 166

Houston, Sam, 17, *18*

Houston and Texas Central Railroad: actions of Eleventh Legislature on debt to
state, 61; economic impact of expansion,

156; land grants confirmed, 61; operations
expanded, 150–51; relief bill, 134

Houston Cotton Mills, 163

Howard, Oliver Otis, 63

Hutchings-Sealy Bank, 162

immigration, postwar, 163–64

Immigration Bureau, 132

Indians, 144

International and Great Northern Railroad:
charter considered by Twelfth Legislature, 133–34; expansion, 151; and state
bonds, 191, 193, 203

Ireland, John: agrarian Democratic leader,
191; arrests U.S. officials, 64; seeks Democratic gubernatorial nomination in 1873,
194

Jury Order: described, 70; enforcement delayed, 75; views of James W. Throckmorton, 72

Jefferson County: employment opportunities for blacks, 167; officials removed, 77;
political violence, 94; social conditions,
165

Johnson, Andrew: reconstruction plan, 7;
declaration end of Rebellion in Texas, 62;
reelection campaign in 1868, local political connections to, 83

Johnston, Albert Sidney, 62

Jones, George W., 47

Keuchler, Jacob, 118

Kendall, William, 167

Kendleton, 167

Kickapoo Indians, 144

Kiddoo, Joseph B., *57;* commander of
Freedmen's Bureau, 56; freedmen, attitudes concerning, 56, 66–67; James W.
Throckmorton, relationship with, 63; labor contracts, instructions regarding, 68

Kiowa Indians, 144, 145

Ku Klux Klan: appearance, 95; Democratic
party connections, 95, 110; election activities in 1869, 110; in election of 1871, 176;
purposes, 110

Lamar County, 117

landlord and tenant bill, 203

Index

Pearre, Charles B., 176
Pease, Elisha M., *76; ab initio,* position on, 90; appointed governor by Charles Griffin, 76; early member of Republican party, 73; gubernatorial candidate, 48; and Liberal Republicans, 184; lobbies Congress against state government, 73; message to constitutional convention of 1868, 89–90; resigns as governor, 112; and Taxpayers' Convention, 175
Petit, Elisha, 127
Pickett, Edward, 128
plantation, 10–11
planters: challenged in postwar years, 165; and Democratic party, 190; resistance to Reconstruction policy, 25; survival rates through war, 16
population: postwar growth, 163; urbanization, 164
Populists, 204
Pridgen, Bolver J. 131
Priest, Mijamin, 131
Pritchett, W. T., 142
public schools. *See* education

Quorum Breaking Incident, 131–32

racial attitudes, 15
Radical Republican faction: differences with Moderate Republicans, 98; moderation of views, 108; opposition to constitution of 1869; origins, 97–98; views of white suffrage, 99
railroads: actions of Thirteenth Legislature, 191; actions of Twelfth Legislature, 131, 133–34; and Democratic party, 152, 194, 202–203; economic impact, 155–56; expansion, 150–52; impact on communication, 152; policies of Edmund J. Davis towards, 112; and prices, 157; social impact, 152; state debts, wartime payments of, 40
Ramsdell, Charles W., 4
ranching, 9–10
Reagan, John H.: opposition to agrarian Democrats, 194; role in Conservative convention of 1868, 83; role in Presidential election of 1868, 83; support for Andrew J. Hamilton, 108

Reconstruction, revolutionary potential of, 8
Reconstruction Acts, 69–70
Redeemers, 194. *See also* Democratic party
Republican compromise movement in 1869, 107–108
Republican party: agrarian appeal, 177, 181; black voters, position on, 73; controls constitutional convention election of 1868, 85; convention in 1867, 75; convention in 1868, 97; convention in 1869, 107; convention in 1872, 185; convention in 1873, 190; election strategy in 1871, 177–78; fragmentation in 1870, 15; Liberal movement in, 172; platform in 1873, 193; racial views of white leaders, 101, 135–36, 178; role in removal of state officials, 75
Republican National Executive Committee, 109
Review of the Laws of the Twelfth Legislature of Texas, 175
Reynolds, Joseph J., *105;* compromise efforts, 107; delays election of 1869, 98; named military commander, 77; oversight of 1869 election, 114–15; restores civil government, 117–18; resumes military command, 106; shifts support to Radical Republicans, 107, 111; support of Moderate Republicans, 103
Richardson, Willard, 40
Roberts, Oran M.: authors history of reconstruction, 205; black testimony, views on, 46; constitutional convention of 1866, delegate to, 43; elected to U.S. Senate, 53; taxes reduced under, 202
Robertson County, 156
Rodriguez, Joseph, 198
Rosenberg, Henry, 162
Ruby, George T., *125;* Colored Men's Convention organized by, 192; Radical Republican ally, 107; Republican state senator, 124; Union League leader, 75
Runnels, Hardin R.: constitutional convention of 1868, candidate for president, 45; intimidation of black voters, 94

San Augustine County, election of 1868, 84
Santanta, 145
scalawags, 88, 127
Sealy, George, 166

Upshur County, 115
urbanization, 164

vagrancy law, 60
Violence and lawlessness: constitutional convention report on, 93–94; explanations of, 35–36; in 1865, 35–36; in 1866, 59, 64–66; in 1867, 77–82; in 1868, 84; in 1869, 115; in 1871, 174–76, in 1872, 182–83; Republican party position on, 93–94; views of Andrew J. Hamilton on, 29; Winfield S. Hancock blamed, 94
Voter registration: in 1865, 31; in 1866, 72–73; in 1867, 78; in 1867–1868, 82; in 1869, 114–15; problems of, 78, 81

Waco Manufacturing Company, 163
Waggoner, Daniel, 161
Walker County, 142
Walton, William: chairman Democratic

state executive committee, 98; fusion with Liberal Republicans supported, 172
Washington County: violence in, 84; voting irregularities in 1871, 182
West, Kench, 141
Wheelock, Edwin M.: editor of *San Antonio Express,* 106; Freedmen's Bureau superintendent of education, 35, 58; supporters Republican compromise movement, 106
Whig party, 16
White, George W., 32
Whitmore, George: defeated for reelection, 182; elected to Congress, 117; resists Republican strategy shifts in 1871, 178
Wichita Indians, 144
Wiley College, 168
Williams, Benjamin F.: assists blacks to secure land, 167; Union League leader, 74
Wood County, 84
Wooten, Dudley G., 205

ISBN 1-58544-361-1

90000